AMERICAN GUERRILLA

AMERICAN GUERRILLA

The Forgotten Heroics of
Russell W. Volckmann

The Man Who Escaped from Bataan, Raised a
Filipino Army Against the Japanese, and Became the
True "Father" of Army Special Forces

MIKE GUARDIA

CASEMATE
Philadelphia & Oxford

First published in the United States of America and Great Britain in 2010, this edition
published 2019 by
CASEMATE PUBLISHERS
1950 Lawrence Road, Havertown, PA 19083, USA
and
The Old Music Hall, 106–108 Cowley Road, Oxford OX4 1JE, UK

Paperback Edition: ISBN 978-1-61200-715-1
Digital Edition: ISBN 978-1-50402-505-8

A CIP record for this book is available from the British Library

Printed and bound in the United States of America

Typeset in India for Casemate Publishing Services. www.casematepublishingservices.com

For a complete list of Casemate titles, please contact:

CASEMATE PUBLISHERS (US)
Telephone (610) 853-9131
Fax (610) 853-9146
Email: casemate@casematepublishers.com
www.casematepublishers.com

CASEMATE PUBLISHERS (UK)
Telephone (01865) 241249
Email: casemate-uk@casematepublishers.co.uk
www.casematepublishers.co.uk

Contents

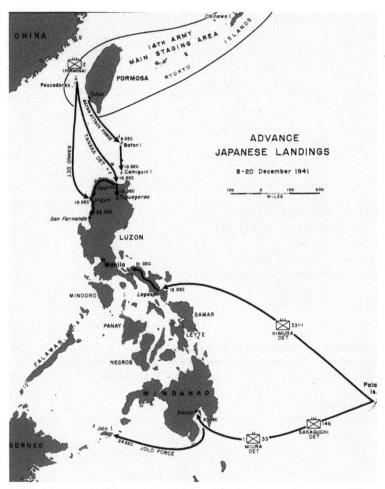

Japanese invasion of the Philippines. The 14th Army landed simultaneously at Aparri and Vigan on 10 December 1941.

Introduction

With his parting words "I shall return," General Douglas MacArthur sealed the fate of the last American forces on Bataan. Yet amongst the chaos and devastation of the American defeat, Army Captain Russell W. Volckmann refused to lay down his arms. Rather than surrender, Volckmann disappeared into the jungles of North Luzon and raised a guerrilla army of over 22,000 men. For the next three years, he led a guerrilla war against the Japanese, killing over 50,000 enemy soldiers. During the interim, he established radio contact with MacArthur's Headquarters in Australia and directed the Allied forces to key enemy positions. Officially designated the *United States Armed Forces in the Philippines—North Luzon* (USAFIP-NL), Volckmann's guerrilla unit decimated the Japanese Fourteenth Army. When General Tomiyuki Yamashita—the commander of the Japanese occupation force—finally surrendered, he made the initial surrender overtures not to MacArthur, but to Volckmann.

Volckmann was also the first to develop the Army's official doctrine of counterinsurgency and to articulate the need for a permanent force capable of unconventional warfare. His diligence in this regard led to the creation of the Army Special Forces. Surprisingly, Volckmann has not received credit for either of these accomplishments. Despite this man's contributions, he remains virtually forgotten by history.

This book seeks to establish two premises. First, it explores how Volckmann's leadership was critical to the outcome of the Philippines Campaign. Had it not been for Volckmann, the Allies would not have received the intelligence necessary to launch an effective counterstrike. Had he not funneled his intelligence reports to MacArthur and coordinated an Allied assault on the Japanese enclaves, the Americans would have gone in "blind"—reducing their efforts to a trial-and-error campaign that would have undoubtedly cost more lives, materiel, and potentially stalled the pace of the entire Pacific War.

Second, this book establishes Volckmann as the progenitor of modern counterinsurgency doctrine and the true "Father of Army Special Forces".*

---

*A title history has erroneously awarded to Colonel Aaron Bank, an Army officer and a former operative in the Office of Strategic Services (OSS).

Volckmann was the principal author of two Army field manuals: FM 31–20, *Operations Against Guerrilla Forces* and FM 3121, *Organization and Conduct of Guerrilla Warfare.* Together, these manuals became the Army's first complimentary reference set outlining the precepts for special warfare and counterguerrilla operations. Simultaneously, Volckmann outlined the operational concepts for Army Special Forces. At a time when U.S. military doctrine was conventional in its outlook, Volckmann marketed the idea of guerilla warfare as a critical and strategic force multiplier for any future conflict. In doing so, he ultimately won the blessings of the Army Chief of Staff and secured the establishment of the Army's first special operations unit: the 10th Special Forces Group.

The story of Russell W. Volckmann commands a unique place within the military historiography of World War II. Military histories of the Philippine Campaign are told predominately within the context of conventional warfare. Several books have been written about MacArthur's triumphant return to the Philippines, the Army Rangers at Cabanatuan, U.S. Sixth Army operations on Luzon, and the Battle of Leyte Gulf. However, the guerrilla war remains largely forgotten. Aside from a few published memoirs, such as *Lapham's Raiders,* and official Army publications such as General Charles A. Willoughby's, *Guerrilla Resistance Movement in the Philippines,* the historiography of the guerrilla war in the Philippines is comparatively narrow. Survey texts on American military history often relegate the guerrilla conflict to only a paragraph or two.

Volckmann himself remains a shadowy figure throughout modern military history. The *Oxford Companion to American Military History* and *Oxford Companion to World War II* have no entries for either Volckmann or the USAFIP-NL. His name is absent from every major biography on MacArthur, and what little history there is on Volckmann is often incorrect or misleading.* Many books cite *Operations Against Guerrilla Forces* and *Organization and Conduct of Guerrilla Warfare,* but do not recognize Volckmann as the principal author. Because field manuals are considered "intellectual property" of the Army, their authors are not credited upon the manuals' release—although the Army does maintain a record of who writes them. For this reason, few know that Volckmann was the driving force behind FMs 31–20 and 31–21. In a dramatic military career that spanned over two decades, Russell Volckmann led one of the most successful guerrilla movements of all time and paved the way for the doctrines used by the Army Special Forces today.

Research for this project began in February 2007. When I made the decision to write a biography on Russell Volckmann, I understood that there would be a narrow selection of adequate secondary sources. As such, my book is composed almost entirely of primary source material.

---

*For example, there are two books that claim Volckmann was in the OSS. This is not true, however, as neither he nor any of his guerrillas ever fell under OSS jurisdiction.

The first step I took in obtaining primary source material was to contact the surviving members of the Volckmann family. My first reference to this end was the United States Military Academy's *Registry of Graduates and Former Cadets*. This is a directory of every West Point graduate from 1802 until the present day. Included with each graduate's entry is a paragraph that gives: (a) date of birth, (b) date of death (if applicable), (c) all active duty assignments, (d) time of separation or retirement, and (e) the graduate's last confirmed address. If a graduate is deceased, the *Registry* gives the names of any known next of kin.

From this, I discovered that Volckmann's eldest son, Russell Jr., also attended West Point. With his name and contact information in hand, I began the research process by conducting a series of interviews with Russell Volckmann, Jr. Aside from the wealth of information he gave me concerning his father's life and career, he informed me that the family had, in fact, retained many of Volckmann's personal effects. Directing me to his son, Christopher, and half-brother, William, he indicated that the family had kept Volckmann's personal papers, letters, and several newspaper clippings. The most important resource, however, was Volckmann's *war diary*. This well-written and thoroughly documented journal is a day-by-day account of his adventures in the Philippines from 8 December 1941 until 16 June 1944.

I then visited the National Archives II in College Park, Maryland. Arriving at Archives in August 2007, I located Record Groups 319, 389, 407, and 496. In doing so, I was pleased to find that there were over twenty boxes of information on Volckmann—including his leadership of USAFIP-NL, his work in creating the Special Forces, and his time as the Director of Special Operations in the U.S. European Command. Record Group 496 included several maps of North Luzon. However, these were drawn from the U.S. Sixth Army Records and, aside from listing Volckmann's guerrilla positions, did not offer anything in the way of battle plans or situation maps.

Continuing my research, I decided to reference the U.S. Army Military History Institute (MHI) at Carlisle Barracks, Pennsylvania. Under the heading of "The Russell W. Volckmann Papers," MHI had seven boxes of material relating strictly to his operations in the Philippines. These were in Volckmann's possession until his death in 1982. Shortly thereafter, the collection was donated by his widow, Helen. Included in this collection are official reports and situation maps of Volckmann's guerrilla units.

Possibly the most salient items in this collection were the *USAFIP-NL G-3 Operations Reports, USAFIP-NL G-2 Intelligence Reports, USAFIP-NL G-3 After-Battle Report,* and the USAFIP-NL radio logs. *USAFIP-NL G-3 Operations Reports* are a collection of all combat reports and records pertaining to actions against the enemy. The *AfterBattle Report*—prepared by General Headquarters, USAFIP-NL—reconstructs the different phases of Volckmann's guerrilla war by synthesizing the combat and intelligence reports. The radio logs contain some 385 radiograms sent to and from MacArthur in Australia. Collectively, these documents provide a valuable look into the thought process Volckmann undertook while contemplating the course of his guerrilla campaign.

Attempting to balance the perspectives of my primary source material, I referenced a handful of Japanese resources. At MHI, I recovered transcripts of interviews and sworn statements from the Japanese generals and colonels whom Volckmann confronted in the Philippines. Aside from General Yamashita, these officers included the likes of Colonel Sotomu Terau, Chief of Staff–19th Tora Division, Lieutenant General Fukutaro Nishiyama, Commander-23rd Division, and Lieutenant General Yutaka Marauka, Commander–103rd Division. Describing Volckmann as a constant thorn in their sides, these flag officers admittedly stumbled over their own frustrations in a vain attempt to shut down USAFIP-NL. These men confirmed the validity of the guerrillas' combat reports and acknowledged that Yamashita had placed a sizeable bounty on Volckmann's head.

Another valuable source came from the files of the Rand Corporation. In 1963, six years after his retirement from the U.S. Army, Volckmann participated in the Rand study panel to discuss the viability of close air support for contingency operations. From the Rand Corporation, I secured a transcript of the panel's proceedings. Volckmann used this opportunity to explain how ground-air operations were indispensable to unconventional warfare. The concepts he articulated on this panel soon found their way into the U.S. Army's air cavalry doctrine during Vietnam.

Finally, at Fort Bragg, North Carolina, I conducted research at the Special Operations Archives at the John F. Kennedy Special Warfare Center. While their archives are comparatively smaller than the ones I had visited previously, there was no lack of relevant material. The Special Operations Archives have one file on Volckmann that contains letters he wrote to the Archives—then known as the "History Office"—over a period of time spanning from 1969–1975 explaining his roles in the Philippines and creating the Special Forces. This file also includes some information about Volckmann's role in developing special operations units for the Eighth Army during the Korean War.

Other primary sources that I encountered included a handful of personal memoirs and Army publications available from the Army Museum System. These included: *We Remained* and *Guerrilla Days in North Luzon: A Brief Historical Narrative of a Brilliant Segment of the Resistance Movement during Enemy Occupation in the Philippines 1941–1945. Guerrilla Days* is an 80-page booklet published by USAFIP-NL Headquarters in 1946, and is the official Army document chronicling the rise of Volckmann's resistance movement. Less than 100 copies of this monograph are known to exist and the master copy rests at the First Division Museum in Fort Riley, Kansas. Memoirs include Robert Lapham's,

Lapham's Raiders, Ray Hunt's, *Behind Japanese Lines,* and other guerrillas who survived the war and have much to say about Volckmann.

After finishing the first round of archival research, I set out to find any of Volckmann's colleagues that were still living. Simply taking into account Volckmann's age—95 years old if he was still living in 2007—this part of my research did not promise to yield any significant information. At first, it appeared as though my apprehensions were correct: Volckmann's sister, Ruth Volckmann Stansbury, tragically passed away the same month that I began researching for this project; Volckmann's brother-in-law, John Stansbury, declined to be interviewed. Cross-referencing other names that Volckmann mentioned in his diary returned only a handful of obituaries. However, a significant lead developed during my research at MHI.

In the Philippines, Volckmann developed a close relationship with Captain (later Brigadier General) Donald D. "Don" Blackburn. Escaping from Bataan together, Blackburn became Volckmann's executive officer in USAFIP-NL and later commanded one of its regiments. I had never found anything significant concerning Blackburn until I came across a 400-page transcript of an interview conducted with him in 1983. As part of an oral history project, MHI commissioned Lieutenant Colonel Robert B. Smith, USAF, to conduct a series of interviews with Blackburn concerning his life and career. Not only did this interview corroborate the information I had previously gathered on Volckmann, it gave the names of Blackburn's immediate family members: his son, Donald Jr., and daughter, Susan. I decided to locate Blackburn's children through a public records search and, in the course of doing so, was shocked to learn that Blackburn himself was still alive and living in Sarasota, Florida.

Contacting the Blackburn family, I secured a visitation in March 2008. Unfortunately, Blackburn had been suffering from Alzheimer's, which diluted much of his memory. However, his daughter granted me access to all of his records. Comprising nearly two whole filing cabinets, Blackburn's collection included a wealth of photographs, letters, war trophies, USAFIP-NL reports, and official duplicates of government documents. I also learned that Blackburn himself kept a diary while in the Philippines. Although his diary started much earlier, it ended at approximately the same time that Volckmann's did. Blackburn tragically passed away on 24 May 2008, nearly two months to the day after completing my visit with him.

The secondary sources that I referenced for this project were largely for the sake of understanding the historical context in which Volckmann operated. Highlights include *The Fall of the Philippines* and *Triumph in the Philippines,* both published by the Army Center for Military History in 1953 and 1963, respectively. *The Fall of the Philippines* provides the background for the American defeat by tracing it to Washington's political neglect and the subsequent impact it had on the Philippines' combat readiness. It also provides a detailed look at the Japanese and American military operations from 8 December 1941 until the Fall of Corregidor. *Triumph in the Philippines* begins with the decision to retake the archipelago and recounts the American conquests of Luzon, Mindanao, and Cebu. Both books are told from a conventional warfare perspective.

Also included is *A Study in Command and Control: Special Operations in Korea, 1951–1953*. Written by Colonel Rod Paschall, it is another publication from the Army Center for Military History. The book does not mention Volckmann, although it makes several references to FM 31–21 as the nexus between the Army's disastrous *ad hoc* approach to special operations in Korea and the establishment of a permanent Special Forces command. Likewise, *Dark Moon: Eighth Army Special Operations in the Korean War* has no references to Volckmann, but tells of the *United Nations Partisan Forces in Korea* (UNPFK) and the Eighth Army's *Special Activities Group,* two organizations in which Volckmann played an integral part.

Other books include *Notes on Guerrilla Warfare: Principles and Practices* by Virgil Ney. Books in this genre do not normally mention Volckmann—if they do, it is only in passing—but provides analyses into the tactics, philosophies, and mentalities of guerrilla warfare.

In all, I have been mindful not to resort to hagiography. Although I believe Volckmann to be a forgotten hero and a tactical innovator, I do not pretend that he was infallible. An innovator of any kind is bound to make mistakes along the way. Many of my primary sources do not portray Volckmann in the most flattering light. Furthermore, none of these sources are without liability.

Volckmann's diary gives a unique first-person perspective and provides a glimpse into the mind of the man himself. Although Blackburn and Volckmann achieve remarkable consistency with their diaries, there are a few discrepancies. For instance, Blackburn recalled meeting certain individuals whom Volckmann never mentioned. In some instances, both men recall a particular incident but do not agree on the date that it occurred—for example Blackburn recalls an event happening on a Friday while Volckmann records the same event happening on a Wednesday. During their trek to North Luzon, both men constantly battled malaria, dysentery, and other tropical diseases. As a result, they may not have always been fully cognizant of their surroundings. Towards the end of Volckmann's diary, his entries become progressively shorter and farther apart. This may be because there was little action to record, but the reader will never know for certain.

Interviews, however, present a much different challenge. As with any subject that occurred long ago, one's memory can—and often does—distort and rearrange the facts surrounding what happened. With the exception of Don Blackburn—who was tragically losing his fight against Alzheimer's—all of the subjects whom I interviewed were of sound mind and recalled their facts about

Russell Volckmann in amazing detail. Furthermore, the recollections of these individuals did not greatly contradict one another.

I believe that the official documents, reports, sworn statements, and other items gleaned from the various archives are relatively safe from refutation. Collectively, these documents tend to corroborate one another—even on Volckmann's missteps and shortcomings as a leader. As mentioned previously, Japanese captives (including several Japanese flag officers) confirm the accuracy of USAFIP-NL operations reports. Radio logs of Volckmann's communication with MacArthur are not one sided. By this, the log-books do not solely contain outgoing messages—all incoming messages from MacArthur are documented as well. Duplicates of these messages are on file at the MacArthur Memorial Archives in Norfolk, Virginia. Furthermore, General Willoughby's aforementioned *Guerrilla Resistance Movement in the Philippines,* a nine-volume report published by MacArthur's Headquarters—Southwest Pacific Area, confirms the dates and times of Volckmann's contact with General MacArthur. Conclusively, I believe that the source material warrants the credibility to support this book's overall thesis.

I give special thanks to all members of the Volckmann family (Russell Jr., Russell III, Bill, Ted, Chris, and Helen) for their help and hospitality. Without their support, this book would never have been written. I also thank the courteous and attentive staff of the National Archives, the Military History Institute, the Special Operations Archive, and the Copyright Clearance Center for their assistance during my research. Finally, I would like to thank the editorial/production team at Casemate Publishers for their patience and professional support.

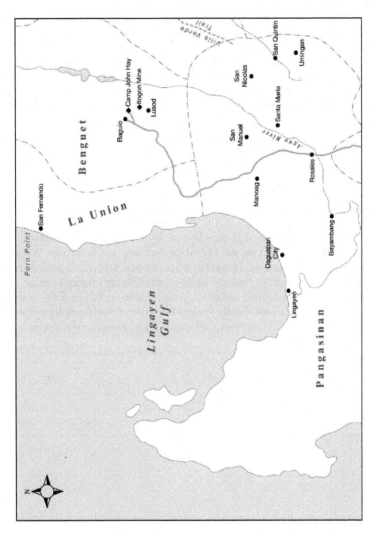

Map of Lingayen Gulf and the immediate vicinity on the western coast of Luzon. The Lingayen beach—from Dagupan City in the east, to the Agno River delta in the west—marks the site of the 11th Infantry's first defensive position.

CHAPTER I

The Road to Luzon

The military career of Russell William Volckmann began on 12 June 1934, the day he graduated from the United States Military Academy at West Point. Prior to his enrollment at the Academy, however, surprisingly little is known about Volckmann's early life. Born on 23 October 1911 in Clinton, Iowa, he was the eldest of three children born to William Volckmann and Hattie Mae Dodds. As the only son in the family, "Russ" enjoyed a childhood that was typical of most boys growing up in small-town Iowa. Boy Scout jamborees, competitive sports, and other vigorous activities punctuated the young Volckmann's life.[1]

From an early age, Russell Volckmann possessed a remarkable fascination with all things military. At the tender age of six, during World War I, he volunteered his services as the unofficial "mascot" for C Company, 133rd Infantry of the Iowa National Guard. C Company's wartime responsibility was to guard the town's bridges over the Mississippi River. Clad in a child-sized khaki uniform and brandishing a toy rifle, Volckmann was a regular sight around the Company Headquarters. With his imagination firing on all cylinders, the young lad would engage in epic battles against pretend foes and cheer wildly as he vanquished one enemy after another.[2]

Developing an appetite for military history, Volckmann spent considerable time reading about the United States Army and its heroic leaders throughout the years. Indeed, by the end of his grammar school career, the young Volckmann knew that he had found his calling. In the spring of 1926, he entered the Shattuck Military Academy—now Shattuck-St. Mary's—in Faribault, Minnesota, an all-boys military school well-steeped in the traditions of the Episcopal Church. Graduating from Shattuck in 1930, Volckmann wrote to Congressman Charles E. Swanson requesting a nomination to the United States Military Academy and entered West Point with the Class of 1934.[3]

Although he was an outstanding cadet at Shattuck, Volckmann did not repeat that same performance at West Point. Graduating 189th in a class of 250, he was a below average student—known more for his golfing and swimming prowess than his academic skills.[4] Despite his class standing, however, he was an excellent soldier. Physically strong and mentally tough, he was drawn to the "rough-and-tumble" world of the Infantry.

On graduation day, as a newly minted Infantry officer, Volckmann requested a duty assignment in the Philippine Islands.[5] A United States Commonwealth at the time, the Philippines offered the best of Army glamour. The tropical climate, expansive beaches, and Manila—the "Pearl of the Orient"—made it one of the most sought after assignments in the U.S. military. However, his class standing made him less competitive for such a popular assignment and he instead received orders to Fort Snelling, Minnesota, then home to the U.S. Army's 3rd Infantry Regiment. After completing his tour of duty as a rifle platoon leader and company executive officer at Fort Snelling, Volckmann attended the Infantry Officer Advanced Course at Fort Benning, Georgia, in the fall of 1937. Shortly thereafter, he received orders to Fort Sam Houston, Texas. Although his "dream assignment" still eluded him, "Fort Sam" proved to be just the stepping stone Volckmann needed.[6]

In the spring of 1940, after returning from field maneuvers with the 2nd Infantry Division—Fort Sam's tenant unit—Volckmann discovered that many of the junior officers in his regiment had received orders to Panama—another exotic outpost. Sensing an opportunity, Volckmann wrote a letter to the chief Adjutant General in Washington, D.C., asking for a reassignment to the Pacific. In doing so, he called attention to the fact that his name had been on the Philippine volunteer roster for the past six years.[7] One week later, Volckmann received his orders.

By the time of Volckmann's arrival, the Philippines Islands were in the midst of their transition to full sovereignty. With the ratification of the *Tydings-McDuffie Act* in 1935, the United States had authorized a ten-year timeline for Philippine independence. By the time of its ratification, however, *Tydings-McDuffie* was little more than a formality. For the past thirty years, the Philippines had enjoyed virtually limitless autonomy: Filipinos elected their own leaders, made their own laws in the Philippine Assembly, conducted free trade with other nations, and enjoyed the full protection of the United States military. Central to the *Tydings-McDuffie Act,* however, was a plan calling for the reorganization of the Philippine Islands' defense scheme.[8] Since becoming an American territory in 1898, defense of the archipelago had been the exclusive province of the U.S. War Department. Now, the Commonwealth Government of the Philippines had to confront the challenge of creating its own defense structure.[9]

The first legislative action taken by the Philippine Assembly in this regard was ratification of the *National Defense Act* (1935). It called for a standing army of 10,000 men and a reserve component of nearly 400,000—anticipated to reach full strength by the summer of 1946. The attendant problem, however, was finding and training adequate personnel. Aside from the Philippine Scouts and the Philippine Constabulary, the Commonwealth had no military tradition upon which to build a standing army. The Philippine Scouts were an American Army unit in which most of the enlisted men and junior officers were Filipino. This well-trained force of only 10,000 men was the closest thing the Philippines had to an indigenous fighting force. The Philippine Constabulary, established in 1901, was the national police force, but their training and organization had always been military in nature.[10]

Calling on Washington for assistance, Philippine President Manuel Quezon enlisted the help of General Douglas MacArthur, the U.S. Army Chief of Staff. Assuming the title "Military Advisor to the Commonwealth," MacArthur set out to create a Philippine Army. To fill the immediate need for officers, MacArthur and President Quezon drew personnel from the Philippine Scouts and the Constabulary. By the end of 1939, despite the enormity of the task and massive budgetary constraints from the U.S. Congress, the Philippine Army had swollen its ranks to 4,800 officers, 104,000 reservists, and developed a standardized curriculum for infantry, field artillery, and coastal defense artillery.[11] However, until Quezon's army could fulfill its projected end-strengths, the U.S. military would continue to shoulder the burden of the Philippines' defense.

American forces in the Philippines fell under the jurisdiction of the United States Armed Forces in the Far East (USAFFE). Commanded by an Army General, USAFFE encompassed all U.S. military assets in the Philippine archipelago.[12] This included American ground forces, the Far East Air Force, the Asiatic Fleet, and the semi-autonomous Philippine Army. USAFFE's mission was simple: continue providing combat-capable units for the Commonwealth's defense and assume responsibility for training the Philippine Army.[13]

Despite these mission parameters, however, USAFFE remained in a deplorable state of combat readiness. In the midst of their isolationist fervor, Congress reallocated defense dollars away from any area that was not considered to be an imminent theater of war. As a result, USAFFE perennially subsisted on less than half of the money and equipment it needed for an adequate defense of the Philippines.[14]

Meanwhile, twenty-nine-year-old Captain Russell Volckmann loaded his family—wife Nancy and their young son, Russell Jr.—aboard the USS *Grant* en route to the Philippine Islands. It was the summer of 1940, and it had been nearly seven years since he put his name on the volunteer roster for the Philippines. Fresh from his tour of duty at Fort Sam Houston, Volckmann welcomed his new assignment to the Pacific. Orders initially assigned him as the commander of H Company, 31st Infantry Regiment. The 31st Infantry was an American Army unit suffering under the same budgetary constraints that had plagued the U.S. military for years. Still, the men of H Company were comparatively better equipped than their counterparts in the Philippine Army.[15]

Volckmann commanded H Company for nearly a year. During this time, he and his men drilled under the Emergency War Plan, which called for H Company to perform extensive maneuvers throughout Southern Luzon. The exercises gave him an intimate knowledge of the southern landscape. Unfortunately, it was knowledge Volckmann would never use, for in July 1941, he was reassigned to a new position in the Philippine Army.

The opportunity that lay before him was one seldom given to a young captain. The Philippine Army desperately needed senior-level staff officers for its newly activated divisions. Normally, the Army gave these billets to Majors and Lieutenant Colonels, but there were simply not enough of these high-ranking officers available to meet the demands for the Philippine defense project.

At first, Volckmann had only a cursory understanding of what his new assignment entailed. He knew that the Philippine Army needed American officers for its higher echelons, and that this would likely be the norm until the Filipinos had sufficient training to take over the command structure. He also understood that Americans like himself would be the minority—all of the enlisted personnel and most of the company-grade officers would be Filipino. Finally, he had no indication where he would be assigned or what his new position might be.

At USAFFE Headquarters in Manila, Volckmann's new orders designated him the Executive Officer of the 11th Infantry Regiment, 11th Division (Philippine Army).* Traditionally, it was *unthinkable* for a captain with only seven years of service to become the Executive Officer for an entire regiment. However, the Army's newfound exigencies had broken down the traditional rank and meritocracy barrier.

Reporting for duty at Regimental Headquarters, however, Volckmann discovered that the Philippine Army was an "army" that existed only on paper. Many of the soldiers spoke little to no English, and their native dialects would often differ from company to company. The language barrier, however, was the least of the regiment's problems. Filipino officers and enlisted soldiers had virtually no knowledge of basic military skills. What little they did know was either wrong, obsolete, or had no practical use in battle. To make matters worse, they carried outdated weapons to which they had no spare parts or ammunition.** The Filipino solider knew little beyond the basics of close order drill and a few marching commands. And most of the officers were political appointees who, in many cases, had less training than the men they were expected to lead.[16]

The 11th Infantry's Table of Organization and Equipment (TO&E) called for a headquarters (HQ) battalion and three combat battalions. The HQ battalion

---

*An "Executive Officer" is the second in command of an Army unit. Volckmann's regiment was one of many that had been recently activated as part of the Philippine defense plan. A regiment normally consisted of two or three battalions, each containing four companies (a total strength of approximately 1,000 men).

**The line companies were equipped with the M1917 Enfield rifle—a mechanically complex and troublesome rifle absent from U.S. inventories since World War I.

United States Armed Forces—Far East (USAFFE)

Sector	Troop Assignment	
	U.S. Army	Philippine Army
North Luzon Force	Force HQ and HQ Co (US) 26th Cavalry (PS) One battalion, 45th Infantry (PS) Battery A, 23d FA (PS) Batteries B and C, 86th Field Artillery (PS) 66th Quartermaster Troop (PS)	11th Division 21st Division 31st Division 71st Division (used as directed by USAFFE)
South Luzon Force	Force HQ and HQ Co (US) HQ Battery, Battery A, 86th Field Artillery (PS)	41st Division 51st Division
Visayan-Mindanao Force	Force HQ and HQ Co (PS)	61st Division 81st Division 101st Division
Reserve Force	HQ Philippine Dept Philippine Division (less one battalion) 86th Field Artillery (PS) Far East Air Force	91st Division HQ, Philippine Army
Harbor Defenses	Headquarters 59th Coastal Artillery (US) 60th Coastal Artillery (AA) (US) 91st Coastal Artillery (PS) 92d Coastal Artillery (PS) 200th Coastal Artillery (US)	

Chart depicting all USAFFE land and air assets as well as the Philippine Army, 8 December 1941. *U.S. Army Center for Military History.*

consisted of an administrative company, medical company, and a heavy-weapons company. The three combat battalions each contained four companies: three 100-man rifle companies and one 96-man machine-gun company. The total strength of the Regiment came to 1,850 officers and men. Aside from his rifle, the Filipino soldier had little to carry. He was issued only one uniform, one pair of shoes, a cotton blanket, and a pith helmet. Other items, such as bayonets and entrenching tools—necessities by American standards—were unheard luxuries in the 11th Infantry. Even the officers had no access to these items.[17]

Volckmann, undaunted by the challenges that lay before him, scoured the countryside for interpreters and began teaching basic infantry tactics to his men.

Indeed, by the end of the summer, the soldiers of the 11th Infantry had mastered some basic commands in English and their tactical skills continued to grow. As the Filipinos celebrated their military benchmarks, however, the Japanese continued their march of conquest. In August 1941, as Japan tightened its grip over the Pacific, USAFFE evacuated all military dependents in the Philippines, including Volckmann's wife and son.* Per the Philippine Army Mobilization Plan, the 11th Infantry Regiment began building its primary defensive line along a five-mile stretch of coast on Lingayen Gulf.[18]

On 15 November 1941, Volckmann received a visit from General Douglas MacArthur, the newly appointed USAFFE commander.** MacArthur arrived at Lingayen early that morning to receive the Regiment's progress report. Volckmann politely voiced his concern over the unit's critical needs. The lack of adequate weapons, clothing, fire support, and transportation were among his chief complaints. The General appeared to appreciate the unit's handicap, but told Volckmann not to worry. Volckmann asked him, "Sir, how do you assess the situation? What are your plans?" MacArthur's response did not inspire him:

> "Well, I'll tell you Russ, I haven't got anything really on paper, yet. I've got it all in my mind, but we really don't have to worry about things at this point. The Japanese have a second-rate navy and about a fourth-rate army, and we don't have to worry about them until around July [1942], or in the summer months, during the dry period."[19]

On the merits, MacArthur's assessment made virtually no sense. The Japanese and their "fourth-rate army" had conquered Manchuria in less than six months. Furthermore, this "second-rate" navy that MacArthur spoke of had taken on—and defeated—the best of Czar Nicholas's fleet in the Russo-Japanese War of 1905. Whatever the basis for MacArthur's assessment, the Japanese were about to prove him wrong.

Before the General departed later that afternoon, he confirmed that the 11th's mission was to defend the five-mile stretch of coast along the Lingayen Gulf. For the final weeks of November, units of the 11th Infantry Regiment continued to drill and maneuver in the sweltering heat. Although it was no easy task, the indigenous soldiers of the 11th Infantry were coming together as a cohesive military unit. Finally, after three months of continuous training, Volckmann earned a three-day pass for Thanksgiving weekend.[20]

---

*Sending Nancy to her parent's home with Russell Jr. in tow, Volckmann promised to write to her as often as he could. The last letter that she received from him was dated March 1942, shortly before the surrender. It would be the last time Volckmann's family would hear from him until January 1945.

**MacArthur had retired in 1937 while serving as the military advisor to President Manuel Quezon. However, in July 1941, President Roosevelt recalled him to active duty and appointed him commander of all U.S. forces in the Philippines.

Relaxing at the officer's club in Baguio, however, Volckmann's weekend was cut short by an urgent phone call from General William Brougher, the 11th Division's commander. According to Brougher, every unit in the Philippines had been put on high alert and all weekend passes had been cancelled. Volckmann was ordered to return to his regiment that same day. With his weekend spoiled and not knowing why the alert had been called, Volckmann hastened himself back to Lingayen Gulf. Upon his arrival, he found no further news from either the Regimental or Division Headquarters.[21] Could this have been just another drill?

The Army was quite fond of conducting these "drills," and Murphy's Law stipulated that an officer's weekend pass always coincided with one. However, the following morning, on Monday, 1 December, Volckmann learned that USAFFE Intelligence had detected a large Japanese naval convoy entering the South China Sea.[22] Volckmann hoped that the alert would pass without incident. Perhaps the Imperial Japanese Navy was on its way to Borneo…or Indochina.

CHAPTER 2

Rising Sun

Arriving at Regimental Headquarters on the morning of 8 December, Volckmann received word that Pearl Harbor had been bombed. By now, it was no surprise that war had finally come, but no one had anticipated a first strike on Hawaii. Volckmann himself could hardly believe it. Why would the Japanese attack Hawaii—over 4,000 nautical miles from Tokyo—when the Philippines were closer and presented a much easier target? Suddenly, it dawned on him: *the entire Pacific Fleet was anchored at Pearl.* Fearing the worst, he knew that the Japanese would terrorize the Pacific if unchecked by the U.S. Navy.[23]

At 8:20 a.m., a mechanical murmur descended over the Regimental Staff Office. Barely audible at first, it grew steadily into a roar that rattled books from their shelves and sent wall clocks crashing to the floor. There was no mistaking that sound: the Japanese had arrived. Running outside, Volckmann stood agape as he counted 60 Japanese bombers thundering overhead. Bypassing Regimental Headquarters, the warplanes continued their flight pattern southward over the horizon. Ten minutes later, the first of their bombs fell on the airfield at Camp John Hay.[24]

The war had begun.

Minutes after the final bomber disappeared from view, the 11th Infantry received orders to occupy their five-mile stretch of coast along Lingayen Gulf. Five miles long and 150 yards wide, this area was larger than what a regiment could feasibly defend. All along the beach, enormous gaps dotted the defensive line. Although ammunition was no longer a problem, the regiment still lacked engineer tools. Thus, to build their defensive enclaves, Volckmann dispatched several parties into Dagupan and the surrounding communities to borrow any civilian equipment available. Items including saws, shovels, garden hoes, and pick axes were used to construct their redoubts. For lack of better building materials, the 11th Infantry made their shelters and pillboxes from wet sand and palm trees.[25]

Volckmann was surprised by the men's newfound sense of urgency. In fact, he had never before seen them work so efficiently. No longer did they have to be encouraged to dig their foxholes and trenches to the appropriate depths—the impending invasion was enough to motivate them. For the next three days, every man on the line worked beyond exhaustion. Occupying the beach with nothing larger than a .50 caliber machine gun, however, Volckmann knew that the odds were not in their favor.

Certainly, they could inflict *some* damage on the Japanese, but Volckmann knew that his men would eventually be overrun. In the best-case scenario, the regiment would have to face only a handful of landing craft and a few Japanese marines. At worst, however, they could be facing an entire naval detachment. A naval task force could take on any composition, but was sure to have at least two gunships, multiple landing craft, and close air support. Whatever the odds may have been, Volckmann worried more for his troops than for himself.

On 10 December, the first elements of the Japanese Fourteenth Army landed near Aparri on the northern coast of Luzon. Simultaneously, another contingent landed at Vigan on the western coast, only 50 miles north of Volckmann's sector. As the Japanese drew nearer to the Lingayen beach, Colonel Townsend, the Regimental Commander, was suddenly relieved of duty and reassigned to a "special mission" in Cagayan Valley. Volckmann never knew the details of this reassignment, but to relieve Townsend now made almost no sense; Townsend was a competent commander and he had certainly done nothing to warrant a punitive reassignment. Upon his departure, he announced that instead of receiving a new commander, he was relinquishing command to Volckmann. As a captain with only seven years experience, Volckmann was now in command of an entire regiment. He felt prepared for the job but wondered why USAFFE had reassigned Townsend so quickly. Ultimately, he feared that the 11th Infantry had been designated a "sacrifice outfit" and that USAFFE would not risk the life of a colonel in such a unit.[26]

As the enemy closed in on Central Luzon, Division Headquarters (HQ) sounded retreat for all regiments in the Lingayen Gulf area. Meanwhile, General MacArthur defaulted on the infamous "Orange Plan," and called for all ground units to make their way towards Bataan.* On Christmas Eve 1941, the 11th Infantry withdrew from the Lingayen beach. Around midnight on Christmas Day, the regiment crossed the Agno River at Bayambang. In his diary, Volckmann recounts an incident that he describes as the bane of every military commander. Before crossing the river, heavy machine gun fire ripped through the silence of the night:

> Seconds after the machine gun firing, which came from the direction of the river, a wave of terrified officers and men (my regiment) were running away from the river. I drew my 45 cal. revolver and yelled to every American officer within hearing to drive every officer and man back to the riverbank. After a

*The Orange Plan was the "doomsday scenario" for an invasion of the Philippines. It called for a last stand on the Bataan Peninsula.

hectic time of what seemed to be hours, we managed to get the entire regiment back into positions along the river. I then found a bugler and ordered "Officers Call" sounded. When all the officers were assembled, I told them that was the first and last time that officers and men of the regiment would retreat without orders. I further made it clear that if ever again I saw an officer running to the rear or failing to do his utmost to stop his men from retreating without orders, I would shoot him on the spot.[27]

Volckmann later found out that the machine gun fire belonged to a trigger-happy American tank crewman.

On 26 December, the Japanese hit the Agno River to the east and west of the regiment's assembly area. With the Japanese now only one day behind him, he knew that time was running out. Although his natural instinct was to turn and fight the Japanese head-on, common sense told him otherwise: he had no idea what sized unit was behind him. At any rate, the Japanese were bound to have artillery support—a luxury he no longer had.

The following day, Division HQ sent word that the regiment was to abandon all heavy weapons and continue southward to a rendezvous point at Paniqui.[28] *Volckmann was livid.* His men had been suffering from supply issues since the day the unit was activated—there was *no way* he was giving up any of their equipment now. They hadn't even traded fire with the Japanese yet. True, his regiment may have been outgunned, but Volckmann knew better than to continue his retreat while combat ineffective.

Fuming over the Division's latest order, he spied a railroad track running north and south through his position. Suddenly, Volckmann had an idea: if the regiment could not carry out the heavy equipment, then a locomotive certainly could. Pleading with HQ, he secured a steam engine with seven boxcars to come in under the cover of night. Arriving shortly before midnight, every square inch of railcar was loaded to capacity. What could not fit on the train was loaded onto the regimental trucks.[29]

At daybreak, the entire regiment arrived at Paniqui where they rejoined the rest of the IIth Division. Ironically, it was here that Volckmann discovered just how lucky his regiment had been. Of the four regiments that comprised the IIth Division, his was the only one still intact.[30] The remaining three, while still functional, had already taken a tremendous beating.

On 28 December, the Division settled into a defensive line astride Highway 13. Extending from the town of La Paz in the west to Zaragoza in the east, Volckmann's sector lay over a three-mile stretch of road. Volckmann received orders from Division HQ to "hold a line north of the La Paz—Carmen—Zaragoza road *until you are licked*" (emphasis added).[31] The adjacent units operating with Volckmann on the line were the 21st Division, which was situated west on Highway 3, and the 91st Division (Philippine Army), that was to the east covering Highway 5 and the Carmen-Cabanatuan sector of Highway 13.

The terrain on which the 11th Infantry found itself was far from ideal. Almost the entire area surrounding La Paz and Zaragoza consisted of rice paddies that had been drained from the previous harvest. Aside from the intermittent bamboo groves, the regiment had no other means of concealment. The main approaches to Volckmann's area came from the north: one road from Victoria to La Paz, another from Carmen to Cabanatuan. The regiment's second battalion covered the Victoria-La Paz route while the third battalion was detached to the 91st Division to cover the area around Carmen and Zaragoza. The first battalion was held in reserve at Barrio Caut, just south of La Paz. This configuration seemed ideal for the time being: the regiment occupied an area that would not overstretch its manpower and there were two whole divisions on either side of it. The other regiments of the 11th Division took up defenses elsewhere in the area.

Volckmann was convinced that the Japanese's most likely avenue of approach would be the road from Carmen. General Brougher, the 11th Division commander, met with Volckmann on the evening of the 30th. After inspecting the regimental defenses, Brougher confirmed that the 91st Division was responsible for the Carmen-Cabanatuan road. Before leaving, the General made it clear that the regiment was to "hold the line at all costs."[32] After a brief meeting with his battalion commanders, Volckmann determined that everything was in good order and turned in for some rest. But what he awakened to the next morning infuriated him.

At daybreak, Volckmann was startled awake by the sound of heavy machine gun fire. What startled him even more was that it sounded so close. Jumping to his feet, it sounded as though his 3rd battalion had made enemy contact around Carmen-Zaragoza. Because 3rd battalion had no wire or radio communications, Volckmann hopped in his command car and drove to their sector. En route, Volckmann wondered why 3rd battalion would be engaged in such heavy fighting. His prediction that the enemy would arrive on the Carmen-Cabanatuan road proved correct, but the 91st Division was to assume the brunt of the assault. From what he could deduce, it sounded as though 3rd battalion was fighting alone. Upon arriving at the battalion command post, he found that the battalion was indeed alone. The 91st Division had withdrawn earlier in the night *without informing anyone.* Volckmann's 3rd battalion had been attached to the 91st Division and yet no one, not even a runner, had been sent to inform them of the move. By the looks of the situation, Volckmann determined that the 91st Division's absence had allowed the Japanese to move farther south, bypass Cabantuan, and hook around to catch 3rd battalion in the rear.[33]

Volckmann scrambled to get reinforcements to the beleaguered 3rd battalion, but Companies A and L were completely cut off and all attempts to make contact with them had failed. The 1st battalion, still in reserve at Barrio Caut, was ordered to launch a counterattack but was decimated by heavy Japanese fire before it could make any progress. To make matters worse, the Carmen-Zaragoza

Bridge had been blown up amidst the confusion, thus denying the battalion its primary escape route. To stem the tide of confusion, Volckmann ordered what remained of 3rd battalion to form a defensive firing line on the bank of the La Paz River. This would provide at least some protection for the regiment's only remaining withdrawal route.[34]

Volckmann's entry for 31 December records the battle in exquisite detail:

> A tank platoon in my area, but not under my command, withdrew and . . . ordered the engineers to destroy the [Carmen-Zaragoza] Bridge. This prevented me from moving my reserve by motor [trucks] to counterattack the Japs in an effort to save Companies A and L. I ordered a platoon of the reserve to move by motors to the bridge east of Zaragoza with instructions to repair the bridge.
>
> As my men began repairing the bridge from one end, the Japs began repairing it from the other end. Giving this idea up, I returned to the west side of Zaragoza where I met Capt. Robinson with one company of the 1st battalion. After giving him the situation, I directed him to counterattack in the direction of Carmen [east]. A lieutenant, with his platoon of tanks, was parked along the road. I asked him if he was interested in joining the 1st battalion in a counterattack. He agreed to join.
>
> I was standing up on the front seat of a Bren Carrier [small utility vehicle similar to a tank] looking down the narrow road toward Zaragoza, watching the progress of the 1st battalion counterattack when I noticed some men dash across the road about 150 yards up. I assumed they were our men but, a few seconds later, my Bren Carrier was plastered with machine gun fire. Automatically, I dropped down into the seat of the Carrier and, at the same instant, my rear gunner opened up with his machine gun. The muzzle of the gun was only inches from my ear and I thought my eardrum had been broken. As soon as the Jap machine gun opened up on us, the tank lieutenant scrambled into his tank. He had no more than shut the turret when a Jap anti-tank gun put a round into the tank...the turret flew open and the lieutenant jumped to ground. The next Jap anti-tank round took the lieutenant's leg off.
>
> Seeing there was no time to organize the counterattack from this point, I ordered K Company [third battalion] to withdraw to the west bank of the Zaragoza River and take up a defensive position astride the road facing east. I then drove the Bren Carrier down the narrow causeway, zigzagging as much as possible in hopes that the Jap antitank gun would miss. The Japs tried hard, but luck was with me—I made [it to the] La Paz [River]...[35]

While organizing the new defensive line, Volckmann's position was suddenly hit by artillery fire. Terrified, he found himself diving for cover into the nearest ditch. As he lay in the muddy wallow, he witnessed the shell bursts flying overhead. Fiery shrapnel landed only inches away from his body—truly a horrific sight. Hugging the ground, his bones rattled with every thunderous explosion as shell after shell pounded the banks of the La Paz River.[36] With every fire adjustment, the rounds inched closer and closer. When it appeared as though the next barrage would blast him from his hole, he poised himself to make a run for it. But just then, the firing stopped. Volckmann could not figure out why, but he had no time to sit and wonder; he had to get his men out of there.

In addition to the artillery nuisance, the 11th Infantry had to contend with an increasing number of enemy dive-bombers. While taking cover from another artillery salvo, he received orders to withdraw to Concepcion. Volckmann acknowledged the order, but knew better than to withdraw right now, for it was still daylight. Any movements now would expose what remained of his regiment to the Japanese aerial patrols. He was certain that if General Brougher were aware of the circumstances, he would agree on a nighttime withdrawal.

Despite uneven odds, the regiment held the lines and inflicted heavy losses on the Japanese trying to cross the La Paz River. At nightfall, the 11th Infantry broke contact and moved out of La Paz toward Concepcion. In the last 24 hours, Volckmann had lost over 300 of his men. Yet, in spite of his tragic losses, he was proud that his regiment had fought valiantly under so many handicaps. By this time, most of the men were without shoes. The uniforms they had been issued the previous summer were tattered and torn, some to the point where they were no longer wearable. Their rifles were only marginally better. More than 500 had broken extractors, forcing those rifleman to use bamboo rods to push out the expended cartridges. The process was time-consuming but necessary considering that the regiment had no spare parts.[37]

Over the following week, the 11th Infantry continued its withdrawal towards Bataan. On New Year's Day 1942, Volckmann ushered in the New Year by ambushing two Japanese columns. While occupying their next defensive position on Mt. Arayat, the first column of Japanese troops came through the adjacent road at about 4:30 in the afternoon. Because they had no forward security elements ahead of their column, the Japanese obviously did not expect to find any resistance around Mt. Arayat. The machine gun teams Volckmann had placed at choke points in the road destroyed the Japanese column in short order. A few minutes later, another column came into the regiment's sector, this time along a railroad track. These troops, too, had no security elements. Just as they had done with the previous column minutes before, the 11th Infantry cut them down in a blaze of gunfire.

By 2 January 1942, the 11th had moved into the town of Guagua. Volckmann was ordered to make this his next defensive enclave. After conducting a reconnaissance of the area and issuing orders to battalion commanders, he began planning for the next withdrawal. It was to be his routine for the rest of the campaign: withdraw, defend a predetermined area, trade fire with the enemy, break contact, and withdraw again—at least until he reached Bataan.

While planning for his next withdrawal, Volckmann was greeted by yet another artillery barrage. Like before, these were 75mm guns but now the shelling continued for over half an hour. As he dove into the nearest ditch, he could not fathom how the Japanese had found him so quickly. After the firing stopped, he discovered that his command post lay right in the middle of three Japanese howitzer batteries conducting coordinated counterbattery fire with one another. Without a moment's delay, he relocated the entire regiment.[38]

The following day, Colonel Townsend rejoined the 11th once again as their commander. His reunion with the regiment was crowned by a heavy Japanese assault—this time with tanks. The armored thrust broke through the 13th Infantry on Volckmann's right flank, and in the process managed to cut off the 11th's main escape route. The regiment had been cut off before, but now they were running from Japanese armor. With Townsend back in command, he ordered Volckmann to find a secondary route under the cover of darkness. Volckmann found a suitable route, but it took the regiment into another position that would not be tenable for long.[39]

At daybreak on 4 January, the regiment hastily dug-in along Highway 7 at Kilometer Post 190 just south of Guagua.[40] For the moment, they had outrun the Japanese ground forces. What they could not outrun, however, were the Zeroes. Throughout the day, dive-bombers pounded the 11th Infantry. Increasingly frustrated by these three-dimensional beatings, Volckmann ordered them to break contact and withdraw under the cover of darkness. This time however, the withdrawal was a welcome change. Instead of being ordered into another defensive position, the 11th was taken off the line and assembled into a rest area.

By now, the men—Filipino and American—looked visibly different. Those who were still alive had been emaciated by only one month of war. Volckmann described them as having drawn and almost ghastly faces. The long periods of sleeplessness, intense combat, and minimal food rations had further diminished their collective health. Several others began showing symptoms of malaria and scarlet fever. For what it was worth, Volckmann still had his health, but his appearance was no better than that of his men. The challenges placed on this young, 30-year-old captain were taking their toll. He had no signs of tropical disease but had already lost several pounds, and had been badly bruised by the tactical environment. Whatever the condition of his body, it was hardly of any importance to him now—the 11th Infantry had arrived in Bataan. This was pleasing, as the defensive lines were now on terrain favorable to the Americans. By the same token, however, Volckmann knew that they had nowhere else to go. Bataan and Corregidor were the end of the line.

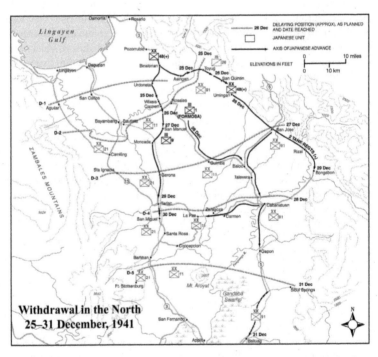

USAFFE's retreat in North Luzon. The 11th Infantry's withdrawal from Lingayen Beach can be traced roughly along Highway 13. La Paz, Carmen, and Zaragoza are visible from the map. This area marks the site of one of the 11th Infantry's deadliest battles.

CHAPTER 3

The Great Escape

Four days in the rest area saw the men beginning to look like their old selves. Smiles and laughter made their way through the ranks, but it would soon be over. The following day, the regiment received orders to occupy a defensive sector along Manila Bay. Though uneventful on the ground, their sector received plenty of bombardment from the air. With the Far East Air Force all but destroyed, Japanese bombers had become a regular nuisance.[41]

During this time, Volckmann recounted a visit he made to the 31st Infantry, where he had been a company commander upon his arrival in the Philippines. It was here that he realized just how miserable his current troops in the 11th Infantry looked by comparison. The men of H Company—whom he had commanded only a few months earlier—looked clean and crisp. The 31st Infantry had not been idle—they were covering the American retreat—but seeing the comparative state of the troops, there was no mistaking that the 11th had received the harsher beating.[42]

On 12 January, General MacArthur convened a meeting of the Division commanders and senior staff, the purpose of which was to assure the impending arrival of reinforcements.[43] MacArthur promised that hundreds and even thousands of troops were on their way. It sounded like great news, but Volckmann recalled his meeting with the General from two months earlier: MacArthur assured him that the Japanese could not possibly strike *until summer 1942.* Then again, he asked himself, "Who was I to question the General?"[44]

Nevertheless, Volckmann tried to remain optimistic. Now that the bulk of American forces were consolidated around Bataan, he was confident that tight communication and common sense would prevail.

Sadly, it was not to be.

On 25 January, he learned that the entire 11th Division would be reassigned further west to the vicinity of Pilar-Bagac. This gave him no worries until he discovered the area where Division wanted to place his regiment. Traveling with a Division staff officer to a point on Trail 7, 2.5 kilometers off the main Pilar-Bagac road, Volckmann learned that his defensive line was to cover over

2,500 yards, or about 1.5 miles. While the distance was not unmanageable for a regiment to defend, the foliage was so thick that Volckmann could barely see ten yards in either direction. Any attempts to cut through the jungle were useless—the foliage was too dense.[45]

How, he wondered, was he supposed to build a defensive line through *this?*

Nevertheless, Volckmann found clearings suitable for his battalions. In his diary, Volckmann documents his frustration with the terrain: although the three battalions now had defensive positions, they were separated by thick patches of jungle. This made them highly susceptible to being cut off and surrounded. What concerned him the most, however, was 3rd battalion.

Per Division orders, he sent them to the Outpost Line of Resistance—over two kilometers away from the main line. Volckmann knew that the order was unwise, and he hated it. The jungle had already separated the elements of his main line. Now, he was expected to send an entire battalion over two kilometers away where—separated by distance *and* heavy foliage—their chances of being cut off suddenly multiplied.

Three days after establishing his new position, Volckmann was on his way to Regimental Headquarters when he ran into elements of the 45th Infantry Regiment (Philippine Scouts) moving off the line. Because they had been assigned to guard the 11th Infantry's left flank, Volckmann wanted to know where they were going. He stopped one of the officers and learned that the 45th had been reassigned to the I Corps reserve farther south. Normally, Volckmann would have taken no issue over the matter, but there was no unit assigned to take the 45th Infantry's place.[46] *This meant that a large sector of the main line was wide open.* Aghast, Volckmann reported the vulnerable flank to Division Headquarters. USAFFE sent the 1st Division, Philippine Army, to replace the departed 45th, but it did not arrive for another two days.[47]

On 30 and 31 January, the Japanese began attacking the Outpost Line of Resistance. Throughout the assault, the outpost units—including Volckmann's 3rd battalion—were driven back into the main line. Meanwhile, Headquarters rejected every appeal Volckmann made to authorize relocation for 3rd battalion. This made Volckmann cringe, as he knew there was nothing more he could do for his outstretched defenders. Even more disheartening was that one of the platoons in 3rd battalion had been captured. Volckmann described the Japanese interrogation techniques with horror and disgust:

> The men were tied to trees and subjected to a session of questioning in a manner in which the Japs were most proficient. Their questions centered on the main battle position, about which our third battalion men had no knowledge, for they had never been on the main battle position. Each question that brought an unsatisfactory reply was followed by a bayonet jab. The Japs finally left all of our men for dead, but some hours later one of our men came to and managed to crawl through the jungle to our lines. He had eleven bayonet wounds to confirm his story.[48]

Finally, on 1 February, the Japanese broke through the main line. For the next 21 days, the 11th and 45th Infantry Regiments, as well as elements from the 91st Division, battled a single Japanese regiment. Although the American-Philippine units had numerical superiority—two of their regiments versus only one of the Japanese—their firepower was inferior. At one point during the battle, the Japanese overran another one of Volckmann's platoons, this time in 2nd battalion. The break created a small pocket in the main line that stood until heavy fighting finally forced the enemy to withdraw.[49] Although they had taken a tremendous beating, the soldiers of the 11th Division could now breathe easier knowing that the Bataan Line had been restored.

By the first of March, the Japanese assault had died down. March was relatively quiet, but the combat of the previous month had taken a heavy toll on the 11th Infantry. By now, they were feeding off plants and animals. Aside from their nourishment, the lack of adequate food affected their performance. Everyone on the line suffered, including Volckmann. Now, only a few hours' work in the tropical heat could turn an otherwise capable soldier into a casualty. Plus, disease within the ranks—a persistent problem even before Bataan—created more gaps in the defensive line.

In recognition of his leadership with the 11th Infantry, Volckmann received a promotion to major. The promotion, however, brought with it another reassignment, this time as the 11th Division's Intelligence Officer. Though unhappy to leave his regiment, the job brought with it more news about the current state of USAFFE ground forces. Unfortunately, none of the reports were encouraging.

Within a week of his new assignment, Volckmann received word that the Japanese had overrun II Corps' main line units. The worst news, however, arrived on the evening of 8 April: the II Corps commander, General Edward King, had surrendered. This meant that the Japanese would be at the 11th Division Command Post *in a matter of hours.* Shortly thereafter, General Brougher ordered the first white flags to be raised.[50]

By now, Volckmann was incredulous. He felt as though all his hard work, and the blood and suffering of his men, had been for nothing. He wondered if "Uncle Sam" expected him to spend the rest of the war in a prison camp—assuming that the Japanese were even taking prisoners. While perusing the possibilities of his fate, he remembered the soldier from 3rd battalion who had crawled back to the main line with eleven bayonet wounds.

Volckmann tried to solicit the idea of escaping and evading the enemy. As Division Intelligence Officer, he had found a glimmer of hope in a report concerning the whereabouts of Colonel John P. Horan, commander of the 43rd Infantry Regiment (Philippine Scouts). While Volckmann had begun his retreat from Lingayen Gulf, Horan found himself in a desperate struggle to impede the Japanese onslaught. As it were, the Japanese expeditionary force that landed at Vigan had cut off USAFFE retreat at La Union Province. What ensued was nearly a total route of the American-Philippine forces, although some units managed to withdraw to the city of Baguio. There, they consolidated under Horan's leadership.[51]

Prematurely, Horan declared Baguio an open city and ordered all remaining units in the vicinity to push southeast toward Balete Pass. Horan had hoped to make Balete Pass a rally point for other USAFFE outfits in Central Luzon, but the Japanese had already occupied the surrounding area. Upon hearing this news, Horan disbanded his *ad hoc* force and withdrew southward into the Zambales Mountains. As the main battle lines continued to move south, the units that Horan had consolidated at Baguio dissolved into the jungle. For the time being, many chose to remain dormant—biding their time against the Japanese. Others, for as long as their supplies and ammunition held out, continued to fight against the enemy's rear echelons.

The latest intelligence reports indicated that Horan was leading a small group of raiders operating somewhere in the northern Zambales Mountains. Volckmann had no intention of joining Horan, but took a keen interest in the units that Horan had left behind at Baguio. Reviewing the intelligence data, Volckmann determined that there were four regiments still in the area.[52] Furthermore, Baguio and Balete Pass were firmly situated in Mountain Province, the largest province in the northern cordilleras and a purported hotbed of American support. The game may have been over on Bataan, he reasoned, but if Volckmann and a few others could escape farther north, they could easily regroup and consolidate with what remained of Horan's old outfit.

General Brougher unenthusiastically told Volckmann that he could do so if he insisted, but Volckmann's fellow officers were even less receptive. They treated him as if he were either overzealous or crazy. "Why try?" they replied. "The Japs will treat us okay."[53] Even if he did run, they were certain that the endless network of spies and informants would eventually intercept him.

Nevertheless, Volckmann told himself that he would rather die fighting than take his chances with the Japanese. He had seen the atrocities of which the Japanese were capable—not only against his own men, but in the headlines chronicling the invasion of Manchuria. However, despite the overall lack of enthusiasm among his peers, he found an ally in Captain Donald "Don" Blackburn.[54]

Since joining the 11th Division in Central Luzon, Blackburn had been the Division Signal Officer. Over the past few months, he and Volckmann had become close friends and often traded combat stories with each other. After listening to the idea of joining Horan's old units, Blackburn cast his lot with Volckmann. Blackburn later recalled the importance of Volckmann's decision to escape this area of North Luzon:

The sparsely inhabited Cordilleras were sandwiched between the narrow Ilocos coastal lowlands bordering the China Sea on the west and the Cagayan Valley on the east. To the south lay the Central Plain. Five principal Igorot tribes inhabited the area—the Benguets, Ifugaos, Bontocs, Kalingas, and Apayaos, whose respectively named subprovinces comprised the larger Mountain Province. The Igorots of this relatively inaccessible and invigorating region had benefited from the early American administrators and missionaries, and their gratitude was evidenced in their kindly [sic] attitude toward Americans. We knew the territory and approached it with confidence in the security and support that it would provide.[55]

It was difficult for the two to make any detailed plans because they did not yet know how the surrender would be constructed. What they did know, however, was that when the opportunity arose, they would escape to the north.

That opportunity arrived on 9 April 1942—the day of the official surrender. By now, all remaining USAFFE units had displayed white flags at their posts. Although recognized as the universal symbol for surrender, the Japanese ignored them. Firing like madmen, they burst through the American-Philippine lines. The previous day, Volckmann and Blackburn had located a northward stream and determined that it would be their best escape route. With the fury of the Japanese only seconds away, both men rolled into the streambed and slowly crawled away from the Division Command Post. Within a few moments, they escaped undetected, concealed by the heavy undergrowth of the jungle. Crawling on their bellies, the pair slowly inched their way out of the Bataan peninsula.[56]

At a snail's pace, they crept through the night. Volckmann stated that "minutes seemed like hours" and indeed, after hours of crawling, both men were exhausted with scrapes and bruises from the rocks in the streambed.[57] The two fell asleep for a few hours but were suddenly awakened by the sound of voices. Volckmann motioned for Blackburn to keep quiet as he strained his ear to determine who stood on the bank of the streambed. Luckily, the voices were not Japanese.

Moving in about 20 yards beyond the streambed, he and Blackburn encountered an American with four Filipino soldiers. The American identified himself as Lieutenant Whiteman. Volckmann invited the young lieutenant into his group, but the four Filipinos insisted that they join as well. Volckmann wanted to keep his traveling party small, but seeing how passionate these Filipinos were to fight the Japanese, he agreed to let them come along.[58]

As the sun rose, Volckmann and his new friends departed for North Luzon. With the enemy behind him and traveling in the opposite direction, Volckmann now had to worry about the garrisons and patrol networks that the Japanese had left behind. However, the Imperial Japanese Army was not the only hazard that lay before him.

Volckmann already knew that several towns unwittingly harbored Japanese spies. Operating under the guise of merchants or traveling businessmen, the so-called "fifth column" had spent considerable time taking photographs and making maps for the Japanese before they arrived. These same spies were no doubt still lingering in the area and likely to be on the lookout for any displaced Americans. Roaming bandits were also a frequent problem. Consisting mostly of petty thugs and other small-time criminals, these bandits often traveled in groups of five. Brandishing pistols, high-powered shotguns, and Bolo knives, they would prey on whatever opportunistic targets they could find—American, Filipino, or Japanese.[59]

Before his escape from Bataan, Volckmann also received a stern warning from General Brougher: if he insisted on escape, there would be no way to reach North Luzon without crossing the Central Plains—territory whose inhabitants were supposedly hostile toward Americans. The most notable of these denizens were the *Hukbalahap,* an amalgamated militia of the Philippine Socialist and Communist parties. The word "Hukbalahap" was an acronym for *Hukbo ng Bayan Laban sa mga Hapon*—literally translated: "The People's Army Against the Japanese." Consisting mostly of tenant farmers and tradesmen, the "Huks," as they were commonly referred to, had been stirring discontent within the Central Plains long before Volckmann arrived and continued harassing the Philippine government well into the 1950s.[60]

All things considered, Volckmann knew it was better to take his chances in the jungle than to rely on the improbable generosity of the Japanese. Armed with nothing more than a .45 caliber pistol and his field knife, he began his tortuous journey into the wilderness.

After regaining his bearings on the map, Volckmann and his crew headed northwest. Because of the dense foliage, however, they could see no more than fifteen feet in any direction. Every step through the jungle was tortuous. The intense humidity left them soaked with perspiration; low-lying branches and rattan vines constantly smacked them in the face and left their uniforms nearly torn to shreds. Since their eyes were limited in the dense jungle, their ears became the only means of security. This proved nearly impossible, though, as every gush of wind and crackle of leaves made determining foreign sounds more difficult. At one point, Volckmann wished they could stop breathing just to lessen the noise pollution.[61]

After they had gone approximately three miles, Volckmann began to recognize the area as a former sector of the 1st Division. Here, they decided to stop and rest a while. Volckmann asked Blackburn to break out some rations and mix it with water. This way they could divide it amongst the seven men in their group. Volckmann knew that food would be a persistent problem. They had plenty of water—the natural stream network provided that—but had no idea how long the emergency rations would last among the seven of them.

After drinking his rations, he reached into his musette bag for the first time since the escape. The day before his departure, Volckmann had had his orderly deliver the musette bag. He always kept it handy and well stocked in case of emergency. The normal packing list included a change of socks and underwear, toiletries, iodine, quinine, first aid items, a rifle cleaning kit, flints, and his map of Bataan. Unfortunately, his orderly had decided to clean out the bag on the day of the surrender and left in it only the socks, underwear, toiletries, and map of Bataan.[62]

Disgusted, Volckmann cursed himself for not double-checking before his departure. Though angered by his own negligence, he took solace in knowing that the most important item still remained: *his map*. Without it, they were as good as dead.

Volckmann pulled out the map and consulted with Blackburn. Neither man knew their exact position, but both knew they were in the old 1st Division area. Aside from the lingering threat of enemy patrols, other concerns included the mines and booby traps that the Americans had set behind them during the retreat. Volckmann had set many of these traps himself and was well aware of their sensitivities; a mere brush might set them off. Weighing the circumstances, however, he determined it was better to brave through the sector than to stay put.

Through the jungle, they came to a trail that the map indicated to be Trail 5. Not keen to the idea of forcing their way through the jungle again, they decided to use the Trail with caution. Their pace remained relatively slow, but it was a vast improvement from their jungle speed.[63]

After a few minutes on the trail, the group spied a Japanese soldier leaning against a nearby tree. Alarmed, the seven of them quickly scrambled for cover into the foliage. Peering at the enemy soldier from underneath a shrub, Volckmann noticed something peculiar about him: *he wasn't moving*. Minutes passed and yet the soldier remained completely motionless. Furthermore, it seemed odd that this soldier was by himself, with not even so much as a squad nearby. Inching his way closer to the unmoving enemy, Volckmann finally realized that the soldier was dead.[64] Obviously, someone had propped him up against the tree. In any case, Volckmann decided to leave the body where it was—for it may have been booby-trapped.

The remainder of their journey on the trail passed without incident, and at sundown they reached the former position of the 12th Infantry Regiment—another unit of the 11th Division. The day's tension had been enough to put all seven men on edge, but tonight the darkness offered no solace. Perhaps still jumpy from his encounter with the dead Japanese soldier, Blackburn found it impossible to fall asleep. At regular intervals, he would awaken Volckmann with reports of enemy sounds. During the retreat to Bataan, both men learned that the Japanese maintained a nocturnal communication system of cricket chirps and whistles. Volckmann convinced Blackburn that it was just his imagination, but a moment later Blackburn woke him up again. Now, he reported seeing flashlights in the distance. At first, Volckmann thought he saw them too: every few moments, beams of lights emerged from the darkness. He soon realized, however, that these "enemy flashlights" were nothing more than the shifting foliage allowing intermittent starlight to shine through.[65]

Try as he may to convince Blackburn, he would not rest until they relocated their position. They relocated only a mere 50 yards, but it was enough to reassure Blackburn and finally put him to sleep.

At dawn, they set out again—this time at a faster pace. Volckmann hoped to cross the former Main Line of Resistance, near the Pilar-Bagac Road, by noon. As they came across what had been their frontline, an eerie sense of stillness came over them. Just a few days earlier these same trenches were bustling with crossfire. Now, they were empty and still. Their dead had been evacuated and the Japanese had done likewise with theirs, but it seemed as though their souls still lingered on the battlefield. The signs of defeat lay scattered everywhere: shell casings, a knocked-out tank—all bitter reminders of the Japanese conquest. Finally, they crossed Pilar-Bagac at Kilometer Post 144.[66]

Continuing in a northeasterly direction, the group began their climb up the southern slope of Mt. Natib. Now on the mountain, they had left the protection of the jungle canopy and the sun beat down on them mercilessly.[67] After only a short time on the slope, the heat, combined with lack of food, began to take its toll. As rations were running out, Volckmann once again turned his mind to the issue of food. There were no farms or villages in the area that he knew of, so scavenging for food would be a "hit-or-miss" affair.

However, on the fourth day of their travels, they stumbled upon an abandoned Japanese bivouac. By the appearance of the site, they could tell that the Japanese had been there only hours before. Whatever the reason for their departure, it had obviously been in great haste. Trash lay scattered everywhere, *but so were leftover rations*. Scavenging rice and dried fish, the group fed on whatever articles they could find. Volckmann commented that some of the food looked so hideous that, under normal circumstances, he never would have eaten it. But given that the seven of them were near starvation, food was food. After scouting the surrounding area to ensure that no other Japanese were nearby, the group settled down for the night.[68]

The next morning, Volckmann set out to find a new course to follow. While at a nearby stream, he spied a field telephone wire that ran northward. He knew that the Japanese had put it there, but then realized that if they were to follow the line, it may lead to more bivouac sites. If the Japanese had left their other sites in conditions similar to this one, the group would have a temporary solution to its food problems. However, the threat of enemy patrols still loomed, and there was the chance that the phone line would lead not to another bivouac site but to an entire garrison. Volckmann and Blackburn discussed their options, but decided that the need for food outweighed the hazard of Japanese patrols. Later, Volckmann would look back on the decision with shame, as he knew it was made by his stomach.[69]

Following the phone line, they arrived at another bivouac. Anticipating the same conditions they had found in the previous one, they broke formation and hurried to the site. Nearly halfway, Volckmann skidded to a halt and stopped the others in the group. *The bivouac was still occupied.* They backtracked quickly and dove behind the foliage. It was a Japanese cavalry troop, about 60 men in total. Though shaken by the close encounter, Volckmann realized that his group had gone undetected. The violent rapids of the nearby river had muffled the sound of their approach.[70]

Cursing himself for the breakdown in discipline, he swore he would never rush another bivouac. Back on the telephone wire trail, they encountered yet another bivouac. Cautiously, they made their way to the site and found it empty. The Japanese had done a better job of clearing this site and, as such, their "pickings here were rather slim, consisting of a little rice and some pretty rotten onions."[71] After the encounter with the Japanese cavalry, Volckmann decided to change course. He estimated that if he went in a more easterly direction, they could avoid the terrain most favorable for cavalry patrols.

By the following afternoon, they had eaten the last of their scavenged food. The newfound need to avoid cavalry patrols took them across the steepest terrain they had yet encountered. Though it gave them an excellent vantage point, it did nothing to solve their food problems nor did it contain any adequate water sources. Eventually, the group spied a native house about a mile downhill from the trail they had taken. Volckmann sent two of his Filipino volunteers to search the house and the surrounding area for food, a task they eagerly accepted. Giving them a few pesos each, he instructed them to approach the house with caution. If the homeowner were present, they were to bargain for as much food as their pesos could earn them. However, it was the last time Volckmann would see either of the two Filipinos—they never returned from the house.[72]

Volckmann never indicated how long he waited for their return, but he eventually resigned himself to the fact that they had deserted him. It was not likely that they had been captured or killed by the Japanese—the native house was less than a mile downhill, and if there had been a struggle, Volckmann and the others surely would have heard it.

The following morning, on 14 April, Volckmann stumbled onto a dirt road in the vicinity of Abucay Hacienda. It appeared nowhere on his map, but he was certain that it was the same road the Japanese had built to coordinate their attack on Bataan. As Division Intelligence Officer, it was a frequent topic among his reports.

After the rough terrain of the previous days' hike, the group decided to try their luck along the road. Volckmann knew it was a dangerous move—fresh footprints and tire tracks indicated that the road had recently seen heavy traffic—but if it offered any relief from the treacherous jungle, he was willing to take the risk.

Relief, however, was short-lived. Not more than a few minutes had passed before the mechanical rumble of Japanese trucks sent him diving into the underbrush. As Volckmann lay in the bushes, he counted 21 trucks as they sped by—all of them filled with troops.[73] Undeterred, Volckmann and the others continued their trek until coming to a fork in the road. As they were discussing what route they should take, Volckmann noticed some movement beyond the bend. Straining his eyes, he could see that it was another Japanese cavalry unit.

The five of them dashed into a nearby sugarcane field. Running furiously through the sugarcane, they became widely separated from one another. Volckmann, Blackburn, and Whiteman eventually regrouped, but the two remaining Filipinos were never seen again. From then on, Volckmann decided to stay off the road. No matter how inviting it may appear, it was no place for three Americans to be traveling.

Exhausted from their latest encounter, the three men laid down for an afternoon rest. Sometime later, a native man approached them—the first civilian they had encountered since the fall of Bataan. Volckmann recounts that the native could not speak English, but they were able to get the message across that they were hungry and needed food. The native man indicated that the group should stay put and that he would be back later. With this, he ran into the jungle and returned one hour later with a young boy at his side. The boy spoke English fairly well and identified himself as the man's son. Offering them some cooked rice, the boy confirmed that there were "many Japs" in the area.[74]

Volckmann asked if there was a safe place nearby where they could settle down for the night. After conferring with his father, the boy replied that they were welcome to stay at their village. Volckmann agreed, but was unsure whether or not he could trust them. Did they really intend to take him to the village, or were they leading him into a Japanese ambush? Whatever the case, Volckmann and his men needed food; it was a matter of life and death—hunger pangs were racking their bodies.

As the native boy led them into the village, Volckmann and the others were relieved to find that there were no Japanese in sight. Perhaps these natives could be trusted after all. Volckmann, Blackburn, and Whiteman spent the remainder of the day recovering from the week's activities. They had barely escaped from Bataan with their lives and were buckling under the intense tropical heat. Scraped, bruised, starved, and exhausted, they were in the worst shape they had been in since the start of the invasion.

To make matters worse, Volckmann was armed with nothing more than a six-round revolver—and he had no spare ammunition. Unlike many of his comrades on Bataan, however, Volckmann had not yet succumbed to any tropical disease. For this he was grateful, but was uncertain how long he could fight it off. The jungle adventures had taken a heavy toll on his body and the tropical heat was slowly tearing down his resistance. It seemed as though maintaining his health would be a greater challenge than evading the enemy. After all, he had seen what malaria, dysentery, and the other assortments of tropical disease could do to a soldier.

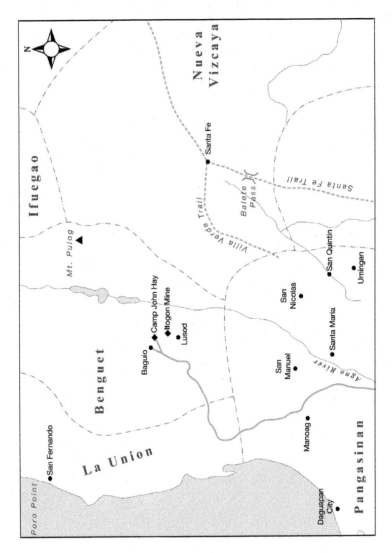

Map of Central-North Luzon. Colonel John P. Horan consolidated his forces at Baguio and planned to make Balete Pass a rally point for other USAFFE units. Visible are the Benguet and Ifugao "sub-provinces" of Mountain Province, where Volckmann would base his operations as a guerrilla.

CHAPTER 4

Northward Bound

After washing their clothes in a nearby stream, the three men departed the village at dawn. Their host agreed to take them around Abucay Hacienda and, before parting ways, Volckmann heartily thanked him for his hospitality. Picking up a northbound trail, they encountered another American: Corporal Bruce, a rifleman from the 31st Infantry who had also escaped from Bataan. Volckmann invited him into the group and, shortly thereafter, they were joined by a Filipino who identified himself as a retired Sergeant of the Philippine Scouts.

As many of the local natives had done, this retired scout had fled the Japanese onslaught. Seeking refuge in the jungle, he had built himself an "evacuation camp" and invited Volckmann to stay with him. These evacuation camps operated on a small network throughout most of Luzon. Their inhabitants came from every walk of life: American businessmen and their families, wealthy Filipinos, tenant farmers, missionaries, school teachers—civilians who had lost their homes during the invasion and fled to the wilderness in hopes of waiting out their Japanese occupiers.

Arriving at the sergeant's camp, Volckmann found it to be nothing more than a quaint little shack with barely enough room for five people. But nonetheless, he appreciated the sergeant's hospitality. Surprisingly, Volckmann entered the camp to find two more Americans: a pair of Army Air Corps lieutenants named Petit and Anderson. Sitting down to speak with his newfound comrades, Volckmann learned the fates of Lieutenant Colonels Martin P. Moses and Arthur K. Noble, two regimental commanders whom he had known in Bataan.

Initially, the pair had been assigned to the 12th Infantry Regiment (11th Division) as battalion commanders. After retreating through Central Luzon, Moses and Noble respectively took command of two other regiments within the 11th Division. By Volckmann's account, both men were competent leaders and had done a fine job during the battle. Since the fall of Bataan, they too had begun their long trek northward.[75] As it were, they had been through the old sergeant's camp a week earlier and found safe passage to the north.

The next morning, Volckmann and Blackburn, along with their new Air Corps friends, hit the trail northbound to Highway 7. After a few minutes on the trail, they encountered another young Filipino. This young man of no more than nineteen years old spoke English fluently and identified himself only as "Bruno." By his appearance and his accent, Volckmann could tell that "Bruno" was not a native to this part of Luzon. Accordingly, he was a member of the Igorot tribe and a corporal in the Philippine Army. Upon hearing that their destination was his native Mountain Province in North Luzon, Bruno insisted that he join them. In exchange for joining the group, he offered his services as a guide.[76]

Remembering the four Filipinos who had deserted him in Bataan, Volckmann hesitated on Bruno's proposition. Yet, if this boy really did know his way around Luzon, he could be a valuable asset. Volckmann agreed to take him on, provided he stay with the group until they reached Mountain Province.

Back on the trail, they arrived at Banban shortly before noon. A small barrio two kilometers south of Highway 7, Banban offered a pleasant respite from the group's travels. At the behest of the barrio chieftain, Volckmann and company were privy to a feast honoring the return of a local son. While enjoying the copious amounts of rice and beef, Volckmann secured a guide to take him across the heavily patrolled Highway 7. Stretching from Dinalupihan in the east to Olongapo in the west, Highway 7 had once been the site of the 11th Infantry's largest defensive line. Now, it was the main thoroughfare into the Japanese naval port at Olongapo.

As the group prepared to cross the highway, Whiteman and Bruce announced their decision to stay behind. Both had come down with debilitating fevers and were too sick to complete the hike. Volckmann hated the thought of leaving them behind, but Bruce insisted that he and Whiteman would be fine after a few days rest. Besides, neither of them wanted to slow Volckmann down. Departing with Bruno, Blackburn, and the two Air Corps lieutenants, Volckmann left the two infirm soldiers in the care of Banban's barrio chieftain. He never saw Bruce or Whiteman again.[77]

On 18 April 1942, Volckmann crossed Highway 7 without incident. He was finally out of Bataan, but what lay in front of him were over 100 miles of swamp, jungle, mountains, and Japanese patrols. Spanning some four and a half months, his journey to the north would be the most painful and excruciating experience of his life. At various times, either he or a member of his traveling party—save Bruno, enjoying his native immunity—would temporarily succumb to dysentery, fever, malaria, yellow jaundice, or beriberi. Until now, Volckmann had come through five months of combat untouched by any tropical disease. Today, however, his luck ran out.

Merely an hour had passed since crossing the road when Volckmann reported feeling weak. Overcome by nausea and diarrhea, his body had begun rejecting all the unclean food he had scavenged. Volckmann's diagnosis: "I came down with dysentery."[78] The Filipino guide who had taken them across Highway 7 diverted the group to a nearby evacuation camp, where Volckmann remained in the care of its chieftain, a man he identified simply as Guerrero. A middle-aged farmer with a family of five, Guerrero had managed a *hacienda* for an American businessman named Demson. Since the war, both Guerrero and Demson fled with their families into the jungle, taking with them only what they could carry. Now, Guerrero, his wife, and their four children resided in hastily constructed bamboo shacks with roofs of cogon grass.

In the entry for 21 April, Volckmann wrote that he remained sick despite the best efforts of the Guerrero family. Nonetheless, Volckmann notes that the Guerreros were the most generous and helpful Filipinos he had thus far met. Aside from the light meals of rice and vegetables, Guerrero's eldest daughter presented Volckmann with a pair of Philippine Army coveralls—the first pair of clean clothes he had worn since Bataan. The family had no medicine to speak of, but the senior Guerrero was well versed in the arts of tribal healing. Brewing some tea made from tree bark, Guerrero presented it to Volckmann, indicating that it would help his dysentery. The concoction was so bitter that Volckmann nearly spit it out, but as of now, it was his only hope to alleviate the disease. Volckmann documented some improvement in his health afterwards, but his strength to perform simple tasks such as walking or standing remained feeble.[79]

It was also at Guerrero's where Volckmann first learned of the Bataan Death March. The stories left him horrified: men who had been his comrades only days ago were now being forced to march without food or water. Those who stumbled were savagely beaten. Men who simply collapsed from exhaustion were shot, bayoneted, or decapitated. The few who actually made it into the prison camps were systematically starved and denied medical attention once they arrived.

Among the more horrific stories included tales of the Japanese peeling the skin from their captives' feet and forcing them to walk through piles of salt. Other prisoners were lined up along the highway and deliberately run over by Japanese trucks racing at full speed. Yet the most frightening stories were those of the Japanese eye gouging techniques: taking a rifle with a fixed bayonet, an enemy soldier would place the bayonet inside of a prisoner's bottom eyelid, and then let go of the rifle. Consequently, as the rifle fell to the ground, the bayonet would eject the prisoner's eye from his socket.[80]

Aside from their astonishing cruelty, what angered Volckmann the most about the Japanese were their seemingly casual and indiscriminate attitudes. There was no rhyme or reason to any of their techniques. In fact, it seemed as though the Japanese were torturing Americans simply for their own amusement.

Painfully, Volckmann recalled the earlier sentiments of his comrades on Bataan—*"The Japs will treat us okay."* How fortunate he was not to have listened.

The following day, 23 April, Guerrero announced that his old boss, Demson, remained in the area and had built a small evacuation camp about three kilometers to the north. Demson's camp lay deeper in the jungle and was farther away from the Japanese patrol lanes.[81] Given the precarious nature of his health, Volckmann would have preferred to stay put. He had, after all, been at Guerrero's camp for only four days and saw little improvement in his health. Nonetheless, he accepted the idea that moving farther away from the enemy patrols would buy him more recovery time in the long run.

Upon arriving at Demson's Camp, Volckmann and his men—Blackburn, Bruno, Anderson, and Petit—were heartily received by their new hosts. Greeted with a meal of rice, tomatoes, and roasted pig, it was the first full meal they had enjoyed in over a month. Demson indicated that he was moving his family—a wife and one son—into another camp near Dinalupihan around the 1st of May, and that Volckmann was free to take over this current location after the move.

Volckmann and Blackburn were deeply impressed by Demson's camp. It was much more elaborate than Guerrero's and consisted of a main house and a cooking hut on the bank of a nearby stream. As with Guerrero's, the Demson compound was made of bamboo with cogon grass roofs. As none of the main trails passed by the camp and the bordering stream offered no easy means of navigation, Volckmann felt relatively secure.

Despite the serenity of the camp, however, his health remained unstable. The tea he had gotten from Guerrero made his dysentery somewhat tolerable, but it did nothing to improve his overall strength. What little food he did consume came only at Blackburn's insistence, who himself was battling a high-grade fever. The Demsons promised to keep Volckmann and his men supplied for as long as they stayed in the area. The family departed to their new camp on 29 April, leaving behind a generous ration of supplies and another roasted pig. With as much strength as he could muster, Volckmann heartily thanked the Demsons for their generosity.[82]

As his body nursed the symptoms of dysentery, Volckmann succumbed to yet another disease: beriberi. In the course of his travels, Volckmann's fare had not included any grains, greens, or native fruits—starving his body of essential Vitamin B. Sensing the change in his condition, the Guerrero girls supplemented his diet with a medley of bread, vegetables, and a delicacy known as *bagong*, or salted fish. *Bagong* was an unappetizing dish that tasted nearly as bad as it looked. Begrudgingly, Volckmann crammed the concoction down his throat, gagging every step of the way.

While Volckmann tended to his own ailments, Blackburn's fever became progressively worse. At times, Blackburn felt as though he would simply explode from the heat building up inside of him. Both men had lost a significant amount of weight. Arriving in the Philippines, Blackburn weighed a healthy 180 pounds. By the day of the surrender, his weight had plummeted to 150 pounds.[83] Petit and Anderson, despite fatigue and nausea, remained relatively healthy. Bruno, however, continued to enjoy his native immunity.

On the night of 1 May, heavy gunfire startled the men from their sleep. It sounded as though a firefight had erupted somewhere to the southeast. A Japanese patrol? Possibly. But Volckmann heard nothing to indicate the use of automatic weapons, which the Japanese were certain to use. Whoever these combating parties were, it sounded as though they were exchanging fire from single-action rifles. Though curious as to the source of the firing, he could tell that it was a great distance away, and thus drifted back to sleep.[84]

The following morning, Guerrero arrived at the camp with a chilling explanation behind the previous night's gunfire: *the Demsons had been robbed.* Bandits had raided the camp and, in the process of stealing the family's valuables, killed Demson's wife and wounded his son. The following day, Guerrero came back with even more disheartening news: a nearby Japanese garrison had heard the same gunfire and was now conducting a search of the surrounding area.[85]

Deciding to hide during the day and return to the camp by night, Volckmann and the others settled into a creek bed a few hundred yards beyond the house. Throughout the day, Japanese gunfire punctuated the long hours of silence. None of the firing came close to their hiding spot, but Volckmann noticed something peculiar about the firing patterns: each flurry sounded as if it were coming from a different direction than the last. It was as though the Japanese were aimlessly circling the countryside, firing their weapons every so often.

Back at the camp by nightfall, the men listened to Guerrero relate what had happened. As part of their effort to investigate the bandit gunfire, the Japanese went down the main trails and fired into every house and evacuation camp they passed before retreating to Dinalupihan. Not a very coherent strategy, Volckmann thought, but at least the Japanese were gone for now.

It remains unclear what became of Mr. Demson and his son after the robbery. Volckmann never mentions him again beyond the entry for 5 May 1942—saying that Demson discontinued sending supplies on this date. Guerrero, in the meantime, supplied the group with whatever useful items he could find. By this time, malaria had settled in alongside Volckmann's dysentery and Blackburn became sick with malaria as well. Nighttime offered no solace as disease-ridden mosquitoes came out in droves. Neither Volckmann nor any of his men had any mosquito nets, and the surgical gauzes with which they improvised were largely ineffective. The rats, however, were far worse—hiding during the day, they would scavenge the camp at night, running across Volckmann as he tried to sleep. Often, he woke in the morning to find that they had eaten holes into his socks, shoes, and extra clothes. To correct the problem, he began suspending these items from the ceiling. Undaunted, the rats began targeting smaller items which they could carry away. They even ran off with Blackburn's toothbrush.[86]

Later that week, Bruno—by virtue of being a native Filipino—secured a travel pass from the Japanese. It permitted him free access to the country without being detained at any checkpoints along the main roads. Using this pass, Bruno would often travel into Dinalupihan for food, supplies, and updates on Japanese activity. On 15 May, the entries in Volckmann's diary abruptly stop and do not resume again until 31 May. He attributed the blank entries to his deteriorating health:

> I have many blank pages this month; it's the same old story most every day. For the first time in my life, I realize the value of health. To my disgust, many of the nights I have almost hoped not to wake up in the morning. I know, if I am to regain my health, I must get strength to get out of this part of the country. To the mountains [of North Luzon]; that is my only chance.[87]

On 1 June, Guerrero once again returned to the camp. Claiming that he had secured a doctor near Dinalupihan, he transported Volckmann and Blackburn by a small sled to an old garage a few hundred yards from Highway 7. There, the doctor—whom Volckmann described as a "quack"—gave them a series of shots. Neither Volckmann nor Blackburn had any idea what the shots were, but given the debilitating status of their health, it hardly mattered to them. Whatever it was they had received from the "quack," it obviously had some effect, as both men were soon feeling better.

The pair remained at the doctor's garage over the next few days with Guerrero returning periodically to check on them. Meanwhile, Petit and Anderson—both of whom had remained at Volckmann's camp—sent word that they were moving north into the Zambales Mountains. Bruno, however, had decided to stay—a decision that Volckmann obviously appreciated. Volckmann, meanwhile, drifted in and out of consciousness but retained enough of his wits to record small entries in his diary.

> 3 June 1942. Nothing unusual. We can see the Japs pass in trucks on [Highway 7]; it is only about 200 yards away.
> 4 June 1942. Awfully hungry for something that tastes like American chow. Feel somewhat better.
> 5 June 1942. Guerrero's children got us some flour. Baked a coffee cake. Turned out pretty well.[88]

By 7 June, Volckmann had returned to Guerrero's camp where he spent the next two weeks convalescing. Day by day, Volckmann recorded new feats as his strength slowly came back to him. By the 15th, he was able to walk again under his own power. Around this time, Petit returned to the camp for the first time since his departure with Anderson.[89] While searching for other Americans, the pair had encountered an evacuation camp run by two brothers named Bill and Martin Fassoth. The Fassoths, Petit explained, were two American sugarcane farmers who had fled to the Zambales when the war began. Since the fall of Bataan, they had taken in a number of American escapees. Their numbers even included an Army doctor who had with him a limited supply of medicine.[90] The camp sounded fascinating and, according to Petit, was only a day's hike from their current location. Petit left later that day, but Volckmann resolved that he would join him at the Fassoth camp as soon as he regained his strength.

But whether he was feeling stronger or not, Volckmann knew he had to keep moving. He hated the idea of leaving Guerrero and his family; they had been enormously helpful and he owed them a debt of gratitude, which he could never truly repay. With their lives interrupted and ruined by the Japanese, the Guerrero family willingly risked themselves and their resources to help these obscure Americans. Despite the burden that looking after two Americans had placed on his family, Guerrero and his children urged Volckmann and the others to stay.[91]

The offering was certainly tempting—over the past month he had grown quite fond of the Guerrero children. But Volckmann politely reminded his hosts that he was a military officer and he still had a mission to accomplish. With that, he graciously thanked them for their hospitality and departed on 22 June 1942. Volckmann later wrote of Guerrero and his family "To these gracious natives we owe our lives."[92]

By this time, Volckmann was feeling relatively well. Back on the trail, they followed a native guide who had been an old friend of Guerrero. Ideally, the hike to Fassoth camp should have taken about twelve hours, but Volckmann had to bypass Pitao because the Japanese had occupied the town. The detour added an additional three hours onto their travel time and took them over the most rugged terrain of the Zambales Mountains. Finally, at around 11:00 p.m., they arrived at Fassoth Camp.[93]

Though Volckmann had made the hike with relative ease, it took a devastating toll on Blackburn. His fever had relapsed before departing Guerrero's camp and now, after hours of continuous hiking, the infirmity had taken Blackburn to his knees. For most of their stay at Fassoth's, Blackburn was nearly comatose.

The Fassoth Camp was an impressive display. Volckmann had never seen anything like it: the dominant feature was a large barracks-like building complete with bunk beds made from bamboo. A working radio picked up station KGEI in San Francisco, broadcasting the first real news Volckmann had heard since the fall of Bataan. There were approximately 80 Americans residing in the camp. Most were enlisted men who had escaped from the Bataan Death March, although eight officers also complimented the group. Just as Petit had described, there was an Army doctor who ran a small infirmary.[94]

Along with the Fassoth brothers, the camp was maintained by a local Filipino named Vicente Bernia. Bernia was one of the few prominent businessmen in the area who had emerged from the Japanese invasion unscathed. He was a major player in the Zambales provincial affairs and the plantation he owned was still operating. The Americans at this camp owed their lives to this man: for as long as the Fassoths had operated this camp, Bernia had kept them supplied with food and medicine.[95]

Bernia was a boisterous man, warm and friendly with a contagious smile. On his frequent visits, he would regale the men with his hair-raising tales of outsmarting the Japanese. Bernia owned a small utility truck, which he used to carry supplies from Manila. When passing the Japanese checkpoints along the main highway, he insisted that the goods were for his plantation workers. When questioned about the mass quantity of his purchases, he explained that the rainy season required him to buy in bulk.[96] It was a plausible story, and the Japanese accepted it. But Bernia, that sly devil, was not satisfied with merely fooling the enemy; he wanted to make the Japanese his unwitting accomplices.

For this, Bernia bought almost exclusively from Japanese bazaars. Arriving at a highway checkpoint, he would present his receipts to the guards and tell them the tale of his "workers' needs." Upon seeing that his receipts were issued by Japanese merchants, the guards—just as Bernia had expected—offered to help him transport the cargo. Thus, the food and other supplies for Fassoth Camp were brought halfway up the mountain by Japanese Army trucks, all under the ruse of supplying Bernia and his plantation.[97]

Although he was a wealthy man, Vicente Bernia could not single-handedly finance the Fassoth operation forever. Using his influence in the area, he negotiated several lines of credit with Filipino merchants in the foothills. In exchange for their goods, Bernia implemented an I.O.U. system; an American officer would sign a receipt promising full reimbursement from the United States Army at the end of the war.[98] Any sensible merchant would have balked at such an indefinite proposal. But if it came from Vicente Bernia, there was no need to question it. Such was the power and influence this man had in the region. When asked by Volckmann what he was getting out of this, his only response was: "When the war is over, all I want is for some soldiers to sponsor me for American citizenship."[99]

The news reports over KGEI left Volckmann wondering if help would ever arrive—Allied forces were on the ropes in North Africa and the Japanese still controlled half of the Pacific. By this time, 26 June 1942, the United States had won a decisive victory over the Imperial Japanese Navy at Midway.[100] Meanwhile, his fascination with Fassoth Camp began to sour. Bernia and the Fassoth brothers had done a fine job maintaining the camp, but they had let the enlisted men run amok, and the officers—outnumbered nine to one—did nothing to reel them in. On the day of their arrival, Volckmann and Blackburn were cornered by Sergeant Red Floyd, a former artilleryman who had become the camp's de facto strongman. Brusque and intimidating, Floyd wasted no time educating his new guests.

"Now look, let's get the name of the game straight, if you guys want to stay here I want you to recognize that there is no such thing as rank. The war is over. If you want to play by our rules, fine. If you don't, you can get out of here. Now, if you don't believe me," he said, pointing to a group of nearby officers, "you go ask those officers. They'll know exactly what I'm talking about."[101]

"If you think that you can do anything about it," he added, "all the weapons around here are in the hands of the noncoms."* Volckmann and Blackburn were speechless. Floyd had taken the Fassoth's humanitarian endeavor and turned it into a cesspool of discontent. By and large, the camp shared Floyd's attitude. Others had simply given up on the war. Determined to get to the root of the problem, Volckmann questioned Floyd about his hostility towards the officers. Perhaps if Floyd had someone to hear him out, it would be the first step towards improving the current state of affairs.[102]

Red Floyd's story began in early May, when Bernia and the Fassoth's were building the camp. According to Floyd, the officers had gone around barking orders while not wanting to do any of the work themselves. Fed up with their laziness and condescension, Floyd and the others rebelled. Outnumbered and outgunned, the officers backed down.

While Volckmann did not approve of the insubordination, the story at least gave him and Blackburn an idea of how to fix things at Fassoth Camp. To ease the tension between the officers and the enlisted men, they had to create an incentive for both sides to work together. Blackburn, who by now was feeling well enough to stand, approached Floyd with an offer to improve the camp's conditions. Floyd was complaining about the dysentery that had taken over the camp when Blackburn chimed in, "If some of the people around here had brains, something could be done about it."[103]

"What do you mean?" Floyd shrieked.

"Well, you're running the camp and there isn't any such thing as a slit trench or a latrine around here. All you do with your 'business' is throw it out of the window. All that great food you cook in there is covered with flies that come off of that stuff, or don't you understand that?" This, Blackburn explained, was the reason why everyone was coming down with dysentery.

"Well," Floyd replied indignantly, "who's going to dig us a trench?"

Seizing his opportunity to bridge the officer-enlisted gap, Blackburn said, "Everybody will pitch in and dig. Now can you get your guys to pitch in? Are you willing to pitch in?" That did it. Both officers and enlisted got to work on digging a network of slit trenches that would keep the human excrement away from the living quarters and, more importantly, away from the food. It was the first time they had accomplished anything as a cohesive group.

Beginning with smaller tasks like cleaning the barracks, they went on to build an entire mess hall as well as a new infirmary. Volckmann, despite his own battles with dysentery and malaria, chipped in wherever he was needed. As the

---

*Noncom (also spelt Non-com) is an abbreviation for "Non-commissioned Officer," referring to enlisted personnel at the rank of Corporal and above.

men regained their trust for one another, they began to distance themselves from Red Floyd's resentful leadership. Soon, the officers resumed control of Fassoth Camp—this time leading by example.[104]

Volckmann spent the entire month of July and the majority of August at Fassoth Camp. While regaining his strength, he finalized his plans for heading north. Blackburn, though still suffering from fever, reported feeling strong enough to finish the trip. Their current location in the Zambales put them over 100 miles southeast from the nearest reported enclave of American units in Mountain Province. If he expected to make it there before New Year's 1943, he would have to leave Fassoth Camp before 1 September. The terrain between the Zambales and the northern provinces was somewhat benign compared to what he had been through earlier, but heavy jungles still dominated the landscape and they were sure to impede his movement. At Fassoth Camp, Volckmann learned from Bernia that two Lieutenant Colonels, Claude Thorp and Peter Cayler, were commanding small groups of USAFFE guerrillas in Tarlac Province, just a few miles north.

Volckmann had known Cayler before the invasion—they met aboard the USS *Grant* en route to the Philippines two years earlier. Taken prisoner at Bataan, Cayler escaped the Death March only after being run over by a Japanese truck. Lying in the road and nursing a broken arm, he was left for dead until a nearby Chinese mestizo family, the Jincos, picked him up. Now living under the Jinco's care, Cayler and his crew, which included four other Americans who had escaped from the Death March, were recovering just fine.[105]

Claude Thorp had been active since the Japanese first landed at Aparri. Prior to the war, he had been the Provost Marshal of Fort Stotsenburg in Central Luzon.* But when Thorp was given the order to vacate his post and join the USAFFE retreat, General King, who later surrendered the Philippine II Corps at Bataan, reassigned him as the Provost Marshal for the Northern Luzon Forces. Thus began Thorp's career as a USAFFE guerilla. By January 1942, Thorp apparently recognized that USAFFE was on the losing end of its struggle against the Japanese. Most records confirm that Claude Thorp submitted the idea of organizing guerrilla units to General MacArthur and, on 26 January 1942, Thorp allegedly received MacArthur's permission to travel out of Bataan and begin organizing an Allied resistance based in the Zambales Mountains.[106]

Volckmann was not certain of either Cayler's or Thorp's exact location. As Tarlac and Zambales provinces had few towns and fewer distinguishable landmarks, he reasoned that he could use Cayler's and Thorp's locations as checkpoints to track his progress on the way to North Luzon. While contemplating his next

---

*A "Provost Marshal" is the commander of all Military Police forces on a military installation or within a certain command.

move, Volckmann was interrupted by the arrival of another Filipino, Sergeant Emilio Gumabay.

Emilio had been a police officer with the Philippine Constabulary prior to the invasion. He had escaped the wrath of the Rising Sun until someone—possibly an old enemy—falsely accused him of collaborating with Americans.[107] Now a fugitive running from the Kempei Tai,* Emilio wandered into Fassoth Camp, offering his services to anyone still interested in carrying on the fight. Unfortunately, guerrilla warfare didn't seem to resonate with anyone besides Volckmann and Blackburn. The tension between the officers and enlisted men had died down, but so had their tenacity for fighting the Japanese. Many had devolved into apathy, content simply to wait for MacArthur's return.

Inviting Emilio into his group, Volckmann explained the situation: he was headed north to Mountain Province, into the Igorot tribal lands. Fassoth Camp had become a reasonably nice place, but the collective apathy of its residents only hastened the need for his departure. Volckmann did not want to stay in the company of lukewarm soldiers. Accepting the invitation to join the group, Emilio mentioned that aside from his duties as a policeman, he was also a shoemaker and a barber. Both skills came in handy, as Emilio offered free haircuts and taught Volckmann to mend the soles of his shoes using tire treads.[108]

On 14 August, Vicente Bernia paid another visit to the camp. Volckmann used the opportunity to ask for a guide to the north and for any more updates on other Americans in the area. Since his involvement with the Fassoth's, Bernia kept a close liaison with other USAFFE personnel in the area. He told Volckmann that Peter Cayler was just outside of Natividad. Thorp's hideout lay in the foothills of Mt. Pinatubo. In response to Volckmann's request for a guide, Bernia offered himself. But first, Bernia insisted that they rest for a few days at his home in Gutad. It was a small town of no more than 2,000 souls, and Bernia's house—one of several that he owned—was the dominant structure. Volckmann, Blackburn, Bruno, and Emilio were treated to beds with clean linen and generous rations of chicken with rice. Tasking a friend to feed his new guests, Bernia informed them that over half of the American prisoners from Bataan had died in the Japanese prison camps.[109]

On the morning of 18 August, Bernia guided the three to Cayler's location north of Natividad, where they remained for the next two days. Volckmann reports that the Jincos had taken extremely good care of him. The family boasted five daughters who were all experienced chefs. With the daughters serving five meals a day, Volckmann and Blackburn gained back much of the weight that the dysentery, malaria, and combat fatigue had stolen from them. Volckmann felt stronger but Blackburn's health remained fragile. He had spent considerable time at Fassoth's recovering, and although Blackburn remained enthusiastic about

---

*Japanese Secret Police.

the mission, the fever attacks had visibly diluted his strength. Nonetheless, even despite Volckmann's suggestion that they wait longer, Blackburn was eager to move out.

Cayler and his men—seven in total—were a jovial bunch. Although they were in good spirits, they were in no condition to conduct guerrilla warfare. Some of his charges were still sick, and Cayler himself had not fully recovered. Furthermore, he said that he was awaiting guidance from Thorp, as he had the "last word" on all guerrilla matters in the area. Volckmann wondered why Cayler would defer to another man of the same rank—or why Thorp would even claim to have control over partisan operations this early. Cayler confided in them, however, that he had lost his confidence in Claude Thorp.[110] According to Cayler, Thorp had already alienated many Americans and agitated the local Filipinos. But his biggest *faux pas* was agitating the nearby Hukbalahap.

Volckmann had never heard of Claude Thorp, and Cayler's description of him did not paint the most flattering picture. Nevertheless, if Volckmann wanted to start guerrilla operations, consulting Thorp might be useful. Thanking the Jincos and bidding Cayler goodbye, the four reached Claude Thorp's camp in the late afternoon of 20 August.

Unlike the Fassoth brothers, Volckmann was not impressed either by Thorp or his camp. He had become quite inactive and, at this point, seemed entirely disinterested in the war. Volckmann found this attitude hard to accept, especially from a lieutenant colonel. He explained to Thorp that they were headed for North Luzon and laid out his tentative plans for conducting guerrilla warfare.[111]

Upon hearing this, Thorp exploded.

He blasted Volckmann and his friends as "interlopers" and declared himself to be the "official" leader of the Allied resistance. Thorp said that before the Fall of Corregidor, he had been hand-picked by General MacArthur to organize the *only* resistance movement in Luzon.[112]

Despite this directive, however, Thorp had done virtually nothing about it. Just as Cayler had described, Thorp alienated local Filipinos and resented the other Americans in his sector. He had snubbed Vicente Bernia—despite receiving 100 pesos from the man—and ignored an offer from the Hukbalahap to combine guerrilla forces. When asked about Moses and Noble, Thorp curtly replied that they had gone north. Apparently, they too had met with Thorp and were greeted with similar hostility.

After two days of fruitless discussions with Thorp, Volckmann asked for a guide who could help him find his way north. Thorp, however, did not know of any guides familiar with the Central Plains area—except for the Hukbalahap. Nevertheless, Volckmann decided to take a gamble and solicit help from a nearby Huk camp. Of course, the possibility lingered that the Huks would shoot him on the spot, but Volckmann desperately needed a guide to help him navigate his way through the swampy lowlands of Central Luzon.

Arriving at a nearby Huk outpost, Volckmann politely asked for any knowledgeable guides to the north. The Huks greeted Volckmann with icy indifference but the inquiry nevertheless produced a stocky young native who offered his services as a guide. The young man, whom Volckmann and Blackburn nicknamed "Kid Muscles," agreed to take them as far as the Hukbalahap district headquarters atop Mount Arayat—the only mountain in the Central Plains of Luzon—in Pampanga Province. From there, they could find a guide with a better working knowledge of the North Luzon landscape.[113]

On the night of 24 August, Volckmann, Blackburn, Bruno, and Emilio departed Thorp's camp with Kid Muscles leading the way. After an hour or so on the trail, Volckmann noticed that they were moving closer to a brightly lit area. Adjusting his eyes to the light, he shuddered as he beheld what lay before him: *this was a Japanese prison camp.* Silhouetted against the nighttime sky were images of barbed wire fence and Japanese guards. He saw no prisoners, as they no doubt had been herded into their barracks for the night. Dazzling searchlights crisscrossed the area from atop the guard towers, frantically searching for any movement beyond the trees. Kid Muscles explained that this was Camp O'Donnell—one of two final destinations for those on the Bataan Death March. Crawling into a nearby drainage ditch, the five men slowly made their way around the prison camp, escaping the beams of light which glided only inches above their heads.[114] How fortunate Volckmann must have felt not to be on the other side of that fence.

In the predawn hours of the following morning, Volckmann arrived at the Hukbalahap headquarters. The hike up the slope of Mount Arayat was no easy feat; the steep grade would have been difficult for even the most experienced mountaineer. Along the way, they were challenged by the Hukbalahap guards at least a dozen times. Every so often, angry voices rang out from the darkness, demanding that the intruders identify themselves. Using Kid Muscles as an interpreter, they explained that they were Americans seeking help from the Huk leadership. Once inside the Huk compound, Volckmann was snatched away by two guards at the front gate. Although it was nearly 3:00 a.m., they ushered him into the home of the Hukbalahap chieftain, Esuebio Aquino.[115]

Militarily, the Huks were among the most ruthless and well-organized guerrilla outfits of the entire war. They fielded their partisans in 100-man units known as "squadrons." Two squadrons made a battalion; two battalions made a regiment. There was no formalized rank structure, although each man was given an assigned task—for example a rifleman or supply officer—and told to report to someone with a higher designated authority than himself. Each squadron was also assigned a political officer who instructed the Huk cadres how to implement Marxist ideas. Volckmann never expressed his opinions on their political ideology, but it is obvious that he respected their military prowess.

As he sat patiently on the floor of the leader's house, he hoped that Thorp's attitude had not caused too much resentment. The Filipinos were proud and passionate people, and to treat them as Thorp had done was neither smart nor endearing. But whatever the extent of Thorp's public relations damage, Volckmann still needed a guide to North Luzon. When Aquino finally entered the room, the faintly lit lanterns revealed a man nearly 60 years old, reserved and ruggedly stoic. He expressed his dissatisfaction with Thorp and lamented their inability to reach a consensus. Nonetheless, he remained open to the prospect of working with Americans. After an hour's discussion, he invited Volckmann and Blackburn to stay at the house and rest for a while; breakfast would be served in a few hours. With that, Aquino silently returned to his room.[116]

The meeting with Aquino left Volckmann feeling somewhat better. At best, he had expected nothing more than a cold and apathetic audience. Now, the Huks were giving him quarter and feeding him, too. Volckmann appreciated their hospitality, but he realized that the Huks had an ulterior motive. Before the war, they had denounced the Americans as evil *capitalistas,* and their diplomatic overtures to Claude Thorp did not reflect a suddenly pro-American attitude. Rather, they saw the war as a political opportunity. Now that they shared a common enemy in the Japanese, the Huks believed that fighting alongside the Americans might lend more credibility to—and propaganda for—their Marxist-Leninist ideologies. Although the Huks were happy to help Volckmann—they even asked him to stay on as a military adviser—they often clashed with USAFFE guerrillas later in the war.[117]

Aquino instructed one of his men to take them as far north as the Huk network extended. Volckmann had no indication of how far that would be, but was nonetheless grateful to have garnered their support. Heading north, Volckmann and the others were greeted at the foot of Mount Arayat by an endless network of rice paddies. Sloshing through the muddy retention ponds, Volckmann recorded the most frustrating hike he had endured since the jungles of Bataan. Every step dragged him down farther and farther into rice-littered muck. Walking along the dikes offered little solace—the footing was so narrow and the surface so slippery that he often lost his balance and went flying back into the muddy water.[118]

Sometime after midnight on 27 August, he arrived at another Huk hideout, this time in the middle of a swamp. As they had done at Headquarters, the Huk staff at this hideout tried to convince Volckmann to stay on as a military adviser. Flattered by the invitation, he again had to remind his hosts that he was a United States Army officer and that his duties lie farther north. After resting a while at the swamp hideout, Volckmann continued north with a new guide.

For Volckmann, Blackburn, Bruno, and Emilio, the swamp would be far worse than the rice paddies of the previous day. At first, the marshy terrain did not drastically impede their movement—until they all sank chest-deep into the water. Squirming through that slimy mess, no doubt fearful of snakes, mosquitoes, and other swamp creatures, they secured a native canoe to navigate their way through the rest of the swamp.

The group finally arrived at the house of an old schoolteacher about one kilometer from La Paz in Tarlac Province. Bypassing La Paz was sure to be a monumental task: it housed one of the largest Japanese garrisons in the province—one that was guaranteed to have a regular dispatch of enemy patrols. Volckmann, however, was more familiar with this part of Luzon, having fought through La Paz and Victoria during the retreat to Bataan. As the final and northernmost Huk operative in the area, the old teacher was obviously uncomfortable at the prospect of housing two Americans so close to a Japanese enclave. Sensing the discomfort of his new host, Volckmann reassured him that he would not stay long and that all he needed was a safe route to the Highway 3 intersection.[119]

La Paz lay along the east-west Highway 13. Highway 13 intersected the north-south Highway 3 only ten miles from Volckmann's current position. He estimated that it would take only an hour to get there, but the evasive route by which the old Huk led them added three more hours of plodding through the swamp. They appreciated the school-teacher's wisdom in wanting to avoid the Japanese, but they were quickly tiring of the savage swampland. Finally arriving at the Highway 3 road junction, Volckmann thanked his host who then darted hastily back into the swamp.[120]

From there, the group traveled up Highway 3 towards Victoria. The move was risky, but the men had seen enough swamps and rice paddies for the time being. Returning to their previous tactics of skirting the main roads, the four would occasionally pass a cluster of two or three farmhouses along the road. This was a common sight throughout Luzon, but what complicated their travels tonight were the farmers' dogs. Volckmann and the others traveled by night, and when passing one of the rural homesteads their arrival was punctuated by a symphony of barking. This was especially frustrating, as the dogs would continue barking long after they had passed the homestead.[121] Volckmann did not worry about the irate homeowners nearly as much as he worried about the Japanese. The sleepy-eyed farmers may have been incensed by their rude awakening, but a nearby garrison might detect the same commotion and dispatch a rifle squad to investigate.

Shortly before dawn on 30 August, they arrived at a house where a farmer and his wife agreed to take them in. Using Emilio as an interpreter, Volckmann related that they were trying to find the safest route around Victoria. The farmer, whose name was never given, knew of a route that would bypass Victoria and pick up a railroad track that ran northeast toward Guimba. When asked for a reliable guide, the farmer happily agreed to show them the way. This pleased Volckmann, as he knew it would save him and his men a considerable amount of time. The level grade of the railroad track was indeed a welcomed relief—Volckmann made excellent time and arrived at the outskirts of Guimba by daybreak.[122]

On the 1st of September, Volckmann arrived at barrio Bagabas, where he encountered the first of Robert Lapham's men. Lapham, like Volckmann and the others, had also escaped from Bataan. Originally under the command of Claude Thorp, he had been tasked to go to the northern part of Pangasian Province to recruit guerrillas. His outfit—the *Luzon Guerrilla Army Force,* as it would later be called—was one of the best-organized guerrilla operations in Central Luzon.[123]

At the time they encountered Lapham, however, he was bedridden with a violent fever. In his immediate company were two individuals: Private Gattie and an African-American gentleman named Bunche. Gattie was an American rifleman. Mr. Bunche was an older man, a veteran of the Spanish-American War who came to the Philippines in 1900 as a cavalry scout. After an honorable discharge from the United States Army, he elected to stay in Luzon, bought a rice plantation, married a Filipina, and now found himself providing food for Lapham's men—much like Vicente Bernia had done for the displaced GIs at Fassoth's Camp.[124]

Despite Lapham's poor health, his camp appeared to be well in order and Volckmann learned from him that Moses and Noble's camp could be reached by a three-day hike. However, Volckmann decided to take a brief respite at Lapham's camp, for his trek through the unforgiving swamps and the frustrating rice paddies had frittered away what little strength he had left. His skin was still yellow from the jaundice he had contracted earlier, and his malaria had since relapsed.[125]

Despite the relapse of his previous maladies, Volckmann remained confident. His goal of reaching Moses and Noble in the Cordillera Central was now only a few days away. Over the previous four months, he and Blackburn had pushed themselves through the most tortuous journey either of them would ever have to make. Narrowly escaping the Japanese, they had been tattered by the jungle and crippled by disease. Travailing through the dense foliage, rocky cliffs, rice paddies, and swamps, they had relied on their wits, sheer luck, and the kindness of strangers.

After breakfast on 4 September 1942, Volckmann departed with Blackburn, Bruno, and Emilio and headed north toward San Nicolas.[126] Their first stop en route to Moses and Noble was the camp of another American, Charlie Cushing.* Now that the dangers of the Central Plains lay behind them, they felt relatively safe amongst the foothills and walked along the trail at a slower pace. The

---

*Charles Cushing later became one of Lapham's lieutenants in the Luzon Guerrilla Army Force (LGAF). He was also the brother of Walter Cushing, the American manager of a Philippine mine who armed his workers and began conducting raids against the Japanese in the early days of 1942 (see Epilogue). Another brother, James Cushing, led a guerrilla force on the island of Cebu. James Cushing was the only brother to survive the war.

newfound sense of security coincided comfortably with the needs of Volckmann's health—with his malaria relapsing, it was best not to force a speedy gait.

At Cushing's hideout, they were met by two other Americans: Herb Swick and Enoch French, both of whom had worked in the local mining industry. Swick displayed the greatest enthusiasm for fighting the Japanese and insisted that he join Volckmann in his quest to find Moses and Noble. Since Volckmann needed all the additional manpower he could get, he admitted Swick into the group. Cushing, meanwhile, told them that Moses and Noble were last seen near Bokod in the Benguet sub-province (Mountain Province). He regretfully had no further information to give, but offered a guide to take them beyond the Agno River Valley.[127]

The Agno River, which Volckmann had crossed nine months earlier, ran from east to west across the island. The point where Volckmann had crossed during the retreat to Bataan was scarcely above sea level. As the river flowed to the Pacific, however, it cut through the Cordillera Central forming the Agno River Valley. Now, Volckmann found himself on the edge of a canyon where the Agno lay over a hundred feet below. His only method of crossing was a primitive cable car. Reminiscent of the aerial tramways in tourist sites, these native contraptions pulled Volckmann across the chasm with surprising ease.[128]

This area surrounding the valley had been one of the few places unmolested by the Japanese. Crossing through Dalaprit on the opposite side of the Agno River, Volckmann and his men spent a grueling three hours trying to negotiate a path to Lusod—a path which took them straight up the side of a mountain. Volckmann knew that the steep grades normally wouldn't have presented this much of a challenge, but the malaria had destroyed his prewar endurance. Every few yards, fatigue would force him to his knees, his body crying out for a few moments' rest.[129] With the level grade of the Central Plains behind him, Volckmann realized he would have to recalibrate his body to the rigors of mountain hiking.

Fortunately, the trail to Lusod led them to the home of a guerrilla contact named Deleon, a former mechanic who had been employed by the local sawmill. Deleon spoke English and happily gave Volckmann the few days rest that he so desperately needed. Deleon informed the group that Moses and Noble were just a few hours north, beyond Mount Lusod in a small barrio called Benning. With Herb Swick leading the way, Volckmann and company enjoyed a slow-paced jaunt around Mount Lusod and arrived in Benning on 9 September 1942.[130]

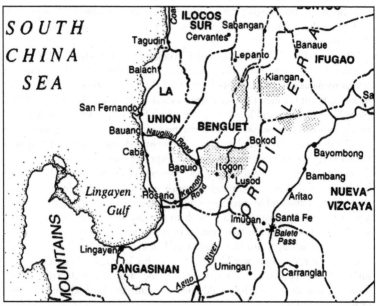

Map of North Luzon depicting the Benguet and Ifugao sub-provinces (Mountain Province). Visible from the map is Igoton (Igoten), home of the Igoten Mines and the site of the disastrous guerrilla raid of 15 October 1942. Also pictured is Kiangan, where Volckmann later built his guerrilla headquarters and solicited help from the Haliap tribe. *Map courtesy of Bernard Norling.*

CHAPTER 5

The New Guerrilla

Benning was a small native barrio, a settlement of cogon-grass houses built upon stilts. Its residents were the Benguets, the southernmost tribe of the Igorot people. The news of Volckmann's arrival in North Luzon obviously preceded him by a few hours, as Moses and Noble stood at the edge of the settlement with a crowd of natives ready to greet him. It was a joyous reunion, for Volckmann had not seen either of them since the fall of Bataan. Moses, Noble, Volckmann, and Blackburn spent the rest of the afternoon regaling one another with tales of their harrowing escape. Despite the treachery of the jungle, Martin Moses had emerged from Bataan in relatively good health. Arthur Noble, however, had not been so fortunate—he had lost sight in his left eye after a rattan vine punctured it.[131]

Over the past few months, Moses and Noble had gathered a wealth of information concerning the state of affairs in the Philippines. Most of the information came from eyewitness accounts, but other reports came through the "bamboo telegraph"—a system of native runners who supplied information from town to town.[132] Moses and Noble had no means of validating the information supplied to them by the "telegraph," but it was often the only source of news available. As the Japanese had taken over the Philippine media, all domestic radio stations and news outlets were no longer trustworthy.

From Moses and Noble, Volckmann learned that Colonel John P. Horan had been captured in the Zambales Mountains. According to the "telegraph," Walter Cushing, the American manager of a local mining company, had armed his mining employees and begun the first Allied resistance in the Philippines. Tragically, though, he had been killed the previous summer. Captain Ralph Praeger, formerly of the 26th Cavalry (Philippine Scouts), operated a small band of guerrillas in the Apayao sub-province. The "telegraph" also indicated that Roque Ablan, the provincial governor of Ilocos Norte, had formed his own guerrilla team. There were also rumors that General Brougher was free and leading a guerrilla force somewhere in North Luzon. Volckmann believed it to be false and, indeed, it was; the Japanese had already captured Brougher.[133]

Also at Benning with Moses and Noble were Captains Parker Calvert and Art Murphy, both of whom had been company commanders in Colonel Horan's 43rd Infantry Regiment. Another one of Horan's men, Captain George Barnett, maintained a guerrilla outfit on the Ilocos provincial coasts.[134] Also in the immediate vicinity were Philippine Army Captains Rufino Baldwin, Manolo Enriquez, Guillermo Nakar, and Bado Dagwa, all of whom were commanding guerrillas—although Moses and Noble gave no indication as to their size, disposition, or any recent activity.

Volckmann's conversation with the colonels then turned to the more serious topic of actions against the enemy. Volckmann enthusiastically gave his estimate of the situation: the environment was an ideal setting for guerrilla warfare—the provincial landscape was remote and rugged, with few roads and a population sympathetic towards the U.S. Moses and Noble agreed, but did not feel that the timing was right. Consequently, they told Volckmann to "take it easy" for the next few days while they formulated a plan.[135]

Slightly disappointed by the colonels' response, Volckmann retired for the evening. His meeting with Moses and Noble had not been very productive. In earnest, Volckmann had hoped for a more aggressive response. The timing may not have been ideal, Volckmann thought, but Moses and Noble—the senior-ranking officers in North Luzon—should have begun developing plans for guerrilla warfare months ago. Nonetheless, Volckmann left the matter for the colonels to decide.

After hearing from Herb Swick that a small American settlement lay in Oding, another barrio only a few miles north, Volckmann and Blackburn decided to make it their unofficial "headquarters" while awaiting the colonels' orders. Swick also mentioned that he knew of a doctor in Oding who could help Volckmann and Blackburn with their recurring bouts of malaria. The following morning, 10 September, Volckmann, Blackburn, Swick, Bruno, and Emilio left for Oding. The path to Oding was not a long trek, but the mountainous trails made it very tiresome. Along the way, Swick told Volckmann about the residents of Oding. The town itself was an abandoned mine settlement where five American families and one Filipino doctor had taken refuge from the Japanese. The Americans had been contract workers with the mining company at Igoten, and the Filipino doctor, Dr. Biason, had been the company staff doctor. Volckmann reported that Biason earned a medical degree from the University of Minnesota and was married to an American nurse.[136]

The camp at Oding surpassed anything Volckmann had expected. Each family had built themselves a small house that drew running water from a series of pipes fed from a nearby stream they had dammed. The most impressive gadget was an automobile generator powered by a water wheel. This apparatus provided electricity for lights and a radio.[137] Volckmann could hardly believe it; these families had created their own power grid. He greatly admired their ingenuity, and their example served him well throughout the rest of his days as a guerrilla.

From 12–15 September, he remained in the Oding area under Dr. Biason's care. Between his malaria shots, Volckmann kept himself busy by listening to radio station KGEI-San Francisco. It was the first reliable news source he had had since arriving in North Luzon. Of late, there had been no exciting news from the Pacific. In the entry for 13 September, Volckmann reports that, "the all out offensive that started last month doesn't seem to be making such headway." And although he enjoyed the families and their hospitality, Volckmann knew better than to stay there any longer. This peaceful camp was no place for two American Army officers to build their guerrilla station—for if the Japanese discovered their hideout, it would force the families to move away from the few creature comforts they had worked so hard to prepare. Blackburn decided to stay over at the camp for a few more days, as he was still in need of more treatment from Dr. Biason's malaria shots, while Volckmann and Swick decided to move farther north to Bokod where Swick himself had established a camp.[138]

After a breakfast prepared by one the Oding families, Volckmann and Swick set out for Bokod on the morning of 15 September. It was an easy three-hour walk and much to his surprise, Colonels Noble and Moses sent him an extra pair of shoes they had taken out of Baguio. From there, the following morning, they set out for Ekip, another barrio farther to the east.[139] Like before, theirs was a three-hour hike, however this time most of it was uphill. Exhausted, they reached Ekip, where they were greeted by two American soldiers and a mining engineer who had established a camp there. Because the camp was situated at a higher elevation—6,000 ft.—the weather was much different than what Volckmann and his group had been accustomed to. Described as a lonely and isolated place in the mountains, the temperature was very cold and the rolling clouds blocked most of the sunlight.[140]

Meanwhile, under Dr. Biason's care—and a steady intake of malaria shots—Blackburn regained his previous vitality. From the "telegraph," Blackburn learned that Moses and Noble had moved from Benning into Bobok and occupied the town's sawmill as their headquarters. As Bobok sawmill was on the way to Ekip, Blackburn decided to report to the colonels' new location for any updates before meeting Volckmann at Ekip.[141]

Arriving at Bobok's sawmill, Moses and Noble informed Blackburn that, effective immediately, they had assumed command of all guerrillas in North Luzon and were planning to launch a guerrilla campaign on 15 October 1942. Listening to the colonels' plans, however, Blackburn noticed that they lacked the necessary amount of thoroughness. The intended participants were scattered all over North Luzon, and the plan gave no mention to the possibility of enemy reprisals.[142] Nonetheless, Blackburn bit his tongue and agreed to inform Volckmann of the plan once he reached Ekip.

The change in climate at Ekip turned out to be good for Volckmann's health. By 17 September, he noted a marked improvement in his condition and was anxious to get back on the trail. That same day, Blackburn joined the rest of the group. He informed Volckmann of the meeting with Moses and Noble at Bobok and delivered their instructions to him: Volckmann was to meet the colonels on 1 October in a barrio called Caraw. For the next two weeks, the colonels' plan was the only topic of discussion between Volckmann and Blackburn. Aside from the lack of thoroughness that the colonels' plans possessed, Volckmann and Blackburn noticed another potential problem: the Agno River. During the rainy season, the Agno was wider, deeper, and possessed a raging current. This was beneficial to the guerrillas, as it created a natural barrier to the Japanese patrols. However, the rainy season had ended and the Agno was rapidly shrinking back to its preseason size, thus denying the guerrillas a critical terrain asset.[143] Nevertheless, both men anxiously awaited their orders. In the meantime, Volckmann enjoyed the newfound abundance of food. Aside from cooking beef and pork, he stretched the bounds of his creativity by making pancakes out of rice flour. Brewing coffee also became a regular occurrence. The Spaniards had introduced coffee to the Philippines centuries ago and it grew well at the camp's elevation.[144]

The next entry in Volckmann's diary, 1 October, documents his meeting with Moses and Noble. As per orders, he went with Blackburn and Swick to Caraw where they found the colonels awaiting them. Just as Volckmann had anticipated, Moses and Noble announced their assumption of command. Dispatches were being sent to all local commanders and a coordinated counteroffensive was to begin on 15 October 1942. His first assignment was to act as Moses' personal liaison and to deliver intelligence reports and other instructions to local USAFFE personnel.[145] Finally, Volckmann was back in the war—this time as a guerrilla.

With the date of the operation confirmed, Moses and Noble set H-Hour at 0100. The colonel's plan was simple in its conception: guerrilla forces would conduct a raid on the Japanese garrison at the Igoten Mines. The main effort consisted of elements commanded by Captain Rufino Baldwin,* formerly of the 14th Infantry Regiment (Philippine Army). Baldwin had commanded an infantry company during the retreat to Bataan and now found himself in charge of a small outfit near Bobok. Baldwin was a talented young officer, one whom Moses and Noble obviously admired. And considering that his group was the one nearest to the Igoten Mines, it stood to reason that the colonels would choose him to lead the raid.[146]

Moses' and Noble's orders to Baldwin were clear: conduct a raid on the Japanese garrison and destroy the Japanese thoroughfare along Kennon Road.

---

*A Philippine Army officer, Baldwin was a *mestizo*—a term referring to those of mixed European and Filipino descent.

In addition to seizing the area surrounding the mines, the raid intended the capture of a Japanese man named Acota.* The nature of Acota's relationship to the Japanese remains unclear—Volckmann indicated that he was a high-ranking Japanese officer while Blackburn identified him as merely a Japanese agent. Whatever his disposition, Acota had become the manager of the Igoten Mines and was universally despised by both Americans and Filipinos; he had taken over the formerly American-run mines and repeatedly gave information on guerrilla activity to the Japanese garrison commanders. It was hoped that the capture of Acota would provide the guerrillas with the names of collaborators along with intelligence on enemy activity.[147]

However, the raid planned for 15 October ended in disaster. Volckmann and Blackburn were not present at the raid, but witnessed it from atop a nearby ridge. Hoping to watch a resounding success, Volckmann and Blackburn saw a tragedy unfold before their eyes. An overzealous guerrilla initiated fire too soon and alerted the Japanese to their presence. With one premature shot, the guerrillas had forfeited the element of surprise.

Scrambling to form a counterattack, the Japanese garrison brutally repelled the guerrilla raid. Aside from their failure to capture the mines, the guerrillas had missed their human target, Acota, which had been their priority. Acota, like the Japanese troops, had been alerted by the premature fire. Dashing for cover, he fell into a nearby ditch where—unfortunately—he had broken his back. Recovered by a small group of Baldwin's men, they quickly discovered that they could not carry him back to their hideout, and in a fit of panic they shot him where he lay.[148] As a result of the disastrous guerrilla raid, the Japanese mobilized all available reinforcements into the area surrounding the Igoten Mines.

The punitive expeditions were about to begin.

A few days after the raid, a sobered Moses and Noble came to Volckmann with a recalibrated plan. The new task that they assigned to Volckmann was to establish a "communication" system with the other guerrillas in the area.[149] Likely, the two colonels had realized that poor communication was partially to blame for their recent debacle. Under their instructions, Volckmann took the initiative to establish a message center at the abandoned Lusod Sawmill Company a few miles east of the Igoten Mines. During peacetime, an open-wire telephone circuit connected nearly every sawmill throughout the province.[150] Using the company's letterhead to type his memoranda and other records, he simultaneously began the process of repairing the telephone line connecting Lusod to other sawmills. Many of the phone lines and terminals were still operable, but several others had suffered collateral damage from the Japanese. The nearest sawmill was located in Bobok, where Blackburn had met the colonels a month earlier before the botched Igoten raid. Since Blackburn had prior service as the 11th Division

---

*Other reports have his name spelt as *Okoda*.

Signal Officer, Volckmann let him take the lead in repairing the phone line from Lusod to Bobok.

Meanwhile, Volckmann busied himself making plans for the next phase of operations. Since the Japanese now had an insurgency on their hands, Volckmann was certain that massive reprisals were coming soon. It was not a question of *if,* but *when.* And when it did come, he wanted to be ready for it. Back at Lusod, Volckmann contacted Deleon, the former sawmill mechanic.[151] Deleon agreed to have the men at the local barrio fix up the sawmill and provide assistance in getting the phone lines operational. Aside from the phone line to Bobok, the Lusod Sawmill Company had terminals connected to Bokod and Dalaprit, two other nearby barrios. Dalaprit, however, was the priority terminal as Rufino Baldwin had recently located his men there.

Encouraged by the help he received from Deleon and his friends in the barrio, Volckmann decided to expand his authority. He sent word to the local barrio leaders instructing them to provide workers and other able-bodied males to assist him in building his guerrilla network.[152] Additionally, Volckmann made requests for food and dry goods via handwritten receipts promising full compensation from the United States at the end of the war. This was a bold and daring move: Volckmann had no idea whether "Uncle Sam" would honor his receipts or if the Filipino villagers would even accept his demands. But if Volckmann acted like an officer of a defeated army, he would be treated as such.[153]

Luckily, the Filipinos responded quickly and eagerly to Volckmann's orders. Signing his handwritten receipts, Volckmann received copious amounts of rice, vegetables, and beef—complemented by a fresh contingent of workers for the telephone line and others awaiting induction into the guerrilla movement.[154] Many of these new recruits were, coincidentally, veterans of the Philippine Scouts and the Constabulary.

On 22 October, Moses and Noble arrived at the sawmill to discuss their future plans with Volckmann. They were going to make their way north to Apayao to establish contact with Ralph Praeger. It was reported that Praeger had made radio contact with Headquarters- Southwest Pacific Area (SWPA) in Australia. If this were the case, the colonels would be able to speak directly to MacArthur and request further instruction. They also planned to give the names of all free Americans under their command in North Luzon. Upon leaving, the colonels instructed Volckmann to continue sending progress reports. However, it was the last time he would see either Moses or Noble again; the Japanese captured both men in June 1943.[155]

On 29 October, Volckmann took Bruno with him to inspect Dalaprit. As it turned out, the pair had to make a treacherous hike through the mountains, as the benign trails and bridges had been destroyed by other guerrillas to impede the Japanese's mobility. Volckmann appreciated the logic but, as of now, the only mobility that suffered was his own. When they arrived at Dalaprit, they were amazed to see Baldwin's camp flooded with evacuees from Igoten. He admired Baldwin for taking them in and postulated what additional manpower the guerrillas could gain from their presence. October 1942 had been Volckmann's busiest month, and although the Japanese had yet to begin their punitive patrols, he was confident that his men would stand firm.[156]

By 9 November 1942, Volckmann had put the finishing touches on his headquarters at Lusod. The phone lines were well established and the natives continued to provide their steady stream of manpower. The "headquarters staff" at the Lusod camp now consisted of Volckmann, Blackburn, Bruno, Emilio, Deleon the mechanic, a young native guide named Atong, and an old native woman whom they nicknamed "Tenny." Tenny earned not only her keep but also the men's admiration for her tireless cooking. Occasionally, their staff included local guards and liaison personnel drawn from the nearby barrios.[157]

Although his camp at Lusod was finally organized, Volckmann would not enjoy the newfound order for very long. The 9th of November marked the beginning of the Japanese counteroffensive. As the Agno River returned to its smaller size, the Japanese contingent at Baguio poured into the countryside. Later that afternoon, the telephone at Bokod reported the Japanese moving south toward Lusod. After falling back to Dalaprit, one of Baldwin's men phoned in to report Japanese movement on the west bank of the Agno River.[158] That put them slightly more than four miles from the Lusod camp.

As soon as Volckmann hung up the phone with Dalaprit, the Japanese greeted him with another artillery barrage. As before, he found himself on the receiving end of another 75mm battery. The shells did not come very close, but close enough to convince him to move his camp. The Japanese had not pinpointed his exact location, but to bring their fire so close indicated that they were aware of his presence. He suspected the work of informers amongst the Filipinos.[159]

The following morning, the phone terminal at Bobok went dead—*the Japanese had cut the line.* Volckmann quickly ushered his staff into a smaller camp higher up the mountain; he was not going to let the Japanese artillery zero in on him, nor risk the enemy attacking his camp at night. Before traveling up the mountainside, Volckmann asked Tenny to go home and maintain her vigilance on Japanese activity. Volckmann indicated that he would meet her back at Lusod the following morning for any updates.[160]

The next morning, Volckmann returned to Lusod where he found Tenny waiting for him. She said that Japanese soldiers had come farther up the mountainside, but estimated that they were still a good two hours away. Volckmann thanked her for the information and asked her to continue monitoring the Japanese. With that, Volckmann departed Lusod with the promise that he would send one of his men to bring her to the new campsite. Shortly thereafter, Volckmann returned to his new campsite where Bruno and Deleon greeted him with news that the Japanese had already reached the Lusod sawmill.[161] It was quite possibly the last news that Volckmann wanted to hear; he had been at Lusod only a few hours before, and now the Japanese were encamped there.

Two hours after sunset, Bruno retrieved Tenny and brought her into the new campsite. Upon her arrival, she gave a full report on recent Japanese activity. A Japanese captain, who had somehow been employed by the sawmill years earlier, was leading the patrol currently occupying Lusod. He was familiar with the surrounding area and, consequently, was chosen to lead the punitive expedition. The captain, according to Tenny, had questioned her at length concerning two Americans: Volckmann and Blackburn.[162]

Both men were speechless—*the Japanese knew their names.* By now, there was no doubt that informers were working amongst the local populace. This complicated things for Volckmann, but for now he had no choice other than to accept it as a part of guerrilla warfare. The vast majority of the Filipinos still disliked the Japanese, but with the enemy commanding greater incentives and materiel, those who "rode the fence" could easily be tipped in the opposite direction. In addition, Japanese torture had a way of making them talk. Success, therefore, lay in exercising caution regarding whom they could trust.

Before determining what criterion they would use in evaluating their allies, Volckmann first had to relocate his camp. The Japanese patrol, and especially their captain, would make life miserable for Volckmann and Blackburn if they stayed in the same place much longer. After instructing Tenny to stay behind and monitor any changes in enemy activity, Volckmann took Blackburn, Bruno, and Emilio on a hike to Sumulpuss.[163] It was a small native barrio that the Japanese had yet to enter. The natives there were friendly and Volckmann eagerly accepted their invitation to sit down for a meal. But while eating his lunch in a small hut, located about 50 yards from the main road, Volckmann noticed some movement from behind the tree line. While he was straining his eyes to get a closer look, an entire column of Japanese infantrymen rumbled around the bend. With their bayonets fixed and wearing full battle regalia, the foot column marched down the main path just outside the barrio. One sidelong glance from a Japanese soldier and Volckmann's game would have been over. Luckily, the column passed without incident—but for Volckmann, this was too close for comfort. He had counted 50 infantrymen by the time the last Japanese rifleman passed by.[164]

After his close encounter with the Japanese column, Volckmann decided to make his way farther north towards the summit of the mountain. The terrain up there was dominated by rainforest and heavy cloud cover—just what Volckmann needed to escape detection. The rainforest provided great concealment and the overcast would dissipate the smoke from any campfires. On the other hand, the dense foliage reminded him of his days with the 11th Infantry in Bataan; he could scarcely see beyond his nose. One hundred and twenty yards above the main trail from Sumulpuss, Volckmann and Blackburn set up camp in a small hut. The hut was deserted and had probably been a Philippine Army aid station at one point.

Over the next five days during 15–20 November, they remained at the hut, lying low as Japanese patrols came within yards of their location. Neither Volckmann nor anyone in the group ever saw a patrol during those five days, but they could certainly hear them. On the morning of the sixth day, however, the Japanese called off their search and began pulling out of the area. As night fell, Volckmann and his group started back toward Lusod, the same direction the Japanese had gone. Realizing that he may encounter a rear guard or backtracking patrol, Volckmann decided to stay off the main trail.[165]

After spending the night at Lusod, the group hit the trail toward Oding, the camp with the industrious American families that they had visited earlier. Volckmann was anxious to see them again and earnestly hoped that they remained in good spirits. Oding, however, was no longer the cheerful hideaway it had been when Volckmann left. During their retreat, the Japanese had passed through Oding and destroyed everything.[166] The proud houses and crude amenities built by these five families had been burned to the ground; there was no trace of any of the camp's former inhabitants.[167]

Maintaining a course along the mountain ridgeline, Volckmann and Blackburn could see various native villages going up in flames. From this vantage point, they could see that the Japanese were crisscrossing the landscape and scorching every village in their path. They settled down for the night atop a ridge overlooking the Bobok sawmill and in the morning, continued northward to their former camp at Ekip. Coming off the ridgeline, they descended into the Bolo River Valley, which had been the region's agricultural nerve center until the Japanese destroyed its crops. Likely, the Japanese had done so as a counterinsurgency measure.

Nearly every trail in the Bolo River Valley bore footprints of the Japanese infantry. The farther Volckmann traveled into the valley, the more devastation he saw—a seemingly endless trail of ruble and burned villages greeted him at every turn. Deeper into the valley, Volckmann and Blackburn encountered a young Igorot who agreed to lead them into Bugias, a barrio that, surprisingly, had been spared by the Japanese. At Bugias, Volckmann learned that his camp at Ekip had been destroyed. The barrio lieutenant also provided Volckmann with a puzzling piece of news: Colonels Moses and Noble had now gone south.[168]

Volckmann pondered over what to do next. Even if he could establish contact with Moses and Noble, his report would not have been a rosy one: units heavily dispersed, phone lines dead, Japanese patrols, villages burned, etc. Furthermore, these were things that Moses and Noble probably already knew. Nevertheless, Benguet sub-province had become a hornet's nest and Volckmann swallowed the bitter revelation that all his hard work had seemingly been undone. To make matters worse, Moses and Noble—for all intents and purposes—had fled to the north and left their guerrillas in Benguet to fend for themselves while the pair tried to track down Ralph Praeger in Apayao.

All things considered, Moses and Noble had not done a stellar job in organizing the Allied resistance in North Luzon. Undaunted, however, Volckmann decided to take matters into his own hands. He still recognized the colonels' authority and remained optimistic that the false starts of October 1942 could easily be fixed. But, for the time being, Volckmann would begin organizing and training guerrilla cadres on his own. This way, when Moses and Noble finally did get back to him, he could present them with a sizeable guerrilla force ready for action. The only question was: *where would he find the manpower and resources for this bold plan?* The recent chaos and devastation throughout Benguet had destroyed any possibility of recruiting guerrillas there. Bruno, however, had an idea: if Benguet had become too hot to handle, Ifugao might be a feasible alternative. Bruno was a native to the Ifugao sub-province, which lay directly to the northeast, and the leaders of the border barrios were relatives of his.[169] Using his family connections, Bruno could cash in a few favors to provide the group with food, weapons, and loyal manpower.

Although the Bugias barrio lieutenant indicated that Moses and Noble were headed south, Volckmann found this counterintuitive. Their only potential communication outlet lay in the *north*—at Ralph Praeger's camp in Apayao. He was certain that this was where the colonels were really headed. After enjoying a rice and pork dinner with the Bugias locals, Volckmann hit the trail for Ifugao. According to Bruno, the quickest way to Ifugao was through the Taboy River Valley. This area was virtually unsettled and previously no white man had ever been there. Bruno, however, knew the area well.

Before stepping off, Volckmann instructed Bruno to inform the villagers that their group was headed south. Of course, Volckmann wasn't really going south, but he had gleaned an important lesson from his early months as a guerrilla: *never tell the locals your true destination.*[170] With informers indistinguishable from friendly civilians, the practice was wise. A grueling hike through Taboy River Valley found the area just as Bruno had described it: sparsely populated. And while trekking through the bottom layers of the jungle, Volckmann and company encountered a nuisance that they had hoped to leave behind in the Huk swamplands: *leeches.* The leeches in the Taboy River Valley were the worst that Volckmann had thus far experienced. Latching indiscriminately to arms, legs, and even their faces, the men feverishly pried leeches from their skin as they entered the outskirts of Ifugao—bleeding profusely every step of the way.[171]

The few natives that did reside in the Valley were more primitive than the ones Volckmann had encountered earlier. Their houses were fewer and farther between, not grouped into barrios as seen elsewhere. While it may have been true that no white man had explored this region, Volckmann could tell that the Japanese had recently been there—their footprints were still fresh on the ground.[172]

The following afternoon the group stopped at another barrio, Pitican. There, the natives welcomed them with a meal of chicken and rice. Unfortunately, Blackburn's malaria had relapsed and his strength was collapsing. Recalling his own bout with malaria, Volckmann felt inclined to let Blackburn stay over at Pitican to get some rest.[173] Bruno, however, interjected that the barrio of Nonpaling was only a day away and that the barrio lieutenant was his cousin. Normally, Volckmann would have balked at the proposal—he had to take Blackburn's health into account—but the Japanese had already found their way into the Taboy River Valley.

Disgusted with the prospect of forcing a sick man to make a one-day hike, he nonetheless encouraged Blackburn to make the trip. It was torture for Volckmann to watch his friend hobble down the trail, barely keeping himself upright with the aid of a walking stick. When the group finally arrived at Nonpaling, Blackburn collapsed. Rushing him into the barrio lieutenant's home, Volckmann appealed for help.[174] Fortunately, Bruno's connections to the Nonpaling leadership made their stay enjoyable. Blackburn was given quarter and plenty of rest at the lieutenant's house, and all were given generous rations of rice and chicken. To Volckmann and his men, this was a welcomed rest. Since being flushed out of Lusod, it was the first chance any of them had to relax.

During the first day of their layover at Nonpaling, Volckmann and his friends were greeted as heroes wherever they went. This warm reception confirmed that the residents were friendly toward the American cause. Though informers could be persistent nuisances, Volckmann was glad to have the Filipinos on his side. Volckmann was amazed at the great faith they placed in Americans, and how much they preferred Americans to the Japanese. What impressed Volckmann even more than the Ifugao's enthusiasm, however, was their ingenuity. The Ifugao were predominantly rice farmers, and they had built their fields into an elaborate system of terraces complete with irrigation and drainage networks. That evening, Volckmann, Blackburn, Bruno, and Emilio were the guests of Bruno's cousins: Graciano, the barrio lieutenant, and Pedro. At Graciano's, Volckmann met a man who he identified as Mr. Herrin, a minister at the Unitarian church in Kiangan, the capital of Ifugao. Herrin was one of the few American missionaries in the area who had continued his ministry despite the pestilence of the Japanese.[175]

After spending the night with Pedro, Volckmann decided to solicit help from the local missionaries. Since the United States' acquisition of the Philippines, Christian missionaries had established permanent bases within the archipelago. According to Herrin, the nearest missionary camp lay only about an hour away and within its walls resided three American women.[176] Two of them, Miss Myrtle Metzger and Miss Lottie Spessard, were missionaries that Bruno had known before the war. The third woman, Mrs. Kluege, was the wife of an American contractor employed with the local lumber industry. Volckmann had heard that her husband, Herman Kluege, was commanding a guerrilla unit somewhere north of Baguio, but had not yet seen him. Miss Spessard, as it were, was a registered nurse and gave what little medicine she had to Blackburn to treat his malaria. After a few days under her care, Blackburn seemed to have his ailment under control. For the remainder of Volckmann's stay in Ifugao, he made it a point to send the ladies any additional food he had.[177]

Although the Ifugao tribesmen were friendly to Volckmann and Blackburn, the presence of two American Army officers within their community made them nervous. To help ease their discomfort, Volckmann began looking beyond Ifugao to garner support from the other tribes in Mountain Province. Across the valley, near the Ifugao capital of Kiangan, lay the Haliap tribe. According to the Ifugao, the Haliap were a throwback to the most primitive denizens of the Philippines: spear-wielding, headhunting savages. The Ifugao people were slightly apprehensive of the Haliap, but what intimidated them the most was the Haliap leader, Kamayong. The Ifugaos characterized him as a fearsome warrior and a tyrant, one who was well known throughout Mountain Province.[178] Despite this intimidating portrayal of the Haliap chieftain, Volckmann had an idea: if Kamayong and his men were indeed as fearsome as the Ifugao described, then the Haliap would no doubt make effective guerrillas. Therefore, Volckmann decided that while keeping his lines of supply open in Ifugao, he would travel to the Haliap country in search of additional manpower.

Meanwhile, Herrin found a solution to Volckmann's recurring problems of food and supply. Using some of his contacts in Kiangan, Herrin had established a line of credit with a local merchant named Formoca.[179] Formoca provided Volckmann and Blackburn with items such as coffee, sugar, and soap. Also, via Bruno's family connections, Volckmann solicited help from two women in Manila who regularly sent him towels, shoes, underwear, and other hygiene products.[180]

By the one-year anniversary of Pearl Harbor, Volckmann had established a new camp outside Kiangan. This "camp" was little more than a small hut, but with some diligence and creativity, Volckmann made the abode livable. He and Blackburn even went so far as to make themselves a carpeted floor from sewn-together cogon grass.[181]

The entire month of December was fairly quiet. They received no further enemy contact and proceeded to spend most of their time regrouping from the previous month. Volckmann busied himself with some light exercise to maintain his strength and fend off the malaria. Over the next few weeks, he received various reports concerning the progress of the war. Some were believable, but others were so farfetched that they had to be untrue. One such report he received from Mr. Herrin indicated that one million U.S. troops landed in China. Another report included a statement supposedly made by President Roosevelt: *"[He] has notified the Japs that if they do not surrender the Philippines by Jan 27th, the USA will attack from North, South, East, and West. President Roosevelt has also ordered all guerrilla warfare to cease in the Philippines until the coming of American troops."*[182] In reality, no such order came from Roosevelt. In any event, Volckmann did not believe it.

As Christmas Eve approached, his thoughts once again returned to his wife and son. His wife, Nancy, and son, Russell, Jr., had been evacuated well over a year ago. In his diary entry for 24 December, he refers to them as "Nan" and "Dutch." Although he missed them terribly, he assured himself that they were doing fine and wondered how long it would be before "Dutch," who was then six, could swing a golf club. Volckmann himself was an avid golfer.

By late December, he still had no contact with the camp at the Lusod sawmill. Herrin's "reports" were among the only news they had concerning the outside world. The following diary entries close out Volckmann's first year of the war:

> 25 December 1942. The American ladies sent us a jar of noodles and wished us a Merry Xmas. We went over to pay them a visit and took them some sausage. Returned here about 4:00 P.M. and had our Xmas dinner—roast duck, mashed [potatoes] with giblet gravy, green beans, rice dressing, coffee, pumpkin pie. Best meal I have had since the beginning of the war [author's note: quite impressive for a dinner behind enemy lines]. Hope Nan and Dutch have a swell Xmas.
>
> 26 December. Chopped some wood today for exercise. At the Xmas celebration in Kiangan, Jap Capt in his speech told the people there was no more war in the Orient; the Japs have superiority in the air, land, and water. Reports indicate there is guerrilla fighting in Bontoc, also five Jap trucks ambushed in Pangasian. Made a chocolate pie today, also some corn bread, turned out very good. The pie crust, which was made of Camote cahoy flour, was very good.
>
> 27 December. Nothing very unusual today. Made corn pancakes for breakfast, also a cake which turned out very good. One of our boys brought in a report that three Americans passed near here and that the Japs were tracking them.
>
> 28 December. Mr. Herrin sent us a note stating Italy has been occupied and that 250,000 American troops have arrived in China (news is supposed to be three weeks old). Reports—Japs ambushed in Natunin, also 50 trucks ambushed in Pangasian. Guerrilla fighting reported going on around Bontoc. Governor of Bontoc killed.
>
> 29 December. Nothing unusual today. Expect some news from Mr. Herrin tomorrow along with some supplies. Made good syrup out of coconut milk and sugar today. Hope to be able to arrange to get direct radio news from the priest in Kiangan.
>
> 30 December. Mr. Herrin returned from Kiangan with news that the U.S. now has a million troops in China. Hope this damn news we are getting is true. Took a hike to the top of mountain north of here. Beautiful country; hope to get some rice wine for tomorrow.

31 December . Took another hike up to the top of the mountain. Don went with me; lay out on the rocks and took a sun bath for about an hour. This past month has been a very quiet one for us. Have not accomplished a great deal in this area yet but have a good start in organizing the Scouts and Constabulary in this area. I certainly hope that before 1943 gets very far underway, they will get some U.S. troops in here. It's going to be hard to keep the confidence of the people if they don't get in here soon.[183]

Thus ended 1942.

CHAPTER 6

The Waiting Game

By the dawn of 1943, Volckmann realized that his options were indeed limited. Without any clear directives from Moses or Noble, it appeared that there was little he could do to improve his situation. December had come and gone, but the Japanese and their friends in the "fifth column" still lurked behind every bend. In response to the disastrous raid on the Igoten Mines, the Japanese launched their first cohesive anti-guerrilla campaign of the war. This included manning garrisons within every city in North Luzon. From these garrisons, ten-day patrols were dispatched on a rotating basis. In addition to the military campaign, the Japanese also enacted a "Plan of Propaganda," which called for psychological warfare.[184]

As with many of the Japanese techniques, their counterinsurgency employed tactics of the lowest common denominator. The Japanese-controlled media ran looping broadcasts of the American "defeat" in the Pacific. Meanwhile, public decapitations, torture, rape, and thievery became the rule of the day as the Japanese took over the once peaceful municipalities of North Luzon. The propaganda machine also utilized local leaders and "puppet officials" to publicly denounce Americans and urge the surrender of those who would dare defy the Emperor's forces.[185] Every war produces its share of homegrown sympathizers—as well as those whose allegiances change with the tides. For Volckmann, the latter seem to cause more trouble than the former. Among the most troublesome was the mayor of Kiangan; one day he would be decidedly pro-American and the next day, decidedly pro-Japanese.[186] Attitudes like his were difficult to decipher. Was it all just a ruse to get the Japanese off their backs? Or were these people merely "fence-sitters," who constantly changed their allegiance depending on which side had the upper hand at any given moment?

Shifting loyalties among the Filipinos could certainly be frustrating, but Volckmann nevertheless needed recruits for the resistance. To this end, Bruno proved to be Volckmann's "ace in the hole." This young Ifugao knew which of his brethren could—and could not—be trusted to help the American cause. Bruno carefully screened any potential recruit whose loyalties may have been questionable.[187] It remains unclear exactly how Bruno knew which individuals could be trusted or what criteria he used in evaluating them, but it is obvious that he had an intimate knowledge of his homeland and the people with whom he shared it. The individuals that Bruno contacted included veterans of the Philippine Army, Philippine Scouts, and hunter and trappers of the more primitive tribes in the Ifugao highlands.

Contacting the local tribe leaders, Volckmann solicited their help in establishing guerrilla camps and keeping his men supplied with necessities. On 7 March 1943, Volckmann consulted with the first of these tribal heads: Tamicpao, chief of the Antipolo tribe. The old chieftain looked much younger than his 70 years suggested. Sharp-featured with a muscular build, Tamicpao and his Antipolos had a more benign reputation than did the Haliap.[188] Neither Volckmann nor Blackburn provided any great detail about their meeting with Tamicpao, but the elderly chieftain pledged his support and offered the guerrillas anything they needed. His one stipulation, however, was that Volckmann not establish any of his camps near the Antipolo's main village.

Tamicpao's reasoning behind this, surprisingly, stemmed from a fear of Kamayong and the Haliap. A long-standing border dispute over a rice paddy complex had put the two tribes at odds with one another. Tamicpao feared that if the Haliap discovered Americans near his village, Kamayong would report it to the Japanese simply out of spite for the Antipolo. Although the Antipolo were the second group of people to express their apprehensions about Kamayong, Volckmann decided to meet the Haliap chieftain anyway.[189]

Despite admonitions from the other Ifugao residents, Volckmann found Kamayong to be a charming and pleasurable man. He was no doubt a strong leader, but he presented a warm and friendly side to those who earnestly sought his help. During the course of their meeting, Volckmann mentioned that Tamicpao had offered his support to the guerrillas. Volckmann also indicated that he knew of their border dispute, but he implored Kamayong to put aside his differences with the Antipolo.[190] At present, the most beneficial thing for all parties was to fight the Japanese. According to Volckmann, the Japanese were a pestilence upon an innocent people. Prior to the war, Kamayong had little contact with civilized Filipinos and even less contact with the Americans. But Volckmann's description of the Japanese and their brutal occupation techniques made Kamayong furious. The Antipolo may have been on the wrong side of Kamayong's sentiments, but he would not stand by idly as his homeland was overrun by such brutality. As leader of the Haliap tribe, he assured Volckmann that his tribal land was safe for their use and that neither he nor his people would betray them to the Japanese. He also promised to restore normal relations with the Antipolo. Oddly enough, Volckmann's stroke of diplomacy provided a lasting peace between the two native factions, for by the time Volckmann departed the Philippines, Tamicpao and Kamayong had become close friends.[191]

Contacting Kamayong proved to be one of the best decisions Volckmann made during his early days as a guerrilla. The Haliap leader kept a close eye on his people, and his influence over them was strong. Indeed, if Kamayong supported the American cause, it was unlikely that an informant would arise from the ranks of the Haliap. Also, the trails throughout the region were sparse and, often, only the Haliap knew their locations. Hence, Volckmann decided to establish his new headquarters in the Haliap lands of Ifugao.[192]

By and large, Volckmann found the Haliap to be a cheerful lot. Their houses and communities were built in a fashion similar to those he had seen elsewhere in Ifugao: on stilts five feet above ground with grass roofs. The only way to gain entrance into each house was by a single ladder in the front. Men were the hunters and warriors while the women tended to domestic and agricultural duties.[193] Rice was their main staple, although livestock—including chicken and pork—often complimented their meals. Volckmann admittedly found many of their customs fascinating. On several occasions, Volckmann became ill and the Haliap doctors would take care of him. He never understood the significance of their healing rituals, but considering the speed with which he always recovered, he did not question their methods.[194]

Throughout April 1943, Volckmann continued to build his headquarters in the Haliap lands of the Ifugao sub-province. At present he had little to work with, yet he brainstormed new ideas while awaiting more updates from Moses and Noble. Volckmann maintained contact with the colonels—both of whom were currently in Apayao with Ralph Praeger—via the "bamboo telegraph." Accordingly, Volckmann discovered that Ralph Praeger actually *did* have a radio set and had established contact with MacArthur's Headquarters, the Southwest Pacific Area (SWPA).[195]

Although the news of Praeger's contact with MacArthur was certainly rousing, the general's only communique stated that USAFFE forces should "lay low" for the time being and avoid direct contact with the enemy.

Not very encouraging, Volckmann thought.

But what other choice did they have? USAFFE remnants in North Luzon were still heavily dispersed and maintained virtually no contact with one another. To make matters worse, the Japanese had intercepted more guerrillas, their "fifth column" continued to grow, and Moses and Noble—the presumed "leaders" of the North Luzon resistance—had not issued any orders since disappearing into Apayao the previous December. In all, the "lay low" advisory did nothing more than restate the obvious conclusions that Volckmann had made months ago.

The waiting game is perhaps what frustrated Volckmann the most. Until Moses and Noble gave him a clear picture of what was supposed to happen, he had no choice but continue waiting. Nevertheless, Volckmann used his downtime productively. The first thing he decided to do was build a communication network with other guerrilla elements in the adjacent area. There were many Filipinos who were eager to help him, but Volckmann wanted to find more of his American compatriots. For this, he sent Blackburn on a reconnaissance mission to re-establish contact with units in the Benguet area. It had been a few months since the chaos of the previous fall had forced Volckmann into Ifugao. Consequently, he wanted to see if any Americans remained in Benguet and get any updates on the Japanese activity there.[196]

When Blackburn began his reconnaissance mission, he departed Ifugao the same way that he and Volckmann had entered—through the treacherous Taboy River Valley. After running through the valley of leeches, Blackburn arrived in Ekip, where the same townspeople who had taken care of him only a few months ago now greeted him with a cascade of disheartening news. Apparently, enemy activity had not quieted down at all: their friend, Daisy Baison—the wife of the Filipino doctor at Oding—had been shot by the Japanese; Herb Swick, who had chosen to stay in Benguet, had been captured; Parker Calvert and Art Murphy were on the run—whereabouts unknown; Charles Cushing had deserted his camp; and Herman Kluege had also been captured. Blackburn did, however, find another American at Ekip. His name was Fish and he had been a lumberman before the war.

Fish had been conducting guerrilla operations in Benguet for some time and knew of some friendly elements that remained in the area despite the recent fury. Offering to take him back to Volckmann's camp in the Haliap highlands, Blackburn told Fish of the idea for a communication network, explaining that his knowledge of the Benguet "friendlies" would certainly be helpful. Hearing this, the ex-lumberman agreed to join Blackburn on the trip back to Ifugao.[197]

Back at the Haliap camp, Fish brought Volckmann up to speed on the events of the past few months. The Japanese had certainly devastated the province, but there were enough friendly outposts left in Benguet to form cadres of a small guerrilla force.

> 4 April 1943. Took Fish over to see the ladies [Miss Spessard and Mrs. Kluege]. He gave them all the news he had.
> 5 April 1943. Fish was going to leave today but stayed over waiting for some supplies from Kiangan.
> 6 April 1943. Fish left with two of our boys [presumably Haliap] to return to his place.

Although he presumably played a hand in coordinating the guerrillas in Benguet, the role that Fish ultimately played in the conflict remains a mystery. He was captured in July 1943.[198]

By the end of April, Volckmann had regular contact with the other USAFFE personnel in the Ifugao and Bontoc sub-provinces. His line of communication with Moses and Noble in Apayao ran through Captain Manalo's area of operation in Kalinga, a few miles north of Ifugao. Manalo was an excellent information buffer, for he relayed messages from other nearby units and from Moses and Noble. The system kept Volckmann up to date on enemy activity, but did nothing to inform him of the war outside North Luzon. Anxious for any news concerning the Allied situation in the Pacific, Volckmann sent a search party into Benguet to locate a radio. They returned with a radio receiver on 16 April and, although the battery died two weeks later, listening to KGEI-San Francisco provided him with the news he had been yearning for. Not all of the broadcasts were encouraging, but at least this news was reliable.[199] Reports included the Allied advance in North Africa and the latest victories of the RAF in Europe.

The progress that Volckmann had made throughout the spring of 1943, however, was about to be reversed. Just as they had done the previous fall, the Japanese were poised to disrupt Volckmann's operation yet again. Little by little, punitive expeditions began to flood the countryside. In early May, Captain Manalo was hit hard by a Japanese expeditionary force. Now on the run, his absence disrupted Volckmann's line of communication. In the north, Ralph Praeger—the only man in Luzon with a functioning radio transmitter—was forced to go off the air and bury his radio.* Meanwhile, Rufino Baldwin had been captured south of Baguio and Major Enriquez surrendered his elements of the 14th Infantry Regiment.[200]

To make matters worse, Captain Manalo's records had fallen into the hands of the Japanese. From these documents, the enemy had supposedly learned the location of Volckmann's headquarters. Although his Haliap hosts were visibly upset by the news, Volckmann knew the details of the records that Manalo had kept—the Japanese may have known that Volckmann was in Ifugao, but they did not have enough information from Manalo's records to pinpoint him in the Haliap tribe lands.[201]

Volckmann knew, however, that it wouldn't stop the Japanese from combing the province. Not wanting to jeopardize his hosts, Volckmann met with Kamayong and asked him to help cache any surplus equipment and records in the event they had to move out. Kamayong instead responded with four pagan priests. This stunned Volckmann: he needed an evacuation plan, not a pagan ritual. Undaunted, Kamayong let the four commissioned priests do their work. He explained to Volckmann that the priests would, after reciting a few incantations, bury a pair of chicken feet on the trails leading to the camp. If a Japanese patrol came upon the site where the feet were buried, they would suddenly become lazy and discontinue their search.[202]

This sounded preposterous, and Volckmann again protested that the surplus equipment needed to be cached. Nothing he could say, however, would alter Kamayong's decision. A Japanese platoon did make its way to the foot of the hill upon which Volckmann's camp was located, but miraculously, when the patrol arrived at the very site of the chicken feet, they changed course and moved down into the river valley. Volckmann never again questioned the pagan priests.[203]

---

*Praeger was captured by the Japanese later that year.

Perhaps the most devastating blow to the North Luzon guerrillas, however, occurred on 1 June 1943: Colonels Moses and Noble were captured just outside of Lubuagan, Kalinga. Returning from Praeger's hideout in Apayao, they sent word to Volckmann to alert him of their pending return and advise him of the increased Japanese activity. Unfortunately, while traveling back toward Lubuagan, the colonels had taken ill and sought refuge in a cave not far from a native barrio. After sending one of their men into the barrio for food and medical relief, he was intercepted by a Japanese patrol. True to form, the Japanese tortured the man until he broke down and gave the exact location of the colonels' hiding place.[204]

Apprehended and beaten, Moses and Noble were sent to Bontoc, where the Japanese garrison commander forged a surrender order with the colonels' names attached:

Bontoc, Mt. Province
Philippine Islands
June 9, 1943

Special Orders

1. I surrendered for the peace and happiness of the Philippines to the forces of the Imperial Japanese Army in Kalinga on June 2, 1943. Since our surrender we have been treated with kindness and generosity and in every case according to the Rules of the International Law.
2. I have been assured by officials of the Imperial Japanese Army that all members of the USAFFE still at large on Luzon, who surrender now, will be treated in the same way and in no case will any of them be tortured or killed.
3. All members of the USAFFE now at large on Luzon are, therefore, hereby "AT ONCE" to surrender to the Bontoc Garrison of the Imperial Japanese Army.
4. We will pray to God for your happiness and peaceful life.

> Signed Martin Moses [signature]
> Martin Moses [typed]
> Lt. Col. Infantry, U.S. Army Commanding
>
> Witness: Arthur Noble [signature]
> Arthur Noble [typed]
> Lt. Colonel, Infantry, U.S. Army[205]

Volckmann would not have followed the order even if it were legitimate. Nevertheless, the capture of these two colonels left Volckmann as the senior-ranking officer in North Luzon. The entire guerrilla movement in North Luzon now rested on the shoulders of this 31-year-old-officer.

CHAPTER 7

Master and Commander

Throughout the summer of 1943, the guerrilla movement in North Luzon had reached its lowest ebb. The Moses-Noble operation, for all its grand intentions, had done little more than send the Allied resistance into further chaos. Now, as the senior officer in North Luzon, it was up to Volckmann to pick up the pieces of their shattered enterprise. Since Volckmann's camp in the Haliap highlands was now "General Headquarters," he devised a numbering system to keep track of his other camps. His current location assumed the title of Camp #1, while Volckmann's men at his outpost back in the Antipolo territory became Camp #2.[206] More numerical designations followed as he brought more camps under his command.

Volckmann would spend the rest of June trying to organize his thoughts. *What do we do now? How are we going to take the fight to the enemy?* But before he could answer any of these questions, this new commander-by-default had a bigger problem to worry about: the Japanese were on their way to Haliap.[207]

Whether it had been the work of informers or just the tenacity of the Japanese, it didn't matter—Volckmann had to clear the area. Hopefully Moses and Noble hadn't broken down under torture and given the guerrillas' location.

> 10 June 1943. The news hasn't changed any. All reports coming in sound bad. Looks like the Japs plan on giving us a good chase. Started spreading rumor that we have left for Benguet. I'm feeling lousy today. They [Haliap] called a couple of witches to pray for me.
> 14 June 1943. Well, the Japs haven't come out yet. Don't know how long it is going to be now.
> 15 June 1943. Japs placed a garrison at Burnay.
> 17 June 1943. Another 50 Japs came to Kiangan from Bontoc.
> 18 June 1943. 80 Japs came to Kiangan from Bontoc.
> 20 June 1943. About 4 P.M., we were notified that the Japs were in the barrio below us. Hid-out our surplus things and went to our hide-out. Made the last part of the trip in the dark; very hard walking.
> 21 June 1943. Japs are still around. The shack that we are hiding in is built like a tent. The roof is made of wild gan leaves (each leaf is about three to four feet across).[208]

When Volckmann evacuated the Haliap camp, he had taken Bruno, Emilio, and Pedro, Bruno's cousin, with him. On the evening of the 21st, Volckmann and Blackburn sent Pedro back to the Haliap village for any further news. After what seemed like an eternally restless night, Pedro returned in the morning with the news that the enemy patrol had finally moved on. Surprisingly, the Japanese hadn't asked any questions and hadn't fired a single shot. Volckmann couldn't be sure what the Japanese were up to—or what they had expected to find in the Haliap lands—but for now, the enemy was gone. Despite the relief, however, Volckmann elected to stay at his "evacuation hut" until he was certain the Japanese were out of range.[209] Although the close encounter had turned out to be a minor affair, it stoked his passions to destroy the enemy once and for all.

Meanwhile, Art Murphy and Parker Calvert had re-emerged on the western end of Benguet and were now sending messages to Camp #2. In other news, Bando Dagwa and Dennis Molintas had likewise reemerged from the wilderness. Dagwa, who had owned a transportation company before the war, had reacquired a few of his buses and offered any mobility that he could to the guerrillas.[210] Other reports flowing into Camp #2 included an update on the 14th Infantry Regiment. When Manuel Enriquez surrendered the regiment, the 14th found itself under the command of Major Romulo Manriquez. Major Manriquez had since herded his elements of the 14th Infantry into small camps throughout the Isabela and Nueva Vizcaya provinces.[211]

By the end of July, the fury of the anti-guerrilla campaign began to die down. Apparently, with the capture of Moses and Noble and the recent failures to apprehend any other high-value targets, the Japanese concluded that the guerrilla movement had lost its momentum and could do no serious harm to the occupation force. Russell Volckmann, however, was about to prove them wrong.

With enemy activity at an all-time low, Volckmann made his move. As commanding officer of the Allied resistance, the first thing he decided to do was reorganize the entire North Luzon command structure. To this point, the guerrillas had only operated within a few isolated bands. Too many guerrillas operating independently of one another had produced many of the problems that Volckmann recognized: there was no effective communication network, no intelligence sharing, no feasible system to protect against informers, and no standard dispositions against the enemy.[212] To have any impact on the Japanese, USAFFE guerrillas in North Luzon had to form a united front. A centralized command structure would establish operating guidelines and synchronize combat operations to have the most devastating effect on the Japanese.

With the "Reorganization Plan of 1943," Volckmann established guidelines covering the organization, communication, supply, and operating principles of his guerrilla force.[213] From what he could estimate, there were four regimental commands left in the area. These included remnants of the 121st, 15th, 14th, and 11th Infantry Regiments.* Determining the whereabouts of these regiments, Volckmann divided North Luzon into five military "districts." The Regimental assignments were as follows:

District 1 —66th Infantry
District 2 —121st Infantry
District 3 —15th Infantry
District 4 —11th Infantry
District 5 —14th Infantry

The 66th Infantry was a composite unit that Volckmann created especially for the occasion. It consisted of three battalions that had previously belonged to other regiments prior to the invasion. During the retreat, 1st Battalion, 43rd Infantry (Philippine Scouts), 2nd Battalion, 11th Infantry (Philippine Army), and 3rd Battalion, 12th Infantry (Philippine Army) were separated from their parent units along the western coast of Luzon. Now within Volckmann's command, he organized the lost battalions into one regiment. Adding together the numerical designations of their former regiments—43, 11, and 12 for a total of 66—he designated them as the 66th Infantry.[214]

Consolidating the five "districts" under one command, Volckmann established the United States Armed Forces in the Philippines—North Luzon (USAFIP-NL). One commander would be assigned to each district, with all units and personnel operating therein reporting directly to that commander. To assist Volckmann in his command duties, he established the General Headquarters, USAFIP-NL, in the Ifugao subprovince. Operating along the same lines as a divisional headquarters, he created staff functions to oversee the administrative needs of his guerrilla force. Each staff section was designated by an alphanumeric code indicating its area of responsibility. The Adjutant (G-1) and his staff were responsible for the maintenance of personnel records and contact rosters; the Intelligence staff (G-2) oversaw matters of intelligence, espionage, and interrogations; G-3 referred to the Office of Operational Planning—the staff with which Volckmann had the most interaction; and supply was the responsibility of G-4. In addition, the general staff also included a section for civil affairs (G-5).[215]

Each district commander was directed to organize a regiment consisting of three rifle battalions with four companies each. Regimental camps would be dispersed throughout each district with no camp larger than company-size.[216] This way, if a camp were raided or compromised, the unit could easily disperse and the damage would be localized to only that camp—not the entire regiment.

---

*These were former regiments of the Philippine Army. The 11th Infantry spoken of here is not the same regiment that Volckmann commanded during the retreat to Bataan.

Volckmann directed that all camps be established away from populated areas and main routes of travel. This dispersion method facilitated secrecy and mobility.

As a corollary, knowledge of the location of each camp was restricted only to members of that unit, those authorized to deal with that unit, and the USAFIP-NL General Headquarters. In giving this order, it appears that Volckmann wanted to create an additional safeguard against the possibility of his guerrillas being captured by limiting the amount of information that the enemy could extract from them. This principle applied to all USAFIP-NL command, technical, and support installations.[217]

As the senior ranking officer in North Luzon, Volckmann had full legal authority to assert command over the remaining USAFFE forces in the area. It was a simple concept in theory, but it did not come without its setbacks and frustrations. Some of the units that Volckmann tried to bring under USAFIP-NL solidly rebuffed him—including Robert Lapham's raiders. Many of them, however, did not. Given the urgency of the war, the guerrilla campaign had to make inroads—and quickly.

Under Volckmann's reorganization plan, Parker Calvert became the commander of the 66th Infantry. Calvert had quite a reputation as a guerrilla. After the Moses-Noble debacle, Calvert directed his small group of Philippine Scouts into Benguet and began conducting raids on Japanese outposts. The anti-guerrilla campaign of 1942, however, destroyed much of his momentum. Like many units operating in Benguet, the Calvert posse was badly dispersed. However, unlike many of his comrades, Calvert was fortunate to have evaded capture and remained alive. Now in command of the newly formed 66th Infantry, Calvert appointed new commanders for each of his battalions.[218]

The 121st Infantry was one of the few regiments in the area that remained intact. In February 1942, Colonel John P. Horan received authorization by radiogram from Corregidor to organize the 121st Infantry. The designation applied to the mishmash of units Horan commanded through Balete Pass.[219] After his surrender, however, the 121st refused to follow suit and continued to hold the Bontoc-Kalinga area until the Fall of Bataan.[220] After Horan's retreat, the fragmented units fell to the command of Captain William Peryam, an American Army officer. He aligned his unit with Moses and Noble but Peryam himself was captured in January 1943.[221] By the end of that year, however, George M. Barnett had assumed command and was now reporting to Volckmann.

Inspecting the regimental camps, Volckmann found the 121st to be among the most well-organized units still operating in Luzon. Despite several setbacks over the previous year, the regiment still retained a moderate degree of operability. The Second District's field hospital, for instance, included a fully functioning dental office.[222] Since Barnett had already been at the helm, Volckmann apparently saw no need in appointing another commander. Barnett was left to command the Second District, USAFIP-NL.

The Third District, encompassing the provinces of Abra and Ilocos Norte, was among the slowest to materialize. Previously, civilian agents enlisted by Volckmann reported a small guerrilla force operating near Laoag, the capital of Ilocos Norte. But Volckmann noticed something peculiar about these supposed "guerrillas": each time that his men made contact with them, the Japanese would come out in force. To Volckmann, this made absolutely no sense—all the appropriate countermeasures were taken to ensure that no information had been leaked ahead of the agents' arrival. Furthermore, Volckmann had regular, uninterrupted contact with guerrilla units in other areas where the concentration of enemy troops was much higher. Concluding that there must have been either an informant or a double agent at work, Volckmann sent Barnett to investigate the area.[223]

Barnett, in turn, detailed the task to one of his lieutenants, John O'Day. An Irish-American, O'Day had worked as a miner before the war. Establishing a patrol base in Laoag, O'Day made contact with the same guerrilla leader whose communications with USAFIP-NL always preceded a Japanese crackdown. A few days after making contact, the situation progressed in the same pattern that it had before: the Japanese came out in force.[224] This time, however, O'Day would not let his guerrillas be driven from the area.

In a shrewd play of tactical ingenuity, O'Day arranged for a meeting between himself and the local guerrilla leader. When the unit arrived, O'Day's men surrounded them at gunpoint and demanded an explanation for the continuous Japanese harassment. Rather than "play dumb" or attempt to make any excuses, the leader made a run for it. O'Day followed in hot pursuit and shot down the leader, and afterwards the surviving members confessed what they had being doing: the Japanese, in attempt to protect their air base at Laoag, had paid a few locals to pose as guerrillas. Under these auspices, they patrolled Ilocos Norte searching for other guerrillas attempting to organize the region. Whenever contact was made with a Filipino-American outfit, the Japanese were promptly notified.[225]

It was a clever trick and it worked effectively until O'Day broke the cycle. With the pseudo-guerillas eliminated, and the Japanese without their indigenous spies, the entire area began to organize rapidly. Borrowing Companies K and M from the 121st, O'Day laid the groundwork for what would become the 15th Infantry. Rob Arnold, a signal officer who had earlier trained Walter Cushing's guerrillas, was appointed commander of the Third District. After Cushing's death, Arnold continued to make his way south. He eventually found his way into the 14th Infantry, which at the time was under Lieutenant Colonel Guillermo Nakar, before joining GHQ, USAFIP-NL in 1943. Together with John O'Day, Arnold expanded the 15th Infantry into a fully operational regiment.[226]

Fourth District belonged to the 11th Infantry. It was among the most troublesome districts to organize because the units were the most widely scattered of any regiment in North Luzon. Furthermore, Ralph Praeger—the man that

Volckmann had wanted to command the district—was already in Japanese custody. Before Praeger's capture, the anti-guerrilla campaign of 1942 had been especially fierce in Apayao. Praeger's men emerged from the debacle relatively unscathed, but the local civilians had born the brunt of the enemy's brutality. Eager for revenge, Filipinos in the Fourth District provinces poured out of the countryside to enlist as guerrillas.[227]

Since Praeger was no longer available, Volckmann turned to Blackburn—a man whose loyalty and capabilities were beyond reproach. Blackburn had heretofore been Volckmann's Executive Officer. Now, he was entrusted with the command of a regiment. As he awarded Blackburn his new command, Volckmann announced his intention to relocate General Headquarters from Ifugao to the La Union province near the western coast of Luzon.[228] With his departure, Volckmann left the task of organizing the 11th largely to Blackburn, his prime directive being to coordinate matters of personnel, supply, and training within the Apayao, Bontoc, and western Cagayan provinces.[229]

It came to pass that the Antipolo and the Haliap—including Tamicpao and Kamayong themselves—provided the backbone of the 11th Infantry's manpower. In fact, more native tribesmen were represented in the 11th Infantry than in any other regiment under Volckmann's command. Organizing the far reaches of the Fourth District proved to be an arduous and time-consuming task—for it was not until three days before D-Day in North Luzon that the regiment was *officially* activated as the 11th Infantry, USAFIP-NL. Its operational area consisted of the Cagayan, Apayao, and Mountain provinces, exclusive of the Benguet sub-province.[230]

The fifth and final district went to Romulo Manriquez and the 14th Infantry. It was the smallest of the USAFIP-NL regiments, but it still covered a sizeable area in the Isabela and Nueva Vizcaya provinces. Rufino Baldwin, who had commanded the largest segments of the regiment, remained in Japanese custody. Major Enriquez—who had previously commanded the 14th—surrendered his command as a "bargaining chip" when the Japanese seized his wife. Romulo Manriquez had been rebuilding the 14th Infantry ever since.[231]

Covering some 15,000 square miles, Volckmann connected the five districts through a synchronized network of intelligence and communication to coordinate strikes on enemy positions. To maintain consistency within USAFIP-NL operations, Volckmann needed an effective communication network. Two things, however, complicated a network created in this environment: the geography and the endless ring of spies. To correct this problem, Volckmann devised a system similar to the one he had operated amongst his small camps in Ifugao. Three east-west and three north-south messenger routes were laid down, linking General Headquarters to each of the district commands. Relay stations were located every four to six hours' hiking distance along the trail. At each relay station, a non-commissioned officer would inspect the documents and credentials of the messenger. If satisfied, he would task someone on his staff to carry the message to the next closet station. Volckmann also devised a series of alternate routes that were ready to use in the event that a primary route was compromised. In addition to handling the flow of information, these routes also moved supplies among the districts. In all, Volckmann's relay system accomplished in two days what would have taken one week with a single messenger. For the remainder of Volckmann's time in the Philippines, nothing along these routes ever fell into enemy hands.[232]

Central to the guerrilla campaign—and perhaps its most critical asset—was the support it received from the local civilians. Even in light of the Japanese brutality, promoting the cause for a resistance movement still required a fair amount of diplomacy. If the Japanese caught a civilian collaborating with guerrillas, it meant certain death not only for the culprit, but for his entire family as well. Also, the Filipinos were collectively a people of limited resources. The wealthy plantation owners and businessmen had much to spare, but these Filipinos were in the minority and the Japanese had already seized most of their assets. Urban Filipinos, for example those who lived in Manila and Baguio, could offer some assistance, but the high concentration of spies, Japanese troops, and Kempai Tai agents meant that these city-dwellers would have to be excessively discreet.

Ultimately, to win the civilians' support, Volckmann had to guarantee two things: (1) that the United States Government would properly compensate them; and (2) that they would be safe from any Japanese reprisal. As mentioned earlier, Volckmann produced handwritten receipts for everything that he received. Later, he retained a Financial Officer on the USAFIP-NL staff whose sole responsibility was to document receipts for all goods and services provided by civilians. After the war, Volckmann made it a priority to ensure that the Army compensated all receipt holders for the assistance they had given him.[233] Throughout most of the war, Volckmann's records referred to individual persons not by name, but by numeric call signs, for example Volckmann's call sign was "1122." Assigning call signs to nearly everyone in contact with USAFIP-NL, Volckmann guaranteed their anonymity if ever his records fell into enemy hands.[234]

A centerpiece of the Japanese war effort was their intensive propaganda. In the spring of 1943, while Volckmann remained in hiding from the previous fall's anti-guerrilla campaign, the Japanese began an amnesty drive. Utilizing such phrases as *Asia for the Asiatics* and *The Greater East Asia Co-Prosperity Sphere,* the program's objective was to induce the local population to cease giving aid to the guerrillas and, in return for cash rewards, supply information about specific individuals and their activities.[235] Meanwhile, the Japanese- controlled media continued circulating denouncements of all things American: America's economy had failed, the United States military had been defeated, and they would never be able to return to the Philippines.[236]

Volckmann hated these tactics but simultaneously admitted being fascinated by them. Never before had he been exposed to this kind of warfare: psychological warfare. It made for a very interesting case study, one that Volckmann documented well. However, he was relatively certain that the propaganda machine would not affect most of his local support.[237]

The Japanese occupation could not erase Filipino support for America so easily. Yet, there were indications that a few Filipinos were steadily buying in to the propaganda. The Japanese could be successful over time if—and only if—they could convince the Filipinos that there was no hope of victory and that America really *had* forgotten about them. That message had already convinced some Filipinos to cast their lot with the Japanese. Hired as spies and informants, they were paid regular salaries by the Kempai Tai and given bonuses for information that led to the capture of American officers. To augment their ground forces, the Japanese also impressed several Filipinos into constabulary units. Although a number of Filipinos voluntarily accepted their conscription, many did so only out of fear.[238]

But however effective their propaganda machine may have been, the Japanese often did more to negate their own success. While trying to win "hearts and minds," the Japanese brutally tortured and killed those who were suspected of aiding guerrillas. These detestable tactics angered many of the Filipinos and hence, the Japanese not only undermined their own progress, they unwittingly gave the Filipinos more reasons to support Volckmann.[239]

Once he had secured the civilians' support, Volckmann then had to determine how he was to use it. The support structure provided by Filipinos fell into two categories: combat support and combat manpower. Combat support persons could either be regular civilians or volunteer guerrillas assigned to non-combat roles. These individuals provided Volckmann's unit with food, water, technical and intelligence support, and other non-combat related specialties. It appears that Volckmann understood that these persons were the ones he needed to bring into his orbit first. Support personnel were critical, as their logistics provided his only lifeline. At the time, no other means existed for obtaining food or supplies. Technical support enabled Volckmann to maintain radio communication with his subordinate commands and, later, with General MacArthur in Australia, while the intelligence network provided Volckmann with continuous "eyes on the ground." Although USAFFE possessed a working knowledge of the North Luzon landscape, it was nowhere near as intimate as the natives who had lived there for generations.

Indeed, the centerpiece of the civilian auxiliary was the intelligence network. Knowledge of the enemy, terrain, and weather were all critical to Volckmann's guerrilla forces. And for intelligence gathering to be effective, it had to be a continuous process. The Filipinos he employed in this regard were indispensable. The Japanese would not normally suspect an average Filipino lingering in the vicinity of their garrisons, particularly since many Japanese outposts were located near settled areas or trading centers. The USAFIP-NL *intelligista* could easily and inconspicuously blend in with a crowd—a luxury that Volckmann and his American cohorts did not have.

Because intelligence operations had strategic implications, long-range planning was critical. The USAFIP-NL G2 files indicate that collecting intelligence centered on five priorities: evaluation of enemy forces and capabilities, interrogation of prisoners, proliferation of special agencies, psychological warfare, and infiltration.[240]

Evaluating enemy strengths and dispositions was the first logical step in conducting the intelligence operation. After being displaced into the mountains by the 1942 anti-guerilla campaign, Volckmann had to assess where the priority targets were and how to coordinate strikes on them. Assessing these targets, Volckmann directed his agents to analyze the largest garrisons, supply points, and infrastructure landmarks that linked the Japanese units together.[241]

Creating special agencies required a little more thought. To effectively promulgate his war plans, Volckmann had to take into account factors beyond the realm of enemy activity. These factors included weather, civilian activity, and the like. To fulfill this need, Volckmann established "watcher" groups to monitor airfields, shipping ports, and the coastline. Airfield watcher stations kept a close vigil on all operational airfields, while port watchers recorded the types and number of ships entering and departing North Luzon ports. Having coast watchers was an old practice from the earliest days of the U.S. Army and, consequently, it seems to be one of the few pieces of conventional doctrine that Volckmann used in the early stages of his guerrilla campaign. Operating in small teams, coast watchers provided information on the principal shipping lanes surrounding Luzon.[242]

Psychological warfare was Volckmann's first line of defense against the enemy propaganda. Years later, he articulated the difference between covert (black) and overt (white) propaganda. Both, he said, were "of great importance in developing and supporting a spirit of resistance in enemy-controlled areas." To counter the enemy's circulation of the alleged American defeats, Volckmann responded in kind with his own newsletter. Two versions went into circulation throughout North Luzon: one to his subordinate units and the other to the civilian communities. The guerrilla newsletters recounted each milestone of the Allied advance in the Pacific, gleaned from KGEI-San Francisco and later, from Volckmann's radio contact with MacArthur. The secondary effects of this newsletter were critical, as it began to sway those who had previously ridden the fence to throw their lot in with the Americans.[243]

Infiltration rounded out the intelligence apparatus as the final ingredient to gain information on the enemy. All other tenets of the intelligence plan were limited in their scope because they could not get within the walls of the enemy's operation.

Infiltrating the Japanese military complex would not be easy but, out of necessity, Volckmann found ways to make inroads. The Japanese's "Bureau of Constabulary" was the most likely avenue of approach. Many of Volckmann's agents found their way into its service and disseminated information on its activities and newest missions.[244] With the Japanese Fourteenth Army employing Filipino civilians for many of its staff and clerical functions, the opportunity for infiltration was ripe.

Combat manpower provided the muscle behind Volckmann's guerrilla force. In fact, the overwhelming majority of his guerrillas were Filipino—displaced members of either the Philippine Army or Philippine Scouts, or natives that Volckmann recruited, such as the Haliap and the Antipolo.[245] For those who did not have a military background, Volckmann devised a curriculum for tactics and drill. To his and Blackburn's delight, they soon discovered that training natives in the art of warfare was relatively easy—for these natives were already accustomed to the Spartan lifestyle and many of them were experienced hunters, well-versed in the arts of tracking and concealment. In all, Filipino support was perhaps *the* critical element to Volckmann's operation.

On 7 October 1943, back at "General Headquarters," Volckmann welcomed the arrival of Dennis Molintas, who together with Bando Dagwa, had come out of hiding from the previous year's anti-guerilla operation. Molintas, a Philippine Army Reservist and former school teacher, commanded a small group of raiders from his hideout in Benguet. He accepted Volckmann's command and agreed that the best thing to do was focus on the training, organization, and security of guerrilla forces. When he asked about when the appropriate time would be for expanding the force, Volckmann replied that that time was *now*.[246] At present, the only thing that he required of Molintas and his charges was their loyalty and continued patience.

About one week after Molintas departed for his camp, Volckmann had yet another close encounter with the enemy. This time, however, the source of the trouble wasn't the Japanese—it was their constabulary.[247] Since the Fall of Bataan, the "Bureau of Constabulary" had been the enemy's best attempt at civil law enforcement. Manned entirely by Filipino conscripts, the amount of trouble that the constabulary could cause depended largely on who their local commander was. If the commander was nothing more than a reluctant conscript—as many of the Filipinos were—then he would intentionally keep his patrol officers away from any guerrilla hideouts. However, if he were a true turncoat, he would cause no shortage of problems. One such turncoat had found his way into the Kiangan precinct and was determined to make his presence known.

When the Japanese declared 14 October as the new Philippine "Independence Day,"* the local officials ordered a celebration in Kiangan and all Haliap were

---

*"Independence" was provisional, pending a Japanese victory against the Allies.

expected to attend. During the celebration, a number of Haliaps—including Kamayong—were seized by the constabulary and taken to a nearby jail.

> 15 October 1943. Spent most of the day answering reports from the west [presumably Calvert]. The radio news we received is only up to the 27th [September]. They sure are moving slow in the Southwest Pacific. Received more reports on the mistreatment of the Haliap people in Kiangan. Method used (a common Jap trick): tie up a man, force his mouth open under a faucet, fill him full of water, then kick him and beat him in the stomach![248]

Furious, Volckmann thought it was another Japanese hit-job. He was surprised to learn, however, that the constabulary had acted independently, and that the seizure of Haliaps had nothing to do with the war.

> 18–22 October 1943. The story between the civil trouble that is going on here at present seems to go back to old tribal troubles. It seems that during the early part of the war, the Haliap people killed a man that was causing trouble. This man was related to [a family in Kiangan]. The Kiangan people rose up, secured arms, and attacked the Haliap. A Captain Jewel (American) stopped the fighting and patched things up.[249]

Since that time, however, tension between the Kiangan residents and the rural Haliap continued to boil. Most recently, the new leader of the Kiangan precinct—identified only as "Beylong"—accused the Haliap of killing one of his relatives. Inciting the old feelings of hatred and distrust, Beylong rallied the Kiangan population against the Haliap. The entry continued:

> The Kiangan people, under the leadership of one Beylong, singled out [Kamayong] and about fifteen other Haliap people and maltreated them severely. The Haliap people even believe the Mayor of Kiangan was in on the deal. It's going to be a job to settle the whole affair.[250]

But settle it he did. And the "whole affair" was quite the double-edged sword. His natural instinct was to launch a raid on the Kiangan jail, execute Beylong, and hang his traitorous comrades.[251] Begrudgingly, however, Volckmann knew that this was a bad idea. Kiangan was too close to the USAFIP-NL Headquarters—and if a local police station went up in flames, the Japanese would comb the area looking for perpetrators. Yet, if Beylong stayed where he was, it would only be a matter of time before his hatred for the Haliap led him to discover the nearby guerrillas.

Kamayong was later transferred to a nearby hospital, where the Mayor of Kiangan brought up a trumped-up charge of assault against him. Apparently, Beylong's accusation that Kamayong had killed his relative wasn't enough to get the Haliap leader out of the way—there had to be some sort of formal charge. Volckmann, already disgusted by the troublesome mayor, wrote him a letter demanding both Kamayong's release and punishment for the reckless constable. But the mayor, true to his Vichy-ite instincts, settled on a compromise: Kamayong would be released, the charges would be dropped, and Beylong would be transferred to another province.[252]

After the incident with the Mayor of Kiangan, Volckmann's diary entries became progressively shorter and less frequent. From that point on, he often wrote only one entry to cover an entire week's activity.

> 25 November 1943. Thanksgiving. No Turkey. Spent the day answering communications from the various units.
>
> 28 November–18 December 1943. The only thing exciting during this period is the offensive on the Gilbert Islands and Bougainville. However, the action on Bougainville has been so slow after the initial landings that it's hard to figure out what they are waiting on. Had report, (reliability unknown) that Col. Thorp, Nakar, and Straughn were taken from Ft. Santiago to Cemetary North Manila—executed. Can't understand why this war in the Pacific is moving so slowly. No action in Burma yet?
>
> 19–24 December 1943. Nothing exciting.
>
> 25 December 1943. Another Xmas in the mountains. Formoca sent us some cigars, a bottle of Chinese whiskey, some cakes.
>
> 26–31 December 1943. Received some pretty good news; New Britain landed on. Rumors also they have landed in Mindanao. So ends another year. I'd sure like to see something come in here before too many months of the New Year pass.[253]

On New Year's Day 1944, Volckmann and Blackburn intercepted a spy near General Headquarters. A few Haliaps had noticed a stranger wandering around the trails close to Volckmann's hideout. He didn't necessarily look suspicious, but none of the Haliap had ever seen this man before. Choosing to err on the side of caution, Volckmann ordered the man to be picked up and brought in for questioning. The following day, Blackburn questioned the stranger until he finally admitted that he was a spy for the Japanese. For this, he was executed on the spot.[254]

The moral of the story was harsh, yet simple: spies and informers were a deadly nuisance and they would be taken care of accordingly. Volckmann knew that if he expected to survive the war, he would have to make the "fifth column" fear *him* more than the Japanese. And he did so by instituting ways to eliminate those who were confirmed as spies.*

Throughout the spring of 1944, Volckmann's diary recorded new feats of guerrilla warfare as he continued to expand his forces, train his men, and coordinate strikes on enemy garrisons and troop movements. However, on 18 June 1944, his diary abruptly stopped. The last entry simply reads:

> The raid on the Philippine Constabulary Co. in Baguio fell through. One of our undercover men got cold feet and exposed the plan. No casualties on our side.**

---

*See Epilogue.

**By the middle of 1944, USAFIP-NL kept a daily record of its activities. Also, the task of organizing a guerrilla army would have undoubtedly left him with little time to keep up a daily journal.

But aside from organizing his forces and planning attacks on Japanese outposts, Volckmann wanted to engage the enemy in open combat; he wanted to take back the Philippines. By raids and ambushes alone, he could no doubt harass the Japanese and possibly, over time, defeat the enemy juggernaut. But this approach would take years to accomplish, and he was bound to run out of supplies long before the Japanese did.

For the first two years of the war, many of the firearms that USAFIP-NL procured came either from local civilians or dead Japanese. Volck-mann's current supply system satisfied his immediate needs but arms, ammunition, and medical supplies—the essential tools for guerrilla warfare—grew scarcer as the war dragged on. Recognizing that he didn't have the resources for a "toe-to-toe" campaign, Volckmann knew that he would somehow have to make contact with MacArthur's Headquarters. Doing so would accomplish two ends: first, it would provide a lifeline to his guerrillas; second, it would provide a means to direct the incoming Allied forces to key positions and facilitate combined operations with USAFIP-NL.[255]

It was a lofty goal, but Volckmann did not lend himself to the notion of guerrilla warfare as a series of "pot-shots" against the enemy while biding his time for MacArthur's return. To destroy the enemy and take back North Luzon, General MacArthur would have to fulfill the two-year-old promise he had made on Corregidor.

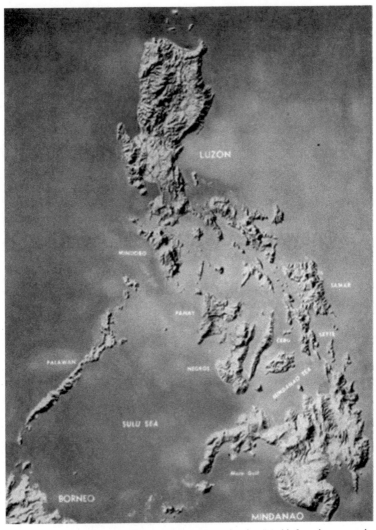

Relief map of Luzon, the largest island in the Philippine archipelago. Visible from the map are the rugged mountains of the Cordillera Central in North Luzon. *U.S. Army Center for Military History*

Russell William Volckmann, 1917. Dressed in his uniform as the C Company "mascot," the six-year-old Volckmann (right) is flanked by childhood friend John Smoller. Coincidentally, Smoller also attended West Point and graduated with the Class of 1934. *The Volckmann Family Collection.*

Cadet Volckmann, U.S. Military Academy, ca. 1932. "Russ," as he came to be known, was popular among his classmates and well-liked by those who knew him. *The Volckmann Family Collection.*

Volckmann's graduating class at the Infantry Officer Advanced Course, Fort Benning, Georgia, 1938. Volckmann stands in the top row, third from right. *USMA Fifty Year Book: 1934–1984.*

Philippine Scouts receive training on a 37mm anti-tank gun. *U.S. Army Center for Military History.*

A wrapper to one of many chocolate bars SWPA sent in its propaganda submarine to Volckmann. The caption near the bottom reads: "This chocolate bar, the ration carried by American soldiers around the world, will give you valuable nourishment. It is fortified with vitamins essential for health and strength." *National Archives and Records Administration.*

Japanese victorious at Bataan.
National Archives and Records Administration.

Elements of the 32nd Infantry Division (US) take up positions on Hill 504, 1 April 1945. As part of the I Corps' assault on Yamashita's southern perimeter, they assisted Volckmann's 14th Infantry Regiment in destroying the Japanese 2nd Tank Division before moving into the Bessang Pass area. *U.S. Army Center for Military History.*

Elements of the 122nd Field Artillery Battalion (USAFIP-NL) fire on Japanese positions during the Battle of Bessang Pass. *U.S. Army Center for Military History.*

A 1940 postcard depicting the Ifugao rice terraces in Mountain Province. This is a representative sample of the rugged terrain in North Luzon. *The Donald D. Blackburn Collection.*

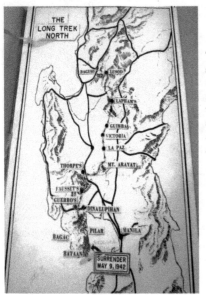

This map, constructed by Volckmann, shows the path of his trek to North Luzon. *Guerro's* (Guerrero's) and *Fausset's* (Fassoth's) represent civilian evacuation camps. Also visible is Mt. Arayat where Volckmann solicited help from the Hukbalahap. *The Russell W. Volckmann Papers, U.S. Army Military History Institute.*

Elements of the 122nd Field Artillery Battalion provide suppressing fire while USAFIP-NL engineers construct a hasty bridge. *The Volckmann Family Collection.*

This map, although crudely titled, shows the activity of Volckmann's regiments as they fought within their respective districts against the Japanese. Visible on the map is the Sixth Army front created by General Kruger as a diversion for the southern forces of Yamashita's defense perimeter. *The Russell W. Volckmann Papers, U.S. Army Military History Institute.*

Volckmann stands with Major General Basilio Valdes, the Philippine Army Chief of Staff, 1945. *The Volckmann Family Collection.*

Volckmann examining the blade of the sword owned by General Osaki, commander of the 19th Tora Division. *The Volckmann Family Collection.*

Volckmann (seated on the far right) sits at the table with General MacArthur and other flag officers to formally accept Yamashita's surrender. *The Volckmann Family Collection.*

Tamicpao, leader of the Antipolo tribe. *The Donald D. Blackburn Collection.*

Undated portrait of Volckmann. *U.S. Army Center for Military History.*

MacArthur Tells Volckmann's Work With Guerrillas

Clintonian, Now Colonel, Heads Forces Which Cleared Japs From Ilocos Norte Province — Killed Thousands of Enemy—Had Been Listed As Missing—Awarded Distinguished Service Cross.

The name of Col. Russell W. Volckmann was added to the list of Clinton World war II heroes who have attained special recognition for outstanding service when Gen. Douglas MacArthur announced that guerrilla forces led by Col. Volckmann had cleared the Japs from Ilocos Norte province, inflicting thousands of casualties while suffering only minor losses themselves.

Gen. MacArthur's announcement was the first official public statement on Col. Volckmann's safety, his name having been carried on the "missing in action" list since the fall of Bataan and Corregidor. His family and The Herald have known, however, for several weeks that he was safe, but security reasons would not permit publication of the definite information.

The announcement yesterday of Volckmann's guerrilla activities on Luzon also carried the news that he was awarded the Distinguished Service Cross on Feb. 21, and has been promoted from major to colonel.

Col. Volckmann is the second Clintonian to be listed among the Philippine guerrilla leaders. Sgt. Joe W. Donnhey having returned from the Philippines only last month after almost three years in that capacity.

Close to the War

Probably no Clinton man has been closer to the war in the Philippines, from the time of the attack, Dec. 7, 1941, the days of Corregidor and Bataan, and continuing through the invasion by our own troops until the present time, than Col. Volckmann, son of Mr. and Mrs. W. J. C. Volckmann, 752 Sixth avenue, South.

Reported as missing in action for three years, Volckmann was awarded the Distinguished Service Cross recently, but has been so busy with his work in liberation of the Philippines that he has not had time to appear before Gen. Douglas MacArthur to receive the medal.

Col. Volckmann leads a band of Filipino guerrillas in Northern Luzon, Gen. MacArthur revealed yesterday in his report of fighting in the Philippines.

According to MacArthur's report, the spaces on the Japanese in the northern mountains was paved by American-led guerrilla forces under Volckmann, who cleared the 2,000-square-mile Ilocos Norte province in the northwestern center of Luzon.

Kill Thousands of Japs

Thousands of Japanese were killed by the guerrillas, armed with modern weapons and aided by U. S. planes, as they drove the last of the invaders from the province, commanding the South China sea, the China coast and the enemy's Formosa stronghold.

Heads Guerrillas

Col. R. W. Volckmann

of Laoag, frequent targets for American bombers, and were only 44 miles from the north coastal air base of Aparri, 490 miles from Hong Kong and 235 miles from the southern tip of Formosa.

The offensive by Volckmann's forces also carried to within 100 miles of American lines on Lingayen gulf, and within 160 miles of U. S. troops pushing up the center of Luzon.

Demoralized the Japs

Volckmann's Filipino forces completely demoralized the Japanese with hit-run tactics in which the guerrillas augmented their American army equipment with razor sharp bolos.

Their method was to silently encircle the enemy garrison, strike swiftly, and then vanish into the jungle before the Japanese could collect themselves for a counter attack.

It is not the first word received from Volckmann, as both his family and The Herald have known. For sometime his part in the guerrilla activities. Announcement of his safety had been prohibited by the War department until the official statement, yesterday by Gen. MacArthur. First actual word came to his parents January 18, in a letter written by him from "The Mountains," October 30, 1944. In this letter, Volckmann briefly informed his parents of his safety, and gave some account of his attitude toward the Japs.

"Although it has been a long time since I have been able to sit down and write you my monthly letter, it seems perfectly natural now that I'm writing this. I know that you have been worried and I hope this reaches you to let you know that God has been most gracious—I'm in the best of health, good spirits and still have a lot of fight left in me.

Only Japs Are Inhuman

"I never thought that there was on the face of the earth a race of people so inhuman as those Japs have turned out to be. Guess that's why I still have so much fight left in me. I don't believe, if I saw this through, that I will ever be able to stand a Jap around me. Oh, well, you don't want to hear all about that.

"Things are looking brighter every day and as the race goes, 'Our last hour to Victory,' I do hope to see you all real soon, it will be the happiest day in my life."

Col. Volckmann mentions in his letter that he had been promoted, evidently from major to lieutenant colonel, since recent stories carry his rank as that of full colonel, but no official announcement has been made of such promotion.

THE CLINTON HERALD

COL. VOLCKMANN GETS SURRENDER OFFER OF JAPS

Col. Russell Volckman of Clinton, commanding Filipino army forces on Luzon, has received surrender overtures from Lt. Gen. Masatsogu Araki of the Japanese army, it was reported by Associated Press today. Col. Volckmann is the son of Mr. and Mrs. W. J. C. Volckmann, 752 Sixth avenue, South.

Other Japanese troops still holding out in northern Luzon, New Guinea and the Solomons have begun formal negotiations to surrender, it was reported.

Officers of the U. S. army's 14th corps on Luzon sent word that emissaries of Lt. Gen. Yoshiharu Iwanaka had begun negotiating with them.

Iwanaka commands the "Geki" force which includes the tattered remnants of the once powerful second armored division; Araki commands the 79th brigade of the 103rd infantry division.

U. S. 14th corps officers said they had learned nothing yet concerning Gen. Tomoyuki Yamashita, diehard Japanese commander-in-chief in the Philippines, who variously has been reported dead, wounded, in flight and leading his troops in their bitter last stand in Luzon's northern mountains.

Isolated parties of Japanese also were inquiring about surrender, and American fliers dropped 775,000 explanatory leaflets in the areas where the Japanese remnants, still several thousand strong, are known to be hiding.

DECEMBER 7, 1945—16 PAGES   *Clinton Herald*

CLINTON'S WAR HERO IS HOME!

First Photo Of Col. Volckmann In U. S.

Magic of Wirephoto Utilized to Bring Clinton Hero's Picture to The Clinton Herald

After his return from the Philippines, Volckmann was highly celebrated by his hometown newspapers, though his contributions were largely forgotten by subsequent historians of the war.

VOLCKMANN FORCE HELPS TAKE LAST ROAD FROM JAPS

Col. Russell W. Volckmann of Clinton was in command of Philippine forces which today helped take from the Japs the last road they held in Northern Luzon, according to a United Press dispatch from there. Col. Volckmann is the son of Mr. and Mrs. W. J. C. Volckmann, 752 Sixth avenue, South.

The road was taken when the 32nd division, driving north from Baguio on Highway 11, made a juncture with Col. Volckmann's Philippine army forces.

The juncture was made 2,500 yards southeast of Cambang village in an 8,000 foot altitude in the Cordillera mountains. The 32nd encountered scattered resistance and many road demolitions. Highway 11 now was secured in its entire length.

The remaining Japanese believed to number possibly 12,000, were pressed into a pocket like an inverted V 16 miles across at its widest part and 21 miles long.

Des Moines Sunday Register   DES MOINES, IOWA, SUNDAY, DECEMBER 9, 1945.—

IOWAN SEIZED 3 JAP ADMIRALS

—SECTION FOUR

Volckmann's Story of Life As Guerrilla

By John Zutt

CLINTON, IA.—The Iowa colonel who commanded America's guerrilla forces in northern Luzon ended the war by capturing three war admirals of the Japanese fleet.

It was a fitting climax to the real Superman exploits, keeping alive in gaunt information the Gen. Russell W. Volckmann, 38.

Don Blackburn on V-J Day, 1945.
The Donald D. Blackburn Collection.

Vacationing in Virginia Beach, 1949. Pictured from left to right are: Helen Volckmann, Russell Volckmann, Ann Blackburn, and Donald Blackburn. The two families remained lifelong friends after the war. *The Donald D. Blackburn Collection.*

CHAPTER 8

Lifelines

North Luzon had been without radio contact since Ralph Praeger went off the air in March 1943. Now, some fifteen months later, Volckmann still had no way of communicating with MacArthur. Under the reorganization plan of the previous year, Volckmann had ordered all district commanders to scavenge any radio equipment they could find. His orders also called for finding radio technicians to build and operate the device. These efforts eventually produced an assortment of radio parts and two technicians from Manila. Volckmann made every effort to provide them the tools they needed, but many integral parts of the radio were still missing, which necessitated all missing pieces to be crafted by hand. The final product, however, was a homemade 75-watt transceiver with enough power to communicate directly with SWPA! To compensate for the lack of electricity, Volckmann secured the device to a water wheel on a nearby stream, thus providing 220 volts of hydroelectric power.[256]

Morale in USAFIP-NL surged to an all-time high. Volckmann's first message to SWPA emphasized the need for arms, ammunition, and medical supplies. When SWPA replied a few days later, they confirmed that:

ONE OFFICER AND FIFTEEN MEN TOGETHER WITH FIFTEEN TONS OF SUPPLY HAVE LANDED BY SUBMARINE ON LUZON. PARTY IS PROCEEDING NORTH OVERLAND TO YOUR HEADQUARTERS.[257]

As it were, the submarine USS *Stingray* had landed on the northern shore of Ilocos Norte near Bangui. Units within Volckmann's Third District (15th Infantry) intercepted the landing party near Highway 3 but recovered only half the tonnage of supplies promised by SWPA. Lieutenant Valera, the officer in charge of the landing party, explained that while consolidating their materiel on the beach, a Japanese naval detachment came within shooting range of the submarine. Fearing detection, the sub commander made an emergency dive and vacated the inlet.[258] This left Valera and his men with half the anticipated supplies and without any means to navigate through the treacherous jungles. How fortunate that the 15th Infantry intercepted Valera before the Japanese did.

Even with half the material that was originally promised, it was nonetheless a boon to Volckmann and his guerrillas. Re-supply meant relief from chronic shortages that had plagued them since Bataan. If the supply chain remained unbroken from now until the Allied invasion of Luzon, Volckmann and his men would no longer have to rely on scavenging from the Japanese or continue borrowing from the local civilians.

On 29 August 1944, Volckmann sent a communique to SWPA outlining the directives he had given to USAFIP-NL.[259] His command policies called for:

1. Harassment and destruction of all enemy lines of communication.
2. Delay and destruction of all enemy troop and supply movements.
3. Destruction of enemy supply dumps.
4. Prevent the enemy from securing food supplies, construction materials, civilian labor assets, and means of transportation.[260]

The message was an indirect effort to discover any tentative dates for the Allied invasion and, hopefully, give MacArthur an incentive to expedite the process. At this point, Volckmann had no idea of when it might come, but he anticipated it happening sometime within the next twelve months. Reports over KGEI confirmed that the Allied push toward Tokyo was gathering steam. Volckmann received no direct answer to the message but instead got a radiogram asking for the locations of principal and alternative rendezvous points for the next incoming submarine. Volckmann consulted with Barnett, commander of the Second District, and radioed SWPA with the coordinates for Darigayos, La Union, and San Esteban, Ilocos Sur, as the respective primary and alternate points. SWPA radioed confirmation of the rendezvous points and set an ETA for 19 October 1944.[261]

On the day of the 19th, however, the submarine was nowhere to be found, and neither rendezvous point had reported any contact. Frustrated, Volckmann again radioed SWPA and demanded an explanation. The answer he received was a vague and apologetic pronouncement that there had been a slight misunderstanding.[262]

A *misunderstanding?* A misunderstanding of *what?* SWPA had already confirmed the location of the rendezvous points and Volckmann had followed the contact procedures perfectly. Nonetheless, Volckmann could do nothing more than negotiate another contact date and hope for better luck. The next submarine, USS *Gar,* had embarkation orders for November. Years later, Volckmann found out that the "misunderstanding" had been between the submarine and the Army Air Forces; the submarine was sunk by friendly fire.[263] On a brighter note, the following day, 20 October, brought news that Allied forces had landed at Leyte Gulf, only 400 miles to the southeast.

Just as before, SWPA confirmed the location of Darigayos and San Esteban as the rendezvous points. This latest submarine carried a party of fifteen men and some twenty-five tons of equipment. Volckmann dispatched Barnett to the alternate rendezvous point while he and Blackburn oversaw the principal site. The situation required much more oversight than Volckmann had originally anticipated: in the overlapping time since the previous submarine, a Japanese garrison had sprung up less than five miles away from the primary rendezvous point. Worse, a Japanese naval base lay fifteen miles to the south and its patrol boats were regularly sighted along the coast.[264]

Beginning ten days prior to the submarine's intended arrival, units of the 121st Infantry kept a close watch over both rendezvous points. Volckmann ordered his men to watch for any unusual changes in the enemy's dispositions. Measures were taken to ensure that every man knew the location of the rendezvous points, the appropriate security measures, signal procedures, and the organization of carrying parties. Two days before contact, Volckmann established outposts surrounding both rendezvous points and ordered one combat battalion to occupy each area. Civilian agents provided some 50 native canoes to ferry supplies to the shore. Finally, the combat battalions covering both rendezvous points were given clear instructions on what to do if either point were compromised by enemy activity.[265]

Yet, despite these efforts, there was still no word from SWPA concerning the protocol for making contact with the submarines. With three days remaining until the anticipated contact date—and still no word from MacArthur—Volckmann decided to travel to the primary rendezvous point himself. Leaving Calvert behind to man the GHQ, Volckmann instructed him to forward any updates received from SWPA during his absence.[266]

Using one of the USAFIP-NL messenger routes, Volckmann began his trip under the fury of a raging typhoon. The torrential rain was certainly enough to impede his movement, but the real trouble began when the deluge turned an otherwise peaceful stream into a raging rapid. With no feasible way to ford it, he had no choice but to sit and wait for the current to subside. During the unexpected layover, Volckmann discovered that things were about to get worse. A runner from GHQ relayed the following message from Calvert:

A CARABAO WASHED OVER WATERFALL AND LANDED ON WATER WHEEL POWERHOUSE. DUE TO NO POWER OUT OF RADIO CONTACT. EVERY EFFORT MADE TO GET BACK ON AIR.[267]

Two days from the submarine's arrival with no official guidance on contact procedures, and now communication with SWPA was lost! Volckmann was terrified at the thought of losing another opportunity to make contact with the submarines. When the storm finally subsided, two days had elapsed since his departure from GHQ. Desperately hoping that another chance had not been lost, Volckmann pushed through the mountain passes and the highland jungles at breakneck speed, finally arriving at Darigayos Cove in the predawn hours of 20 November. Greeted by Major Cubas of the 121st Infantry, Volckmann received up-to-the minute information on activity around the rendezvous points.

He was satisfied with the control measures already in place but Volckmann still had no way of determining the submarine's whereabouts.[268] Relief finally came in the form of another messenger from GHQ: Calvert had somehow managed to fix the radio and was once again trading wires with SWPA. Confirming the submarine's arrival date on 21 November, SWPA indicated that between 0600 and 0800, USAFIP was to:

> DISPLAY ON BEACH TWO HUNDRED METERS APART TWO WHITE DISC TWO METERS IN DIAMETER WITH A SMOKE SMUDGE FIRE MIDWAY BETWEEN DISC. REPEAT SAME SIGNALS FROM 1600 TO 1800. AT 1630 COMMANDER SHORE PARTY PUT TO SEA IN A SMALL SAILING BOAT FLYING A CHINESE FLAG. IF NO CONTACT IS MADE PRIOR TO DARK DISPLAY THREE LIGHTS VERTICALLY FROM THE MAST OF THE SAIL BOAT STOP.[269]

Volckmann could hardly fathom the utility behind these measures. Nothing could be more conspicuous or certain to get the enemy's attention.[270] Although he hated these instructions, Volckmann knew that they were the only means to coordinate with his outside supplier. The unexpected radio damage had undoubtedly cost him any possible buffer time to protest. An ETA on 21 November meant that the submarine was already en route and its skipper would not be expecting any deviation from SWPA guidelines. Volckmann had no choice but to follow the signal procedures, although it remains unclear what prompted these contact procedures or why SWPA assumed that Volckmann would have two white discs and a Chinese flag in his possession. Volckmann had a makeshift Chinese flag sown together but how he obtained the white discs remains a mystery. It is possible that the supplies recovered from the first submarine included kits for signaling future skippers.

After setting up the specified signals, Volckmann returned to the rendezvous point at Darigayos Cove. In the distance, he noticed a large Japanese naval convoy heading south. This convoy was soon picked up by a group of what appeared to be dive-bombers. Since the Far East Air Force had been demolished three years earlier, Volckmann thought that the planes, too, were Japanese. But suddenly, the bombers swooped down in unison and began pounding the ships—*the planes were American!* Volckmann was ecstatic as he watched six Japanese cruisers sink beneath the waves. The excitement, however, was short-lived; within a few hours, the Japanese had dispatched a network of patrol boats to scan the area for any survivors of the ill-fated convoy.[271] This increased activity surrounding the primary rendezvous point was no doubt aggravating for Volckmann. Conspicuous signals and enemy garrisons on either side of their position certainly gave Volckmann enough to worry about. The last thing he needed now was an increased naval presence to further jeopardize their chances of contacting the submarine. Unfortunately, Volckmann had no other option than to wait and see what the

Japanese would do. It was still possible that the activity may die down before the *Gar* would come within sight of Darigayos. For the time being, however, Volckmann decided to stay put.

By the following morning, it seemed as though the enemy patrols had dispersed. Volckmann was about to order his men to occupy the beach when, all of a sudden, a Japanese patrol boat came in from the south! At first it appeared as though it might bypass their position, but then suddenly it made a sharp turn straight for the cove. Volckmann tried to keep his composure: perhaps the boat would not stay long; patrol boats normally carried no more than 20 men, so this was likely just a foraging party.[272]

Volckmann's assessment proved correct: sixteen men dismounted the patrol boat and scavenged the native huts beyond the shore. The party left after only an hour and, once out of sight, Volckmann ordered his signal crew to occupy the beach. It appeared that the mission was to be a success, but his men had no more than reached the shoreline when the sound of rifle fire broke through the quiet air. Startled by the sudden burst of automatic rifles, Volckmann's shore party scrambled for cover. Volckmann was staggered. *Who could be firing on his men?* The answer came as a Japanese patrol emerged from the jungle and established a beachhead right on top of the rendezvous point.[273] He could hardly believe his eyes. *How did an entire patrol slip past his observation posts?* Bristled with anger, Volckmann decided to wait the Japanese out.

The afternoon hours came and went. As daylight turned to dusk, the Japanese began settling down for the night. Dejected, Volckmann sent a radiogram to SWPA indicating the primary point had been compromised. He ordered his units surrounding Darigayos to stand down and return to their base camps.[274] Now, all Volckmann could do was hope that Barnett would have better luck at the alternate rendezvous point. One failed attempt at contacting the submarine was aggravating enough, but two consecutive failed attempts might discourage SWPA from sending any more submarines entirely.

Arriving back at GHQ, however, Volckmann's despair over the submarine issue was put to rest by news that Barnett had made contact with the *Gar* at the alternate point. Overjoyed by the success, Volckmann radioed the news to the other USAFIP-NL stations.[275] The impact of the submarine's arrival spread beyond Volckmann's network. For the first time since the beginning of the war, civilians were coming out in droves to assist Volckmann any way they could.[276] Indeed, a newfound sense of enthusiasm ripped through the echelons of USAFIP-NL. From this, it was evident that the second stage of Volckmann's enterprise was reaching critical mass. Now that help had arrived from the outside world, USAFIP-NL would have the means to effectively stand "toe-to-toe" with the Japanese.

Barnett arrived at GHQ only a few days after Volckmann, with the *Gar's* landing party in tow. Giving a full account of the skipper's story, Volckmann learned firsthand just how troublesome the enemy beachhead had been. As it were, the submarine had initially surfaced off Barnett's point at San Esteban. The skipper, thinking that he had correctly surfaced at the primary rendezvous point, made contact with Barnett assuming him to be Volckmann. Politely informing the errant skipper that he had missed his mark, Barnett climbed aboard the submarine and guided them farther south to Darigayos Cove. Arriving shortly after nightfall, Barnett spotted the campfires set by the Japanese on the beach. Assuming the fires had been set by Volckmann, Barnett and two of the submarine's crew landed on the side of the cove. Only yards from the beachhead, however, they realized that the fires were manned by the Japanese. While en route back to San Esteban, they received the radio message from SWPA indicating that the primary point had been compromised. Volckmann recalled that "the skipper had been tempted to radio back: WE FOUND THAT OUT FOR OURSELVES."[277]

This landing party delivered more critical specialists than Volckmann had ever had before, including technicians trained in meteorology, demolition, and radio maintenance. Aside from delivering arms, ammunition, and other combat assets, they also provided an impressive display of radio equipment. This in turn allowed Volckmann to establish radio nets within each of the five districts.[278]

On 30 November, while GHQ busied itself coordinating another contact date, Manriquez's men in the Fifth District recovered the greatest source of enemy information that USAFIP-NL had yet to find. A Japanese liaison plane, carrying a number of high-ranking officers, had crashed in Nueva Vizcaya. Stripping the plane for any pertinent intelligence, the 14th Infantry gathered a series of papers from a conference held by General Tomiyuki Yamashita. As the newly appointed commander of all Japanese forces in the Philippines, he had reorganized the entire defense of Luzon.[279]

Apparently, Yamashita understood that Luzon was the critical juncture of the Philippine Campaign. He admitted that Japanese ground forces could not withstand the superiority of American armor.[280] Therefore, to minimize that advantage, he would consolidate his forces within the mountains of North Luzon.

The reconfiguring of the Fourteenth Army defense occurred throughout the summer and fall of 1944, and culminated in January 1945. As a result, six army divisions settled into the mountain landscape and Yamashita relocated his headquarters to Baguio. Not coincidentally, the puppet government also moved its capital from Manila to Baguio.[281] These events confirmed what Volckmann had seen in the documents from the plane; it was clear that the Japanese intended to make North Luzon their last defensive stronghold.

Two more submarine contacts were made in December 1944. The first shipment, arriving on 12 December, proved to be a huge disappointment. Instead of the arms, ammunition, and medical supplies that were so vital to Volckmann's enterprise, they opened the crates to find nothing but propaganda items: cigarettes, rubber stamps, and candy bars bearing the words "I Shall Return." Frustrated by the futility of this nonsensical cargo, Volckmann radioed SWPA with an appeal not to send any more propaganda material. SWPA did not reply but the message appeared to have some impact, for the very next submarine arrived with 25 tons of military equipment and not one ounce of propaganda.[282]

At the same time, Volckmann began the painstaking task of determining a proper landing site for the invasion of North Luzon. The burden was enormous, as the success of the Allied landing hinged on Volckmann's ability to select an area that would not be saturated with enemy defenses. The Yamashita defense plan relocated most of Fourteenth Army inland but a few coastal defense batteries still remained. Naval gunfire and close air support could dispatch these in short order, but the risk of collateral damage was too high. There were other considerations, too. Volckmann had to direct the landings to a spot that would allow the easiest access to the USAFIP-NL supply lines.

Based on the intelligence assessments provided by his scouts and district commanders, Volckmann settled on Lingayen Gulf. Reports estimated that activity surrounding the gulf had died down significantly since the start of the war.[283] Volckmann knew the area well; it had been where he and the 11th Infantry had built their first defenses in 1941.

Conferring with Calvert, Volckmann studied the intelligence overlay and cleared the message to MacArthur:

> FROM VOLCKMANN TO MACARTHUR
> THERE WILL BE NO REPEAT NO OPPOSITION ON
> THE BEACHES[284]

For the next 48 hours, Volckmann had little else to do but wait for the Allied landings and hope that he had made the right decision in selecting Lingayen Gulf. The Gulf area was devoid of enemy activity, but if his correspondence with SWPA were intercepted, Yamashita would not hesitate to deploy his holed-up forces to the beach.

The suspense finally ended on 9 January 1945, when Volckmann received the following radiogram from MacArthur:

> OVER ONE HUNDRED THOUSAND AMERICAN TROOPS LANDED
> BETWEEN SAN FABIAN AND LINGAYEN ON THE MORNING OF
> 9 JANUARY 1945. THE COVOY WHICH COMPOSE OVER 700 SHIPS
> WAS 80 MILES LONG. THERE WAS LITTLE OPPOSITION TO THE
> LANDING WHICH WAS PRECEDED BY A PAY AIR AND NAVAL
> BOMBARDMENT[285]

From his Headquarters, Volckmann could see the ships entering Lingayen some 50 miles away. Although he had promised no resistance on the beaches, MacArthur obviously deferred on the side of caution and precipitated the landings with a hail of naval gunfire. Official confirmation of the landing included orders placing Volckmann's guerrillas under the U.S. Sixth Army's command.[286]

Reassignment to Sixth Army began one of the greatest transformations in Volckmann's resistance movement. The supply issues had largely been solved by the submarines, but now Volckmann had additional manpower and a permanent logistics base. Until now, USAFIP-NL operations had been limited to raids and ambushes. While these operations covered a large area and inflicted some losses on the Japanese, he still did not have the wherewithal to stand "toe-to-toe" with the enemy in a prolonged battle. Now that the Sixth Army had arrived in North Luzon, however, the guerrillas' fortunes were about to change.

To organize the joint effort between USAFIP-NL and Sixth Army Headquarters, Volckmann arranged for a PT boat to take him to the Lingayen landing site. Picking him up at Darigayos Cove, the PT skipper delivered him to General Walter Krueger, Sixth Army Commander. Coincidentally, Volckmann had served under Krueger some five years earlier when the latter commanded the 2nd Infantry Division at Fort Sam Houston. The two had met previously but Volckmann was unsure whether the general would remember him after their brief meeting years earlier. Emphatically recalling the then-Captain Volckmann from years past, Krueger listened intently as the guerrilla commander gave his report on the Japanese strengths in North Luzon.[287]

The general seemed perplexed by Volckmann's assessment. If the numbers and capabilities that Volckmann reported were correct, the general said, then why weren't the Japanese pushing the Allied landing party back into the sea? Volckmann's reply was simple: the Japanese had dug their defenses into the mountainscape; they were expecting "Uncle Sam" to dig them out inch by inch.[288]

Aside from pledging the Sixth Army's support, General Krueger gave Volckmann full authority to deal with the Army 308th Bomb Wing and instructed him to contact Admiral Forrest B. Royal, commander of Amphibious Group Six, who would henceforth take responsibility for the rest of Volckmann's resupply needs. Before doing so, however, he would report to General Douglas MacArthur.[289] Arriving at MacArthur's office, Volckmann came face-to-face with the general who had abandoned him some three years earlier. Rather than giving Volckmann an admonishment for refusing the surrender order, MacArthur congratulated him on a job well done and promoted him to Colonel![290]

With MacArthur's blessing, Volckmann climbed aboard the next PT boat inbound for the USS Rocky Mount, the command vessel of Admiral Royal. Once on board the flagship, Volckmann began discussing his resupply options. Now that the Allied armada had an anchorage in Lingayen Gulf, the submarines would no longer be necessary. Darigayos Cove had previously been a rendezvous point for SWPA submarines, and since it was relatively close to the main body of Royal's fleet, the two men agreed that Darigayos would be the optimal supply point. After settling his affairs aboard the Admiral's flagship, another PT boat would take Volckmann back to Lingayen beach where he would go to the Headquarters of the 308th Bomb Wing.[291]

His meeting with the Headquarters Staff of the 308th produced a lengthy discussion on the means of communication and coordinating air strikes. According to Volckmann, air support in North Luzon had its own unique challenges. Heavy cloud cover over most of the region ruled out the possibility of sustained high-altitude aerial reconnaissance. To offset this disadvantage, Volckmann drew out detailed plans to have his men direct low-altitude bombers around the mountains to their targets via two-way radios. This made Volckmann among the first in the Pacific theater to exploit the concept of *forward air controllers*. In a true display of tactical ingenuity, Volckmann devised a unique method of air-ground communication. Since not all of the USAFIP-NL camps had radios to communicate with one another, Volckmann devised a quicker way for them to communicate with the Sixth Army and his own General Headquarters. The result was an information retrieval device that operated in a manner not dissimilar from the way an airplane landed on an aircraft carrier. Retrofitting the aircraft of the 308th with large hooks on the underbelly of the fuselage, Volckmann instructed the pilots to fly their aircraft to the site of a USAFIP-NL camp. The pilots would then swoop down over the campsite so that their retrieval hooks would catch an encased message that hung from a wire suspended between two poles.[292]

Departing the 308th Headquarters, Volckmann boarded an L-5 liaison plane to fly him back to GHQ.[293] Although he was leaving the safety of American lines, he took great satisfaction in knowing that the campaign to retake North Luzon was about to begin.

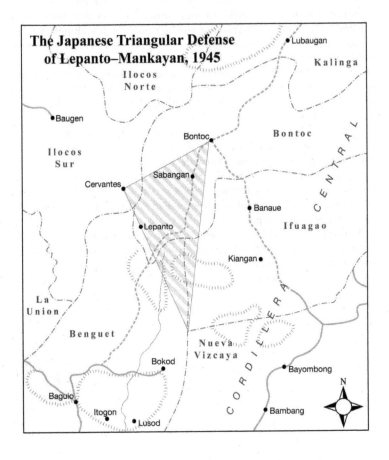

The Japanese Triangular Defense of Lepanto–Mankayan, 1945

CHAPTER 9

Combat Operations

Combat operations of USAFIP-NL fell into three distinct phases. The first phase lasted from the middle of 1943—the date of Volckmann's "Reorganization Plan"—until the arrival of the U.S. Sixth Army at Lingayen Gulf on 3 January 1945. The next two phases overlapped one another: the second phase, from 3 January to 15 August 1945, saw the regiments of USAFIP-NL fight within their respective districts in open combat against the Japanese. The third and final phase of operations lasted from about 1 June until Yamashita's surrender on 1 September 1945. In this phase, three regiments of USAFIP-NL—the 121st, 15th, and 66th Infantry—fought together as a Division-sized element under the U.S. Sixth Army.[294]

The first phase of combat operations covered the longest period. As mentioned previously, as of 1943–44, Volckmann knew that neither he nor his guerrillas possessed the resources to engage the Japanese in open combat. As a result, Volckmann divided his early operations into two categories: intelligence gathering and subversive activities, both of which took place simultaneously.[295] As he made plans to contact MacArthur and arrange for resupply, Volckmann directed his men to engage in a number of guerrilla activities. These included sabotage, demolition, and small raids on Japanese garrisons. The objective, as Volckmann saw it, was to put the occupying Fourteenth Army on the defensive and erode the Japanese combat power *before* the Americans arrived to retake North Luzon.

Volckmann's decision was important for two reasons. First, a united guerrilla front would draw Yamashita's priorities away from the North Luzon coastal defenses and, consequently, from any incoming Allied naval task force. Second, Volckmann's operations would undercut the means by which the Japanese could repel the Allied invasion. Reviewing his options, Volckmann concluded that the Japanese supply system was his priority target. The Japanese had the numerical advantage, but Volckmann apparently knew that he could offset this advantage if he destroyed their means to continue the war. If the Japanese had no ammunition, their rifles would be useless; if they had no fuel or usable trucks, they would lose their mobility; and if they had no food or replacement parts for their equipment, their army would wither and die. Next, Volckmann set his sights on the North Luzon infrastructure. Training the local Igorots and Ilocanos in the art of demolition, Volckmann targeted the road and bridge network over which the Japanese moved their troops.[296] This, however, presented Volckmann with a unique challenge: he had to devise a method of demolition that would impede the Japanese movement without hindering his own or that of U.S. conventional forces once they arrived. During the course of the invasion, the Japanese had put their engineers to work building road and bridge networks to connect their garrisons and improve existing trails, with detours to their supply caches. The solution that Volckmann devised—or so it appears—was to target the Japanese service roads and leave the main highways alone for the time being. Drawing upon conventional military principles, the third leg of Volckmann's guerrilla strategy included the use of raids and ambushes on Japanese garrisons.[297]

The first phase of combat operations can be told through the messages sent between GHQ and the various district commands. Missions varied in their scope, intensity, and outcome, but they shared the common thread of guerrilla warfare on the rise in North Luzon.

19 September 1944
Subject: ENEMY CASUALTIES
To: 1122 [Volckmann]

1. For your information, my units had unavoidable engagements with the enemy and had inflicted the following casualties on the enemy's part.

A platoon of "B" Co. met Jap patrols (50) in Aludaed, San Juan, La Union and engaged them. 4 Japs killed and no casualty on our part. September 5, 1944.

On September 10, 1944, "A" Co. wrecked a train with 60 Japs killed and wounded.

On September 11, 1944, a platoon of "D" Co, while having its daily training, met Japs (20). 7 Japs killed and no casualty on our part.

On September 12, 1944, the Japs tried to chase the "D" Co...36 Japs killed and 8 wounded. Captured from the enemy 1 Garand rifle, 6 Enfield rifles, and 85 rounds 30 Cal. 2 killed and 6 slightly wounded on our part.

—2-121-113[298] [Major Diego Sipin,
CO, 2nd Battalion, 121st Infantry]

9 October 1944
Subject: Mission
To: 1-66-113 [Parker Calvert, First District, USAFIP-NL]

1. This is to inform that the mission to ambush Japs patrol at KP [Kilometer Post] 68 & KP 69 was very successful. The officers and EM [enlisted men] fought like fools and devils. In spite of the fact that we did not have BARS

[Browning Automatic Rifles], we have given the heaviest blow to the enemy with less than 20 rifles. The enemy were caught [so] unprepared that the Japs were not given a second to fire with the machine gun and rifles. The Japs did not fire a single ammunition. They dropped from the trucks like drunken men.

2. The following listed hereunder were captured from the enemy:

One (1) machine gun, US aircool, cal.30

Four (4) machine gun belts filled with cal.30 ammunition

One (1) machine gun box

Six (6) Jap rifles (long)

Five (5) Jap bayonet

Twenty (20) Jap helmet

Four (4) Japs garrison belts

Many hundreds of cal.30 ammunition

Many hundreds of Japs ammunition

3. Detailed report will be submitted later including report of the other group posted at KP 60.

4. We are proceeding slowly toward home because of heavy load.

(Sgd) (3-1113-L-1120)[299]
[unidentified guerrilla call-sign]

In another report dated 17 November 1944, men of L Company, 3rd Battalion, 66th Infantry (First District) set out on a mission to cut telephone wires and to ambush a Japanese patrol. The men of L Company succeeded in disabling the wires, but their ambush turned sour when the patrol called in reinforcements from a nearby garrison. Outgunned and overmatched, the guerrillas fled. Although the enemy patrol had won the day, USAFIP-NL claimed the lives of six Japanese soldiers and eight kilometers worth of telephone wire.

Other encounters, however, were not so successful. In a report from the Third District, a planned raid on the town of Bangui, a proJapanese town and hotbed of enemy spies, ended in disaster. At 2:30 a.m. on the morning of 29 October, a platoon from the 15th Infantry attacked the town to seize three of its most wanted spies: the mayor, the city treasurer, and a police sergeant. The residents, in a fit of panic, stormed the Japanese garrison for protection. But amidst the darkness and chaos of the predawn debacle, the Japanese opened fire on the townspeople, mistaking them to be guerrillas. In all, 300 civilians died. Hand-to-hand combat ensued as the enemy garrison fought the 15th Infantry until daybreak, when two Japanese fighter planes were called in to strafe the area. USAFIP-NL suffered no casualties that day and even apprehended their target spies, but what had begun as a simple "snatch-and-grab" mission resulted in a destroyed town and over 300 dead civilians.

Volckmann had no doubts that his men could wear down the Japanese, but to have the kind of catastrophic impact that he desired, he would need a lot more resources and much more time. His operations frustrated Yamashita to no end, but even with the resupply from SWPA submarines, Volckmann could not possibly destroy every bridge, ambush every column, or raid every garrison. To destroy the Japanese completely meant that MacArthur had to fulfill the "I Shall Return" promise.

As USAFIP-NL peeled away at Yamashita's combat power, the worried "Tiger of Malaya" began to re-evaluate his predicament. As the Allies advanced on all fronts throughout the Pacific, the Rising Sun diverted more of its combat assets away from the Philippines. This left Yamashita with few options for resupply and fewer options for additional manpower. To correct these deficiencies, Yamashita thought it best to use the terrain to his advantage. He was still relatively unaccustomed to the mountainous jungles, but he obviously saw the utility in what they could provide for his defenses.

Volckmann, meanwhile, kept a close watch on the Allied progress—not just over the radiograms from SWPA, but from the radio station KGEI in San Francisco.[300] News of the Allied landings in the Marshall Islands, New Britain, and the Marianas all meant one thing: U.S. forces were tightening their grip on the Empire of Japan. Yamashita, undoubtedly aware of the same news, began to mobilize his forces inward.

Yamashita's new defense scheme reflected a simple idea: if the Allies wanted a fight, they would have to dig him out inch by inch. He withdrew nearly 150,000 troops into the *Cordillera Central* of North Luzon and ordered them to set up their defenses high within the mountains. The rugged landscape negated the use of everything that gave American forces their superiority (i.e. tanks and mechanized infantry). Yamashita could now command the initiative—or so he thought.[301]

Forcing Yamashita out of the mountains could be done but not without enormous casualties and loss of life. Volckmann's native guerrillas knew every square inch of the terrain, but the incoming Allies had no such luxury. With no probable means of aerial reconnaissance available, the Allied cause would have to rely on Volckmann to provide intelligence on Japanese positions and the surrounding terrain. Without it, U.S. conventional forces would be walking into a bloody stalemate as they tried to pry the Fourteenth Army from their mountainous redoubts.

From 9 January until 15 August 1945, Volckmann directed each of the USAFIP-NL regiments to fight within their respective districts, each obtaining strategic goals that collectively led to the defeat of Yamashita's forces in Luzon. Meeting with General Kruger, Volckmann outlined the situation in Luzon and the requirements needed to defeat the Japanese.[302] Aside from the obvious necessity for more arms and ammunition, Volckmann would need his forces supplemented by conventional infantry and air units. The first utilization of Sixth Army assets in this regard began with an attack on the southern end of the Yamashita perimeter.[303]

Lepanto-Mankayan Operations (66th Infantry)

The Sixth Army landings at Lingayen beach put U.S. forces geographically closest to the 66th Infantry Regiment. As the U.S. I Corps began to attack the enemy's southern flank—thereby diverting Yamashita's attention—Volckmann sprang into action. With a fresh contingent of rifles, machine guns, bullets, and artillery pieces—courtesy of the Sixth Army—Volckmann began the planning phase for the 66th Infantry's assault against the enemy enclaves in the area surrounding the Highway 11 road juncture.[304]

The Japanese had built a triangular defense bounded by Bontoc, Cervantes, and the Loo Valley—with Highway 11's Kilometer Post 90 being the southernmost apex. This area was collectively known as the Lepanto-Mankayan region, so named for the two prominent mountain ridges that dominated the area.

Lepanto-Mankayan represented one of the most strategically important regions in North Luzon, and as such the Japanese defended it for four reasons: (1) it was the gateway into the Loo Valley, known as the "Japanese breadbasket"; (2) in addition to the rich deposits of manganese and iron, the area was home to Luzon's largest network of gold and silver mines; (3) Lepanto-Mankayan housed the largest cache of Yamashita's reserve weaponry; and (4) as indicated in the 66th Infantry's combat reports, Lepanto-Mankayan guarded the approaches into Ifugao, where the enemy had determined to make their last stand.[305]

In 1941, only a small, unimproved road connected the town of Cervantes to the Lepanto-Mankayan pass. When the Japanese invaded, they converted the trail into a hard-surface road to transport copper from the Lepanto mines. Of late, this road had become the primary defensive line on the Japanese position and, consequently, it became a priority target for the USAFIP-NL. Going up against Volckmann's guerrillas were the elements of the 19th Tora Division and the 58th Independent Brigade.[306]

The planning phase for the Lepanto-Mankayan assault began with Field Order #27, issued by Volckmann himself. The order called for the assault to be conducted in three phases: (1) the initial artillery preparation and demolition, (2) the ground assault, and (3) consolidation around the Japanese perimeter.

The assault began with coordinated artillery fire on key enemy positions. Because Volckmann knew that the 19th Division and the other units guarding Lepanto-Mankayan were motorized, he anticipated that they would mobilize their troops via the road and bridge network to defend the precious mines. This realization is where the demolition aspect came into play: as artillery fell on the Japanese, Igorot demoli- tionists would simultaneously blast the thoroughfares, rendering them impassable. This action, in turn, would isolate the Japanese elements and prevent them from reinforcing one another.[307]As the main body of the 66th closed in on the enemy, rear guards would stay behind and occupy the same area that had once been the Japanese perimeter. With guerrillas now occupying the perimeter, American conventional forces could move in to secure the mines.

When the ground assault began, elements of the 15th Infantry occupied the area surrounding Cervantes, the westernmost apex of the Lepanto-Mankayan defense. This allowed the 1st Battalion, 66th Infantry the freedom to move southeast toward Lepanto proper while 2nd secured the communication and supply routes south of Highway 4. The 3rd Battalion, meanwhile, occupied their hastily constructed redoubts in the area surrounding Mt. Namandaraan. This arrangement guaranteed enclosure of the Japanese; escape would not be easy. Of course, "escape" was not what the Japanese had in mind.

As 2nd Battalion soon discovered, the Japanese were prepared to fight to the death. Several assaults launched by 2nd Battalion to destroy the garrisons immediately north of KP 90 were repelled. One such garrison, about 500 yards southwest of the Mankayan Ridge, successfully repelled nine consecutive guerrilla assaults. Aggravated, the CO of 66th called for air support. In the course of their nine disastrous attempts to unseat the Japanese garrison, 66th Infantry scouts determined that there was a nearby field gun giving fire support from a hilltop only a few hundred yards from the enemy outpost. While Allied planes and guerrilla artillery strafed the hilltop gun site, 1st Battalion moved in to catch the enemy garrison off guard. After the gun was silenced, 1st Battalion launched "a perfectly timed assault, closely supported by 60 mm mortars and knocked out the Japanese stronghold."[308]

With this latest garrison destroyed, the entire left flank of the Japanese defenses collapsed. A few raids and skirmishes, involving small arms and light mortars, continued sporadically as the 66th Infantry pushed eastward through Lepanto proper to the Bontoc side of the Japanese defenses. Finally, on 20 July 1945, the last of the enemy-guarded mines fell to the 66th Infantry, bringing the siege of Lepanto-Mankayan to a close.[309]

The 66th Infantry's destruction of the Lepanto-Mankayan defense was important for several reasons. The Japanese had taken three years to build this compound and made it one of the most fortified positions in North Luzon. Now that the area had fallen to the guerrillas, it effectively siphoned off the largest mineral reserve in North Luzon. Consequently, Yamashita could no longer secure shipments of the precious metals to his Emperor. Also, the Lepanto-Mankayan weapon caches had been wrested from Japanese control. The U.S. military considered it bad form to use captured enemy weapons, but Volckmann and his guerrillas had no concern for such formalities. The smorgasbord of grenades, automatic rifles, and bayonets were fair game. And each battalion of the 66th Infantry enjoyed the fruits of the captured Japanese arsenal.

San Fernando-Bacsil Operations (121st Infantry)

Farther north of the Allied landings, in the area surrounding the villages of San Fernando and Bacsil along the coast of La Union, the 121st Infantry directed their attention toward the 6,000 Japanese troops led by Colonel Hayashi. This hodgepodge force was a conglomeration of Marines and four combat regiments taken from the 19th Division.[310]

The Japanese 19th Division had landed at San Fernando earlier in the war. Now, in anticipation of the American landings, the Division had withdrawn the bulk of its forces to Baguio, leaving Hayashi only a few elements with which to defend his coastal areas. Unfortunately for Hayashi, the naval bombardment that screened the Allied landings on Lingayen Gulf had rendered most of the Japanese forces at Bacsil and San Fernando impotent. Consolidating what little equipment they had left, the Japanese contingent built their redoubts into a system of terraces so steep that USAFIP-NL would have found itself literally *climbing* to meet the enemy.[311]

At the beginning of the assault on the San Fernando area, 1st Battalion, 121st Infantry deployed its guerrillas along an east-west front situated a few kilometers north of the village. The 3rd Battalion occupied key positions from the La Union coast, stretching as far east as Highway 3 and the interior barrios of the province. "The holding of this east-west line blocked all Japanese intentions and movements to push beyond the San Fernando enclosure."[312] Meanwhile, 2nd Battalion—in conjunction with the U.S. 123rd Infantry—laid along the rice terraces to the south of Hayashi's main defenses. Bloody skirmishes and a fight for attrition would no doubt punctuate this battle. However, to neutralize the enemy's well-placed redoubts, Volckmann looked to the third dimension.

Building on the *forward air controller* concept, Volckmann devised a way to overcome the heavily fortified terraces. Coordinating his efforts with the Army 308th Bomb Wing and elements of the 24th Marine Air Group, Volckmann supplied his ground liaisons with twoway radios connecting them directly to the pilots overhead. Every time the 121st Infantry called in an air strike, they would display a series of white panels visible from the air. These panels would indicate the forward edge of the battle lines as a safeguard against fratricide. Once the pilot acknowledged recognition of the white panels, Volckmann's ground liaisons would direct the plane to its target.[313]

The flight leaders of these bombing runs, after confirming the location of their target, would make a "dry run" on the mark. After completing the initial bombing runs, the pilots would then come in on strafing runs (i.e. a low-altitude fly-by punctuated by machine gun fire on a target). On the final prearranged strafing run, the pilot would give a signal to the ground forces, like dipping his wing, as a sign for the guerrillas to rush the enemy target. Simultaneously, the bombers would come in on a fake strafing run to deceive the Japanese. With their heads to the ground in fear of another violent machine gun strafing, the Japanese could not see USAFIP-NL ground forces scaling the terraces to assault their positions.[314]

The outcome of the San Fernando-Bascil operation was important not so much for what it contributed to the Japanese defeat—although destroying this Japanese contingent was no meager accomplishment—as for what it contributed to the future of military air-ground operations. Although air-ground tactics similar to Volckmann's had also been used in the European Theater, the modern incarnations of air support and forward air control tactics more closely resemble those employed by USAFIP-NL.

Ilocos-Tangadan Operations (15th Infantry)

The 15th Infantry, under the command of Colonel Rob Arnold, mobilized his troops against the Japanese in Ilocos Norte at the northernmost extremities of Luzon. At first, Volckmann directed the 15th Infantry to carry out missions similar to those of the other regiments. Arnold's men began the fight with a 100-mile demolition route along Highway 3. Special Order #129 from GHQ read:

1. Maximum demolition of bridges, culverts, and defiles between Laoag and Vigan; between Narvacan and Lagangilang;
2. Destruction of every wire communication;
3. Destruction of ammunition, fuel, and other supply dumps;
4. Destruction of planes concealed in dispersal areas;
5. Destruction of convoys and troop trains; and
6. Encouragement of patriotic people under local leadership to unleash maximum violence against the enemy.
7. Power lines, railroad tracks, and stations will only be destroyed upon order.[315]

In January 1945, Arnold was facing over 4,000 enemy troops within his district—the highest concentrations being in Cabugao, Laoag, and the Gabu Airfield. By this time, however, the main highways and service roads had been demolished—courtesy of Arnold's men—and vehicular traffic had come to a standstill. This in turn isolated the prominent Japanese garrisons from one another.

The 15th Infantry began their initial assaults during the second week of January 1945. The ensuing campaign for Ilocos-Tangadan would last nearly five months, culminating in May of that year. The offensive in Ilocos Norte targeted three garrisons, each within the towns of Bangui, Burgos and Batac. Intelligence from GHQ indicated that the enemy's heaviest armaments within the Ilocos provinces were in Ilocos Norte. These included some 18 anti-aircraft guns and at least one 155mm artillery piece.[316] Since the demolition of the previous fall had rendered the highways useless, the Japanese had no choice but to flee on foot, abandoning any weapon that could not be shouldered. Because their motorized assets were no longer useful, the fleeting Imperial soldiers left behind countless heavy guns and artillery pieces—all of which fell into the hands of Volckmann's guerrillas. The methodical destruction of the isolated Japanese garrisons led Volckmann to cast his eyes on a new target. Now, instead of strictly going after Japanese ground forces, he wanted to bring down their air forces as well.[317]

The Imperial Japanese Navy Air Service operated a massive airfield out of Ilocos Norte near the town of Gabu.[318] With a regular reception and dispatch of long-range bombers and transports, Volckmann undoubtedly saw the strategic opportunity that lay before him. An Allied airfield behind enemy lines would serve two functions: it would provide a landing zone and staging area for American bombers heading to Japan, and also provide a faster means of resupply for USAFIP-NL and the Sixth Army. By 9 February 1945, this idea had become a reality as the 15th Infantry captured the airfield at Gabu and converted it into an Allied landing zone.

By the end of the initial assaults in Ilocos Norte and the capture of the Gabu Airfield, the 15th Infantry had claimed the lives of nearly 3,000 enemy soldiers. The terrified Japanese, undoubtedly aware that they were running out of time, retreated into Ilocos Sur, joining their comrades in Cabugao and Tangadan. "On their heels were the 1st and 2nd Battalions of the 15 th Infantry."[319] These two garrisons were the southernmost enemy strongholds in the Third District. Cabugao was a relatively small outpost but Tangadan housed over 2,000 enemy troops under the command of General Araki. On 1 April, the 2nd Battalion began its assault on Cabugao. The *After-Battle Report* described the situation as a "see-saw affair," with guerrillas cresting the garrison only to be beaten back by stubborn resistance.[320] However, on 7 April, Companies C and G entered the town with no enemy resistance whatsoever.[321]

It was clear that the Japanese had used the defense of Cabugao as a stall tactic to reinforce the garrison at Tangadan. The mountainous citadel had hence become the focal point of the Japanese resistance in northwest Luzon. Tangadan lay situated along a series of hills, "bristling with guns of various calibers."[322] The elevation gave the Japanese an excellent vantage point and their fields of fire covered any approach to the garrison. Fortunately for the guerrillas, however, a combination of dry river beds and tall grass on the hills surrounding the complex allowed safe passage for advancing troops. The mission to take Tangadan was a critical one. The Japanese could not be allowed to escape as they had in Ilocos Norte and at Cabugao. If they did so, their next rendezvous point would most likely be Cervantes, right at the edge of the Lepanto-Mankayan defenses. The 66th Infantry, which at the time was planning its initial raids on the Lepanto mine network, certainly had enough on its plate. If more enemy troops arrived to reinforce the mines at Lepanto-Mankayan, it would certainly make life more difficult for the guerrillas trying to shut down Yamashita's mineral outlet.

Beginning around the 10th of April, the three battalions of the 15th Infantry occupied their assault positions for the final raid on Tangadan. Each battalion divided its companies into assault and reserve elements. Reserve elements ensured that no enemy would retreat beyond the perimeter established by the guerrillas. After nearly fifteen days of air strikes, artillery barrages, mortar fire, and hand-to-hand combat, Tangadan succumbed to the guerrillas of the 15th Infantry.

14th Infantry Operations

Meanwhile, the 14th Infantry was steadily enjoying the fruits of the I Corps' advance in the south. The new battlefront was certainly a distraction for Yamashita's forces but, unfortunately, the I Corps fighting did not seem to be making much headway. In fact, it looked as though the I Corps front had devolved into a relative stalemate. Although this development was hardly encouraging, it proved to be a blessing in disguise.

Yamashita apparently realized that if an entire American corps were fighting its way through the mountains, he would have to lend his heaviest firepower to the beleaguered southern perimeter. Unfortunately, the only heavy armor assets he possessed were elements of the 2nd Tank Division.[323] Releasing them to repel the I Corps assault meant that Yamashita would have to compromise the "stay-put" aspect of his defensive strategy.

As the smallest of the USAFIP-NL regiments, the 14th Infantry needed to conserve its resources. As such, Volckmann directed the 14th Infantry's regimental commander, Major Manriquez, to limit his operations to the area surrounding Highway 4.[324] For Yamashita to get his armor moving to the beleaguered southern perimeter, he had no choice but to use the same Highway 4 that the 14th Infantry knew intimately. Thus, using the regiment's anti-armor weapons, including mines and bazooka teams, the 14th Infantry destroyed Yamashita's only armor asset.[325]

This defeat took away the only real maneuver asset that Yamashita had left in the area south of Baguio. Judging from the USAFIP-NL situation maps, the 2nd Tank Division provided the only means of cover for the approaches into the Ifugao and Bontoc sub-provinces (Highways 4, 5, and 11). In this regard, Yamashita could deploy his Type 89 and Type 97 battle tanks to either destroy or severely delay any American infantry wishing to gain access to his headquarters through Ifugao.[326] However, with his tank units destroyed by the 14th Infantry, "The Tiger of Malaya" had lost his best line of defense.

11th Infantry Operations

The 11th Infantry—now commanded by Don Blackburn—covered Cagayan, Apayao, and Mountain provinces, the largest operational area of any regiment within USAFIP-NL.[327] Volckmann gave Blackburn considerable leeway in managing the regiment. Volckmann's primary directive, however, was to deny Japanese access to the Cagayan River Valley. As in Lepanto-Mankayan, the Cagayan River Valley was a "breadbasket" region whose farms had been commandeered by the Japanese.[328]

The easiest way into the valley existed through two cities: Mapayao and Aparri. Both were agricultural centers and had roads offering easy access to the valley's rice plantations. Aparri, however, seems to have been the priority target—and Volckmann was not without reason to make it so. Aparri was the last Japanese naval port into North Luzon and was also where the Japanese landed in 1941.[329]

Viewing the situation, Blackburn saw several potential problems. To corner the enemy, the 11th Infantry would have to push northward through the valley and make their way through its narrow confines into Mapayao.[330] This maneuver would give Blackburn the initiative, but it would also give more flexibility to the Japanese. Aparri was the enemy's last outlet to Tokyo, and they were guaranteed to put up a fight for it.

To affect their assault on Aparri, the 11th Infantry employed elements from USAFIP-NL's organic artillery battalion.[331] Placing these 105mm guns at key redoubts, Blackburn targeted the farmhouses-turned-Japanese command posts. This bombardment would take out as many resources as possible *before* the Japanese retreat began.

As the Japanese retreated from Blackburn's hail of artillery fire, two battalions of the 11th Infantry swooped down in a pincer-like movement to prevent the enemy from reaching and fortifying Aparri. However, due to one of the battalion commander's lack of tenacity, a rather large contingent slipped through to Aparri. The resulting siege of the city lasted approximately three weeks. Assisted by the 1-511 Airborne Infantry Regiment, the 11th Airborne Division, which had parachuted in behind enemy lines to assist USAFIP-NL, Blackburn's men cleared Aparri and the surrounding area of Tuguegarao, thereby shutting down and closing access to the enemy's last operational naval port in Luzon.[332]

Bessang Pass and the Final Push

The Battle for Bessang Pass represents perhaps the most decisive engagement for the USAFIP-NL. By the time USAFIP-NL began concentrating its forces on Bessang Pass in June 1945, the Japanese Fourteenth Army was in its last throes. Crippled by the collective action of Volckmann's regiments and the newly arrived Sixth U.S. Army, Yamashita put everything he had into making his last stand at Bessang Pass.[333]

Bessang Pass was the narrowest part of Highway 4 heading east into the Cordillera Central. In recent months, USAFIP-NL intelligence had reported that Bessang Pass had become the back door to Yamashita's command center.

Activity along the Pass and the surrounding countryside seemed to confirm this observation: the Japanese fortified their redoubts with artillery and dug a sophisticated network of tunnels, trenches, and pillboxes.[334]

After winding down their operations in San Fernando, the 121st Infantry, which was the closest of Volckmann's regiments, was the first to arrive. The Japanese, however, would not give up Bessang Pass without a fight. Nearly two and a half weeks of combat between the 121st Infantry and the 19th Tora Division ended in a bloody stalemate. Volckmann soon realized that taking Bessang Pass and rousting Yamashita from his hole would require more than one regiment. Beginning on 15 June 1945, Volckmann pulled the 15th Infantry and elements of the 66th Infantry into the 121st Infantry's staging area outside of Bessang Pass.*

For the next two weeks, the three regiments engaged in the fiercest fighting Volckmann had ever witnessed. The battle, in many respects, became an artillerymen's game. In a desperate stroke to bolster his defenses, Yamashita concentrated the last of his functional artillery pieces on the ridges surrounding Balete Pass. What the Japanese lacked, however, was the ability to coordinate infantry-artillery operations. As their men remained bunkered down in their trench networks and pillboxes, they had no means of employing forward artillery observers to gauge the proximity of enemy formations. Before firing their rounds, the Japanese artillerymen simply calculated a hypothetical trajectory and fired into the fog, not taking into account any possible terrain features that would offset the desired impact. Volckmann, on the other hand, saw his artillery as a critical maneuver asset. With each advance on the territory surrounding Bessang Pass, Volckmann's men would relay the distance and elevation of a particular target back to the "gun line."** This process made it easier for American artillery to zero-in, neutralize, and severely weaken the Japanese enclaves. In contrast, Yamashita's howitzers fired blindly with hopes that a round would make impact on an enemy patrol.[335]

As his men worked their way up the last occupied ridges surrounding the pass, liaison scouts noticed the Japanese withdrawing from the area surrounding Bessang Pass. Their direction of travel meant that they were withdrawing closer toward Yamashita—no doubt in an attempt to protect their leader's hideout. More importantly, it meant that their positions at Bessang Pass were no longer tenable. As the Japanese retreated from their Bessang

---

*At this time, the 11th Infantry remained in the midst of securing Aparri and the surrounding area. The 14th Infantry, meanwhile, moved in to occupy the Lepanto-Mankayan mines so the 66th Infantry could partake in the Bessang Pass campaign.

**Artillery term referring to every howitzer committed to support a particular ground operation.

redoubts, Volckmann greeted them with another artillery salvo. Although estimates vary, it is likely that only half of the enemy's retreating force made it to their next rally point.[336]

The Battle for Bessang Pass was critical to the campaign, largely because it broke down the back door to Yamashita's Headquarters. Although the worst of the fighting was still to come, the fall of the Pass signaled the end of Yamashita's reign in North Luzon. It was scarcely 25 miles from Bessang Pass to Yamashita's Command Center, and the bulk of his forces had already been destroyed.[337] Furthermore, at this point, there was no hope for Yamashita to receive any assistance from the mother country. The fortifications at Bessang Pass had been his last stall tactic. Now, it was only a matter of time before the Americans would burst their way through Cervantes and Bontoc en route to his headquarters. Taking these two towns would not be overly difficult, but the accompanying terrain meant a slow and methodical approach for the Americans, as there were no roads in this part of Mountain Province and very few trails.[338]

Cervantes sat along Route 4 approximately 1,000 yards from Bessang Pass. Occupying Cervantes took nearly two weeks to accomplish, but was a critical milestone because it blocked access for Japanese reinforcements along Route 4. Following the capture of Cervantes, the USAFIP-NL Division (referring to the three regiments fighting together) worked in concert with the U.S. Army's 6th and 32nd Infantry Divisions to storm the enemy contingent at Bontoc. Pacifying the last municipality between the Allies and Yamashita, USAFIP-NL occupied its final attack position. Together with the 6th and 32nd Infantry Division, Volckmann's guerrillas formed a circular perimeter around the last enclave of combat-capable Japanese forces.[339]

With the encirclement of Yamashita's defenses complete, Volckmann's guerrillas attacked from the north and west while the 6th and 32nd Divisions closed in from the east and south, respectively. The Japanese fiercely fought over every square inch of this land until the official cease-fire came down on 15 August 1945. By the time Emperor Hirohito accepted the terms of surrender, USAFIP-NL had fought its way over 7,000 feet of elevation and came within a mere five miles of Yamashita's Headquarters.[340] Had the Empire of Japan not surrendered, it is likely that Yamashita's men would have fought to the death. Nevertheless, Yamashita chose to respect the Emperor's wishes and emerged from the cordillera to face the consequences of surrender.

When the "Tiger of Malaya" finally came out of the mountains, he made his surrender overtures not to MacArthur, but to Volckmann. Over the previous year, Yamashita had developed a begrudging respect for the USAFIP-NL. He knew Volckmann by name and had issued one of the largest bounties in the Philippines on his head. Now, after his failed attempts to crush the resistance movement and defend Luzon from the Allied advance, Tomiyuki Yamashita ordered his troops to lay down their arms.*

Over a period of three years, 1942–45, and commanding a guerrilla force of over 22,000 men, Volckmann's guerrillas killed over 50,000 enemy troops. USAFIP-NL accomplished these figures while losing less than 2,000 of their own.[341] For his efforts, Volckmann earned the Distinguished Service Cross, the nation's second highest military honor.[342]

---

*Yamashita was later tried and hanged for war crimes, as were many of his subordinate commanders.

CHAPTER 10

After the Fire: 1946–1948

For Russell W. Volckmann, the first two years following the Japanese surrender were nearly as chaotic as the war itself. Since 8 December 1941, he had been in a relentless struggle to survive. Harrowing escapes, debilitating sickness, and the ever-present fear of the unknown had been his daily lot. Yet, Volckmann had emerged victorious: the commander of among the greatest irregular armies of all time. Quietly, however, he was a tired soldier, eager to make his way back home. By September 1945, it had been some four and a half years since he had seen his family.[343]

Meanwhile, Nancy Volckmann and her young son, Russell Jr., had spent the last four years hoping that he was still alive. The pair had been evacuated five months before the invasion and knew nothing of what the next four years might hold. Upon their departure from the Philippines, Nancy and Russell Jr. settled in Arlington, Virginia, where she took a clerical job with American Airlines. While raising her young son, Nancy kept in contact with Volckmann's parents for any news regarding her husband.[344] The last she had heard of Volckmann was a telegram delivered to his father, William, indicating that his son was "Missing in Action." Throughout his time in North Luzon, the War Department had no idea whatsoever that Volckmann commanded an army of guerrillas, for he officially remained "Missing in Action" and by 1945, was presumed dead.[345]

The first letter that Volckmann sent out after the Fall of Bataan was dated 20 October 1944, and did not arrive at his parents' house until three months later.[346] Although it is not certain, he may have used his contact with the SWPA submarines to post his letter from Australia. On 15 January 1945, the Clinton *Herald*—Volckmann's hometown newspaper—reported the first news of Volckmann's status, indicating that he was alive and that his wife had received news of her husband's whereabouts from an "undisclosed source." Regardless, for security reasons, the War Department gave no comment on Volckmann's letter and maintained that he was still officially considered "Missing in Action."[347]

Before Volckmann could come home, however, there were several items that required his attention. Now that Yamashita had surrendered, Volckmann had to begin the long administrative process of delivering his records to the United States and chronicling his activities for the Army Adjutant. Then, there was the question of Yamashita himself. The "Tiger of Malaya" had seen the best of his forces diminished by an enemy that constantly lurked in the shadows. The more pressing issue on his mind, no doubt, was the punishment that he would have to face for the crimes he and his men had committed. Yamashita, the man who had boldly proclaimed that *he* would dictate the terms of peace to MacArthur, now faced a military tribunal. Among the crimes of rape, pillaging, and the cruel treatment of USAFFE prisoners, Tomiyuki Yamashita's march to the gallows seemed all but certain. Since Volckmann was a material witness to the war crimes of the Japanese, he was subpoenaed to appear at the tribunal and give sworn statements of the atrocities that he had seen.[348] Perhaps more importantly, however, Volckmann was obligated to reconstruct the phases of his operations against the Japanese so that the Army could have a verifiable record of his actions and a safeguard against fraudulent claims from the enemy.

To meet this requirement, Volckmann began work on two booklets. The first, titled *G3 After-Battle Report,* gave a reconstructive narrative of actions against the enemy from the Allied landings at Lingayen Gulf to the Japanese surrender. The second booklet was titled *Guerrilla Days in North Luzon.* Published by Volckmann's Headquarters in La Union Province, it was much shorter in length than *After-Battle Report.* Nevertheless, *Guerrilla Days* provided the Army with an accurate and in-depth overview of the evolution of the North Luzon resistance. As an additional measure, Volckmann included information on the other guerrilla leaders that arose in the early stages of the conflict, for example Walter Cushing. Concurrently, Volckmann assigned certain USAFIP-NL personnel to interview the Japanese generals and other high-ranking officers that he had recently defeated in North Luzon. After being assured that the war was over and that their candor was imperative, these Japanese subjects recounted their engagements with USAFIP-NL and—with begrudging respect—admitted that Volckmann's tactics had outfoxed them.[349]

In accordance with the original *Tydings-McDuffie Act,* the United States still had a promise to keep. Although the Japanese had impeded the progress towards independence, the Filipinos were ready to take control of their own country. Picking up the pieces of the shattered Philippine Army, however, would not be easy. The Japanese had destroyed nearly all of their equipment and several more items remained unaccounted for. Amid the chaos of December 1941, Philippine Army quartermasters had abandoned their supply depots to join the USAFFE retreat. American-Philippine guerrilla units, including Volckmann's, had since foraged these unmanned depots to recover any available arms and ammunition. Despite the grim task of rebuilding the Philippine defenses, Volckmann remained slightly ahead of the curve. The United States Armed Forces in the Philippines-North Luzon was roughly the size of an

American Army division. Since the amalgamated regiments of USAFIP-NL were already Philippine Army assets, Volckmann suggested converting his force into a new division of the Philippine Army. Before the Army would let him do this, however, they granted him a 45-day furlough to visit his family in the United States.

Beginning on 30 November 1945, Volckmann began the long journey back to Clinton, Iowa. The last time he had seen his hometown was in 1940, shortly before his departure to the Philippine Islands. Prior to receiving the letter of 20 October 1944, William Volckmann buried himself in the day-to-day operations of his furniture business, desperately hoping that his son was still alive. Now that the mystery was over, he hurriedly prepared for his son's homecoming. Meanwhile, Nancy and Russell Jr. boarded a train westbound from Arlington. Even Volckmann's sister, Ruth Volckmann Stansbury—whose husband John was currently serving with the U.S. Army in New Guinea—arrived in Clinton for the occasion.[350]

Arriving at Hamilton Army Air Field in Novato, California, a flood of reporters from the Associated Press greeted the new colonel on the tarmac. Anxious to avoid the excessive publicity, however, Volckmann hurried himself past the throngs of newsmen and prepared to board the *Statesman,* a chartered ATC plane en route to Chicago. Unfortunately, due to an engine malfunction, the plane was grounded on the tarmac. Rather than have his homecoming delayed, Volckmann made other arrangements and boarded a TWA flight to Kansas City.[351] After four days of seemingly endless connecting flights, train rides, and virtually no sleep, Volckmann finally arrived in Clinton. Ironically, Volckmann had arrived in his hometown on 7 December 1945, the fourth anniversary of Pearl Harbor.[352]

Stepping off the train at the Clinton Depot, Volckmann enjoyed the tearful reunion he had been longing for. Rushing to greet him was his now nine-year-old son, Russell Jr. He had been a lad of only five when he and his mother evacuated the Philippines. Uncertain as to whether or not he would ever see his father again, the young Volckmann recalled that, "My reaction was excitement and joy. We went for several years without knowing."[353] Minutes later, Nancy Volckmann reunited with her soldier-husband. It was a joyous ride back to Volckmann's home at 752 Sixth Avenue South. Greeted by his father, Volckmann received a warm embrace and a simple question: "Are you hungry, Rusty?"[354] That night, the family—William, Russell Sr., Russell Jr., Nancy, and Ruth Stansberry—enjoyed one photo op after another, as everyone in town was bustling about the return of Clinton's war hero.

Volckmann remained in Clinton with his family throughout Christmas and into January 1946. Unfortunately, it would soon be "back to business." Boarding an Army air transport, Volckmann bid his family goodbye as he departed, once again, for the Philippines. This time, however, there would be no imminent war on the horizon. The enemy had surrendered and America was now at peace with the Empire of Japan. He gave his assurances to Nancy and Russell Jr. that he would return within a few months, just as soon as he transferred control of USAFIP-NL to the Filipinos.

The process of transfering authority of the guerrilla regiments to the Philippine Army was a lengthy one. There were a number of issues that Volckmann had to tackle. Chief among them was taking an inventory of weapons and equipment, as well as coordinating pay issues with the Philippine government. Since many of Volckmann's guerrillas were members of the Philippine Army, Scouts, or Constabulary, they sought back pay for their service against the Japanese. Guerrillas that had no military service prior to the war but now sought to join the Philippine defense community also required compensation. Since the Fall of Corregidor, USAFFE and the Philippine defense apparatus had become military non-entities. Consequently, they had no means to continue their financial operations. Furthermore, during the occupation, the only monies circulated throughout the Philippines were the Japanese war notes—which were worthless currency now that the Emperor had surrendered.

The task of sifting through the Philippine Army's bureaucratic minutia, however, became easier for Volckmann after the Philippine elections on 23 April 1946. The president-elect was none other than Manuel Roxas, with whom Volckmann had unwittingly earned a close friendship. Roxas had quite an interesting political career. As a Philippine senator and reserve officer in the Philippine Army, Roxas had been captured on Corregidor and impressed into the new puppet government as the chief economic advisor. Undaunted by his *de facto* captivity, Roxas fed intelligence to Allied spies operating in Manila.[355] Upon hearing of Volckmann's daring escapades in North Luzon, Roxas penned the following letter:

> PHILLIPINE SENATE
> Manila
> July 31, 1945
>
> My dear Colonel Volckmann:
>
> I take this opportunity of the visit of Capt. Felix-berto M. Verano to Camp Spencer [Volckmann's Headquarters] to write you and express my profound admiration for the most gallant and successful leadership of the guerrilla forces in Northern Luzon. Throughout the Japanese occupation, I have tried to keep informed of your activities and did everything I could to aid and support your command. All the Filipinos are deeply grateful to you and will never forget the service that you rendered not only to the United States but also to the Philippines. If there is anything that I can do to help in obtaining for you and the forces under your command the recognition that is due to you and to them, as well as any assistance that you believe just and fair to the widows and orphans of your dead soldiers, I shall be very glad to exert my efforts in their behalf.

I am very anxious to meet you and extend to you personally my warmest congratulations. If you should come to Manila at any time in the near future, kindly let me know so that I may arrange a meeting with you.

Yours Truly,

(Signed) Manuel Roxas[356]

Seizing the opportunity, Volckmann solicited help from Roxas throughout the unit's entire conversion process. Then, on 14 June 1946, the organization formerly known as the United States Armed Forces in the Philippines—North Luzon completed its transition from guerrilla force to a division of the new Philippine Army. To commemorate the occasion, President Roxas officially declared the 14th of June "USAFIP-NL Day." The affair of transforming his guerrilla outfit into a division of a professional army ended victoriously, but it would not be the last time Volckmann would call upon President Roxas for help.[357]

Returning to the United States in July 1946, Volckmann assumed the duties of Assistant Chief of Staff—Army Personnel Division, Washington, DC. During this time, Volckmann began work on a project known as the Guerrilla Recognition Program. By this time, many of the guerrillas' receipts had been redeemed. Now, however, more individuals began lobbying the Philippine government with claims that they, too, had been guerrillas and had not been properly compensated. The Guerrilla Recognition Program set forth guidelines for evaluating claims in order to prevent fraud and abuse of the system.[358] Accordingly, a supposed guerrilla unit would have to establish the following: (1) a record of service with definite timeframes, (2) proof that the unit maintained ongoing opposition to the enemy, (3) that the activities of the unit materially contributed to the defeat of the enemy, and (4) that there was a definite organization to the unit. Using these criteria, the Army validated the claims of many of the guerrillas while discrediting those who attempted to cheat the system.[359] Meanwhile, Volckmann began the arduous journey through the Army's rehabilitation program. The tropical diseases that Volckmann had acquired in the Philippines now lay dormant, but to prevent any future relapses, the Army put him through an endless cycle of blood work and phased medicine before issuing him a clean bill of health. Indeed, Volckmann spent more time at Walter Reed Army Hospital than he did at the Personnel Division offices.[360]

In the midst of his physical turmoil, Volckmann soon encountered a problem of a different kind: after nearly thirteen years of marriage, Nancy wanted a divorce. At first, Volckmann could hardly fathom it: for thirteen years he had been a devoted husband. Perhaps the four years of separation during the war had taken its toll, or maybe she had gained a newfound sense of independence. Whatever Nancy's reasons may have been, Volckmann knew that if she no longer wanted the marriage, it was better to let her go than to embroil himself in a fight he couldn't win. Thus, while making his arduous roundtrips to Walter Reed,

Volckmann endured the legalistic hassles of divorce papers and asset division. Their divorce was finalized on 17 August 1947.*

In January 1947, less than six months into his tour at Personnel Division, Volckmann received a summons from General Dwight D. Eisenhower, Army Chief of Staff. It appeared as though a problem had surfaced in the Philippines in the wake of Volckmann's departure. During the war, Volckmann had authorized—out of military necessity—the elimination of enemy spies and collaborators. Now, it seemed as though his tactics were coming back to haunt him.

When the families of the executed collaborators broke their silence, they lobbied the Philippine government to punish those responsible for the deaths of their loved ones. Don Blackburn recalled that Volckmann "explained the situation to Eisenhower [who then] dispatched him back to see MacArthur. Ike wrote a note to MacArthur which Volckmann carried, saying that he felt these cases should be quashed."[361] Later that week, Volckmann boarded a plane to Tokyo, where General MacArthur had assumed command of the American occupation forces. Arriving at MacArthur's Headquarters, the general's aide-de-camp instructed Volckmann to sit down and write a "staff study" on the situation before meeting MacArthur.[362] *A staff study?* Volckmann and his comrades had just become the targets of a war criminal witch hunt—and the General wanted him to write a staff study? Thoroughly irritated, Volckmann complied with the order and wrote a four-page staff study before being ushered into the general's office.

Sitting across the desk from MacArthur, Volckmann watched the general peruse over the staff study he had completed only minutes ago. Chuckling, MacArthur promptly threw it in the wastebasket.[363]

"Russ, tell me what the problem is," he said.[364]

Volckmann explained the situation to MacArthur and said that there should be no reason why anyone should stand trial for eliminating enemy conspirators. MacArthur took out his pen and notepad and drafted a memo to General James E. Moore, Commanding General of the Philippine Ryukyu Command: "Let Russ Volckmann explain it all to you, and let him write the ticket. I agree that we shouldn't allow these things to continue."[365]

---

*Although they were married for nearly thirteen years, surviving family does not recall many details about their marriage or courtship. Nancy purportedly met the young Cadet Volckmann circa 1932 when she was an art student in Philadelphia. It is possible that Nancy's sister (who was engaged to one of Volckmann's classmates) arranged the meeting. Nancy and Russell were married on 25 August 1934. Russell Jr. (b. 1936) was the couple's only child. Volckmann later married Ms. Helen Rich, with whom he had two children: William (b. 1954) and Edward (b. 1961). They remained together until Volckmann's death in 1982. Nancy, too, later remarried although she had no further children.

Returning to the Philippines, Volckmann sought to cash-in his last favor with Manuel Roxas. Delivering MacArthur's memo to General Moore, Volckmann then set out for the Presidential Palace in Manila. Together, Roxas and Volckmann produced an amnesty proclamation that read, "Any act performed in furtherance of the resistance movement should be exonerated."[366] While the amnesty act proved beneficial to the Americans, (indeed, no American ever came to trial), it had mixed results for the Filipinos. Many of the Filipinos were being pulled into the court system, which obviously cost the Philippine government more time and money than it could feasibly devote to the project. Subsequently, President Roxas created "amnesty boards," which would travel around the country to hear the charges levied against Filipino men and officers. Amnesty boards were unique in the sense that they did not require a lawyer, and initially they fell beyond the country's jurisprudence. The accused would go before the board, plead their case, and "if it looked as though their actions were in furtherance of the resistance movement, amnesty was granted."[367]

But as Blackburn conceded, the amnesty system was flawed and rather ambiguous. For example, if a Filipino were charged with executing a certain collaborator and replied, "Yes, I did it because he was an informer," then that was enough to exonerate him. However, if he said, "I was directed to execute him by Captain John Smith [hypothetical name]. I was carrying out his orders," or some other phraseology, the case would be thrown to the Philippine courts.[368] Under that system, many Philippine guerrillas who had served under Volckmann ended up in prison, although some were never convicted legally. Distraught by these results, Volckmann and Blackburn sought to accomplish something from the American side of the Pacific. In June 1947, both men paid a visit to the Honorable Kenneth Royal, Secretary of the Army. If Americans were being implicated in the amnesty trials, then perhaps the U.S. government could create a sufficient diplomatic solution to exonerate any Filipino who had killed upon the orders of an American commander. The result was an amnesty proclamation signed by Secretary Royal stating:

> Due to the fact that the military situation in the Philippine Islands, during the period of Japanese occupation, prevented the orders of the recognized guerrilla commanders and their duly appointed subordinates from being confirmed or made a matter of record, all orders of the former said recognized guerrilla commanders as shown by the official records of the United States Army in the Philippines. Such orders having been issued on the grounds of the absolute military necessity for maintaining discipline among their guerrilla forces, and for the security of such forces concerning the elimination of persons aiding or abetting the enemy in the time of war during the period, 8 December 1941, to 15 August 1945, both dates included.[369]

The proclamation was officially signed and notarized on 12 August 1949. But the proclamation only turned out to be a half-victory. Volckmann and Blackburn had offered to return to the Philippines to testify on behalf of those charged. However, their well-spring of support with the Roxas Administration no longer existed—Roxas had passed away the previous year. Further complicating the matter was the U.S. State Department. As it were, the Secretary of State's legal experts "cried foul" on the grounds that the amnesty proclamation violated some issue involving international jurisdiction.[370] Thus, Secretary Royal's amnesty proclamation became a worthless document.

Nearly a decade later, however, the matter came to the attention of the new Philippine President, Ramon Magsaysay. Magsaysay himself had been a guerrilla in Western Luzon and, upon hearing of the legal plights of his comrades, immediately sprung into action. Sometime in the 1950s, Ramon Magsaysay met with Blackburn to discuss the matter: all cases were to be reopened and accompanied by fact-finding missions to determine whether those guerrillas currently in prison had acted on the orders of an American officer. Magsaysay, however, was not oblivious to the darker side of human nature. At one point during his meeting with Blackburn, the Philippine President said, "Look, so many of these cases of murder were not really aiding and abetting the resistance movement."[371] With this, Blackburn couldn't have agreed more. He conceded that some of the Filipinos under USAFIP-NL had vindictively used the opportunity to eliminate their personal enemies. These wayward guerrillas may have escaped the legal system with a simple reassurance that their personal enemy was an informer. But these same guerrillas had inadvertently incriminated themselves by killing not only their adversaries, but killing their families as well. Blackburn and Magsaysay could find no reason why killing a toddler or bayoneting someone's wife could have furthered the resistance movement. Thus, Magsaysay's task was to separate fact from fiction and weed out the murderers from those who had killed in the line of duty. Neither Volckmann nor Blackburn ever knew the outcome of the Magsaysay project, although some USAFIP-NL guerrillas eventually regained their freedom.[372]

After surviving four years of continuous combat, Russell Volckmann had returned home to a wife who no longer loved him, angry families of deceased collaborators, and an Army medical system that occupied nearly every minute of his day. Yet in spite of these personal setbacks, Volckmann remained optimistic. If he had survived the jungles of North Luzon, he could certainly survive whatever obstacles the peacetime Army threw his way.

In the early months of 1948, Walter Reed finally stamped their seal of approval on Volckmann's medical file and dismissed him from their outpatient clinic. Concurrently, his service at the Personnel Division drew to a close and Volckmann received orders to report to the Infantry Center at Fort Benning, Georgia. General Eisenhower had an important job for him to accomplish.

CHAPTER 11

A New Kind of Fighting

Volckmann's most significant contribution may lie in what he accomplished *after* the war. Upon his arrival in the United States, Volckmann reflected on the lessons he had learned over the past four years. Nothing in his professional training had prepared him for the kind of combat he had seen in the Philippines. In fact, guerrilla warfare existed nowhere in U.S. Army doctrine. The reasons were numerous: traditional military minds did not understand nor appreciate the art of guerrilla warfare, calling it "illegal and dishonorable."[373] Professional armies were expected to meet each other in contests of fire and win by attrition. Many also regarded guerrilla warfare as a tactical aberration. It represented nothing more than untrained, undisciplined rebels who could be disposed of in short order by a superior force. However, the success of the Philippine guerrillas had shown military leaders otherwise: unconventional forces were indispensable to obtaining strategic goals. When Volckmann began the process of closing down USAFIP-NL and overseeing the reorganization of its organic components into a new division of the Philippine Army, he began to promote the idea of establishing a permanent force structure capable of unconventional warfare. Ultimately, he wanted to parlay his knowledge into something that future servicemen could use.

Historically, the Army had been relatively successful in using conventional means to fight guerrillas. Therefore, the principles of counterinsurgency and guerrilla-style warfare remained nothing more than an afterthought within the larger bodies of conventional doctrine.[374] But as the Army found itself participating within the various insurgencies that erupted after World War II—the Greek, Chinese, and Philippine civil wars—Volckmann's ideas suddenly gained new traction. Volckmann knew of the emerging "Cold War" and the shift in military doctrine that accompanied it. With contingencies focusing on a possible war with the Soviet Union, the idea of having to fight enemy guerrillas working alongside conventional forces seemed a viable threat. After all, the same Soviet partisans who contributed to the defeat of the Nazis could just as well be used against the Americans.

Consequently, Army Chief of Staff General Dwight D. Eisenhower commissioned Volckmann to write what would become the Army's first official counterinsurgency doctrine.[375] While the Army pondered over what to do in regard to establishing "special operations" forces, they concluded that writing a doctrine for combating guerrillas was a good place to start. The result was Field Manual (FM) 31–20 *Operations Against Guerrilla Forces,* released in September 1950. Written exclusively by Volckmann, it was the result of nearly a yearlong writing campaign (1948–49). Writing FM 31–20, Volckmann analyzed the tactical gaffes of the Japanese and pondered what methods an army could use to defeat a guerrilla like himself.

Drawing from his own experiences, Volckmann used FM 31–20 to show the "characteristics, organization, and operations of guerrilla forces." This was done to provide the readers with a better understanding of guerrilla nature and the underlying factors that foster guerrilla movements. FM 31–20 focused on two manifestations of guerrilla warfare. The first included conflicts "conducted by irregular forces (supported by an external power) to bring about a change in the socio-political order of a country without engaging it in a formal, declared war." The second covered operations by irregular forces working "in conjunction with regularly organized forces as a phase of a normal war"—just as the USAFIP-NL had done a few years prior.[376]

Volckmann conceded that rarely would a guerrilla movement succeed without the support of the *local population* and a *third-party conventional force.* Both represented the only lifelines a guerrilla movement had to continue its operation. Without support from the local population, a guerrilla's only reservoir for recruits and labor would not exist. And even though a guerrilla movement could produce its own network of spies, propagandists, and paramilitary personnel, their long-term supply and logistical needs were best fulfilled by conventional forces.[377]

However, the more important topic for Volckmann was how to undermine the very factors that led to insurgencies. By this, Volckmann knew that "preventing the formation of a resistance movement is easier than dealing with one after it is formed." Preventing a full-scale insurgency, he claimed, could be accomplished by plans "based on a detailed analysis of a country, the national characteristics, and the customs, beliefs, cares, hopes, and desires of the people." Volckmann did not claim to be a politician but called on commanders to build a rapport with the local population by restoring law and providing humanitarian relief.[378] This had been a critical error of the Japanese during the war. Instead of restoring the law, they instituted their own—even in areas where there was no overt resistance to the occupation. Humanitarian relief was conspicuously absent from their operations as they burned, raped, and plundered entire villages.

Once the proper political framework had been established, the theater commander's first priority would be to develop an effective intelligence apparatus.

Operations Against Guerrilla Forces called for more intelligence assets than would normally be given to conventional forces. Psychological warfare specialists and counterintelligence personnel were also called upon to weave through the indigenous cultural dynamics.[379]

FM 31–20 outlined three stages of counterguerrilla operations: The first was to isolate guerrillas from the civilian population. The second was to deny them any external support. Volckmann emphasized the importance of cutting off external aid as he knew that, had his guerrillas not been resupplied by the U.S. Sixth Army, it would have taken USAFIP-NL much longer—possibly years—to defeat the Japanese. The third and final stage called for the destruction of guerrilla forces.

To accomplish this, FM 31–20 envisioned three types of offensive action: "encirclement," "surprise attack," and "pursuit." According to Volckmann, encirclement represented the most effective way to isolate and destroy guerrillas. Once the guerrillas had been isolated by encirclement, commanders could use one of four methods to eliminate all resistance within the enclosed area.

1. A "tightening encirclement" in which all forces move in and shorten the perimeter.
2. A "hammer and anvil" technique that consisted of one attacking element advancing while the other stayed in place waiting for the fleeing guerrillas to be driven into their path.
3. Splitting an encircled area in two and destroying either one in turn.
4. Conventional assault against fortified positions.

Whatever method a commander might use during the encirclement phase, Volckmann emphasized that it would not be easy. However, he stressed the importance of small-unit operations throughout counterguerrilla warfare. Small infantry units would employ scouts and guides—drawn from the local population—to direct them to a guerrilla outpost and attack either at night or at dawn.[380]

Pursuit, the third offensive tactic, represented what regular forces would likely find themselves resorting to in counterinsurgency warfare. If guerrillas escaped either *encirclement* or *attack,* the *pursuit* option guaranteed their final destruction. Volckmann did not outline specifically how it should be done, but he made it clear that small units linked by artillery and close air support would pound the guerrillas incessantly.[381] The Japanese had failed to do this in Luzon. Artillery miscalculations, the lack of coordination among infantry teams, and the virtual absence of Japanese air support guaranteed their demise.

Among the grandest mistakes that Volckmann had witnessed from the Japanese were their frequent troop rotations. This deprived their soldiers and commanders an opportunity to adjust to the local political and military climate. Volckmann not only warned against this but also advised any regional commanders to coordinate their efforts with one another. One of the worst mistakes they could make would be to allow guerrillas safe passage from one sector to another.[382]

Although he designed FM 31–20 from an infantry perspective, Volckmann contended that close air support and ground-attack aircraft were vital to counterguerrilla warfare. However, the existing methods of air support were inadequate to meet these demands. Recalling his meetings with the 308th Bomber Wing in the Philippines, Volckmann promoted the same ideas that he had used to employ his forward air controllers in coordinating air strikes.[383] By the time Volckmann wrote FM 31–20, however, the Army Air Forces had become the United States Air Force. Now its own separate branch, the Air Force assumed all responsibility for employing forward air controllers, but nonetheless traced many of their doctrinal precepts to Russell Volckmann.* And although fixed-wing aircraft largely became the Air Force's responsibility, it did not impede Volckmann's contributions to Army Aviation. FM 31–20 was the first manual in Army history to forecast the viability of employing helicopters in counterinsurgency warfare.[384] Concepts set forth by Volckmann in this regard laid the foundation for the modern air cavalry.

The concepts detailed in FM 31–20 set the precedent for all future counterinsurgency doctrine. It synthesized military principles into a comprehensive doctrine that could easily be adapted to any situation. Moreover, it outlined the tactical dispositions that American forces would use in Vietnam. Subsequent editions of the manual, including those that became the operational basis for infantry units in Vietnam, merely recycled the same principles that Volckmann had written earlier.** Even today's counterinsurgency manual, FM 3–24 *Counterinsurgency,* regurgitates the same concepts and tactics Volckmann wrote over 50 years ago.

As Volckmann's manual went before the Army review board, the first conflict in America's Cold War began. With the goal of reuniting the Korean Peninsula under Communist rule, the North Korean People's Army (NKPA) stormed across the 38th Parallel on 25 June 1950. Though officially termed a "police action," the Korean War pitted the United Nations, led by the U.S., against the Communist forces of the NKPA and later, the Chinese Army. In October 1950, one month after publishing *Operations Against Guerrilla Forces,* Volckmann was on his way to Korea via Tokyo.

The Korean War represented a unique opportunity for Volckmann. Throughout the conflict, unconventional warfare occurred in two overlapping phases. In the first phase, spanning from June 1950 until fall 1951, U.S. conventional forces conducted counterguerrilla operations against the NKPA

---

*Recall Volckmann's participation in the Air Force-sponsored Rand study.
**FM 31–15 *Operations Against Irregular Forces* and FM 31–16 *Counterguerrilla Operations,* published respectively in 1961 and 1967.

irregulars. The second phase of unconventional warfare, from January 1951 until the cease-fire in 1953, saw the U.S. Eighth Army develop its own "special operations command" to conduct guerrilla warfare behind enemy lines. The North Koreans made extensive use of guerrilla units during the first year of combat. From a military standpoint, NKPA guerillas served two functions: (1) their tactics could offset the superiority of American maneuver forces; and (2) while camouflaging themselves within the local population, NKPA partisans could work to undermine American ideology. The irony of the situation was not lost on Volckmann, for the NKPA strategy was nearly identical to the plan he had developed against the Japanese a decade ago.

As North Korean partisans wrought havoc on American assets, the newly appointed Army Chief of Staff, General J. Lawton "Lighting Joe" Collins, scrambled for a cohesive plan to neutralize the enemy guerrillas. Among the most significant problems caused by NKPA irregulars were their attacks against lines of communication and rear areas. The hastily devised solution from the Chief of Staff thereby included a directive to all in-theater units—as well as those tapped for deployment—to receive instruction on counterguerrilla techniques.[385] When the stateside units began their predeployment training, they utilized the only literature available on counterguerrilla operations: Volckmann's FM 31–20.

Meanwhile, General Douglas MacArthur, now the commander of UN forces, pondered his next move. He was confident in handling the conventional aspects of the war, but dealing with the NKPA partisans brought to mind an aspect of warfare that he had hoped to leave behind in the Philippines. Admittedly, he had never been a fan of irregular warfare or the "special operations" concept.[386] Nonetheless, during his days at SWPA, he had feverously supported the USAFIP-NL and had even been quoted as saying that the guerrillas were indispensable to the outcome of the campaign. Whatever the genesis of MacArthur's reservations towards unconventional warfare, he nonetheless approved of the creation of special Army units to combat enemy guerrillas.[387] However, creating the framework and the operating principles for these units could not be done without the help of someone more knowledgeable in the ways of guerrilla warfare. Recalling the young officer who had radioed him from North Luzon years earlier, MacArthur gave simple instructions to his staff in Tokyo: *find Russ Volckmann and get him in here.*

At the start of the Korean War, the U.S. Army had no command apparatus for special operations. In fact, the term "special operations" had yet to gain widespread acceptance throughout the military. In response to North Korean partisans, the Army simply created a series of units geared for counterguerrilla or "behind-the-lines" activities. Most of these units fell under jurisdiction of the Eighth Army G-3 Miscellaneous Group, although the Far East Command did retain its own, organic special operations unit.[388]

When Volckmann arrived in Tokyo to report to Eighth Army Headquarters, he met with Colonel John H. McGee,* the hastily appointed Director of Special Operations for the Eighth Army.[389] Weighing in with his assessment of the situation, Volckmann emphasized the need for small-unit tactics and mobility. The elusive nature of the guerrillas would be consistent regardless of what country or ideology to which they swore their allegiance. North Koreans, however, would be especially problematic. They were united not only by a common ideology—in this case, Communism—but an ideology that was now shared by two of America's newest enemies: the Soviet Union and the People's Republic of China. The ideological link could spell disaster if it translated into material support. Volckmann also knew that the biggest concern—outside of destroying the guerrilla's combat capabilities—was to keep them away from civilians. Considering that NPKA had a better grasp on Korean culture and language, enemy partisans would undoubtedly have the upperhand in turning the population against Americans. In the early days of the conflict, when America appeared to be on the losing end of the war, a fear of the South Koreans' receptiveness to Communist ideology was not completely without merit. A priority for all special operations, therefore, lay in building a rapport with the local civilians.

While still assigned to Eighth Army Headquarters, MacArthur appointed Volckmann the Executive Officer of the Special Activities Group (SAG)-Far East Command.** SAG was an interesting conglomeration of U.S. Army Rangers, Marines, and other South Korean personnel commanded by Colonel Louis B. Ely, a veteran of the OSS. As Executive Officer, Volckmann's responsibility lay in planning and conducting guerrilla activities behind NKPA lines. SAG conducted numerous patrols during the first year of the Korean War, and became especially adept at nighttime operations. "The unit screened refugees, destroyed villages and buildings that could be used by [enemy] guerrillas, and provided medical treatment to civilians. Its effectiveness was enhanced by the provision of radios down to the squad level and the establishment of an extensive intelligence network in conjunction with local authorities and Korean and American intelligence services."[390] Unfortunately, Far East Command dissolved the Special Activities Group in April 1951, concurrent with the Army's disestablishment of Ranger companies and all "ranger-style units." Accordingly, the Army decided "to provide Ranger training to the Army as whole, rather than by relying on special formations."[391] Still, the Army, in conjunction with the CIA, continued to organize and lead South Korean and disaffected North Korean partisans behind enemy lines. By the end of the

---

*McGee had also been a guerrilla in the Philippines, serving under the command of Wendell Fertig on the island of Mindanao.

**The U.S. Far East Command was the next highest echelon above the Eighth Army.

war, these guerrillas were collectively known as the United Nations Partisan Infantry in Korea (UNPIK).[392]

In all, Volckmann did not approve of the methods he saw in Korea. During his time with SAG, Volckmann ran into many of the same problems he had encountered with USAFFE nearly a decade earlier: supply issues, unclear mission parameters, and indecisive leadership in the higher echelons. Also, the manner in which the military approached unconventional warfare was largely *ad hoc*—they had merely thrown together a special operations command for the occasion. Volckmann knew that "reinventing the wheel" with special operations for every war was dangerous and unproductive. What the Army needed was an unconventional force of its own.[393] Although Volckmann had floated the idea as early as 1946, the only progress he made was the Army's acceptance of FM 31–20 as a guide to train conventional forces to combat guerrillas. Relying on FM 31–20 wasn't a bad start, but the blunders he witnessed in Korea confirmed his belief in the need for a permanent special operations command.

The Eighth Army special operations tactics were another point of contention. Statistically speaking, their operations were a success: by the end of 1951, UNPIK had confirmed 9,095 enemy KIA, captured 385 prisoners, captured or destroyed over 800 pieces of enemy equipment, and claimed the destruction of 49 bridges and 22 railroads.[394] But Volckmann had noticed that UN partisan assets were not being used properly. Over half of their engagements had been in open combat against enemy forces. Conversely, only eleven percent of their activity had been dedicated to sabotage, and less than three percent directed against enemy lines of communication along the eastern coast. As Colonel Rod Paschall poignantly remarked, "the partisans had devoted most of their energy and efforts into killing the troops of an enemy that had an almost inexhaustible supply of manpower."[395] Meanwhile, the task of cultivating civilian support was left to conventional assets and third-party civil agencies, for example the UN Civil Assistance Command. While it was commendable on behalf of the guerrillas to engage the enemy in open combat, it was not the operational context to which they were best suited. According to Volckmann, guerrillas were best geared towards subversive activities (counterintelligence, sabotage, etc.) and were optimized for open combat only when directly supported by conventional forces. Certainly, UNPIK had done a fine job in meeting the latter requirement, but they had paid too little attention to the subversive activities needed to wear down the enemy's supply and logistical apparatus.

There were several reasons why the Eighth Army employed the guerrillas in this manner. First, guerrilla operations were kept as a "staff activity." The Eighth Army kept partisan operations under the supervision of its G-3 Miscellaneous Group. "Since the G-3 could only recommend and not command, there was actually no chain of command for partisan operations."[396] Second, because special operations remained a staff function, Eighth Army Headquarters never devised a coherent plan for the employment of guerrillas. In the early stages of the war, the existing plans executed under Colonel McGee's leadership were often confounded by the bureaucratic friction between G-3 and the Eighth Army Command Group. Meanwhile, SAG, under the jurisdiction of Far East Command, operated within its own microcosm and often duplicated the efforts of the Eighth Army partisans. Third, guerrilla operations depended heavily on naval transport and seaborne delivery into their areas of operation. This condition not only limited the guerrillas to a "coastal tether," it put their operations at the mercy of competing naval requirements.[397]

Volckmann also did not agree with the heavy emphasis on Ranger formations. Volckmann had no objections to the Ranger doctrine or their tactics, but in the realm of special operations, Ranger capabilities were only part of the equation. Covert raids, ambushes, rapid deployments, and extractions—revered tenets in the Ranger tradition—were indispensable to the special operations concept. However, the Rangers did not prescribe the training necessary to accomplish the *strategic* goals of the special forces, for example building rapport with local civilians and working to exploit local sympathies to American ideology.

Volckmann did not remain in Korea very long. After less than six months into his tour, he sustained a critical injury and was evacuated to Walter Reed Army Hospital.* Though frustrated by his removal from Eighth Army operations, it proved to be another step that would solidify his legacy within the U.S. Army Special Forces.[398]

---

*The details of his injury are unclear, although the Volckmann family indicates that it was a relapse of a severe stomach ulcer he had acquired in the Philippines.

CHAPTER 12

Special Forces

The overtures to develop a special warfare doctrine began with the dissolution of the OSS in 1946. Despite the success of Allied guerrillas in World War II, there remained a strong tide of resentment against the establishment of "guerrilla-style" forces. This bureaucratic resistance arose from the conservative-minded military officers who felt that conventional means were sufficient for combating enemy partisans. Furthermore, these conservative military minds appeared to be growing in number. Indeed, by 1947, even the Joint Chiefs of Staff had expressed their doubts about the feasibility of "special forces." With FM 31–20, however, the Army seemed to have reached a solution that satisfied both sides of the special operations debate. The manual outlined methods guaranteed to dismantle guerrilla forces while still using conventional assets and not relying exclusively on special formations.

The prevailing wisdom dictated that although "the United States should provide itself with the organization and means of supporting foreign resistance movements," a civilian agency would be sufficient to handle all aspects of the job—including the training, organization, and management of guerrilla units.[399] After all, why should the Army concern itself with the "unconventional" aspects of warfare when the Army's designated functions were conventional by nature? Thus, in 1947, the newly formed Central Intelligence Agency (CIA) took control of all "special warfare" operations—a term it included under the umbrella of counterintelligence and espionage activities. Although the CIA never adequately defined the term "special warfare," the agency adopted the broadest possible interpretation—deciding that their authority rested over the entire planning, organization, and training of indigenous guerrillas.[400] Although the actual deployment of these guerrillas would be an Army responsibility, the CIA had effectively made guerrilla warfare a paramilitary—and therefore, ultimately a civilian—responsibility. However, the Korean War and the Army-CIA boondoggle in the special operations field sparked a renewed interest in guerrilla-style units and their tactics.

In the early days of the Cold War, however, the Army's only study apparatus for "special operations" existed under the Office of the Chief Psychological Warfare (OCPW). A small office tucked away in the bureaucratic jungles of Washington DC, the OCPW was an autonomous study group that reported directly to the Army Chief of Staff. Psychological warfare as a military discipline, however, was woefully ill defined and OCPW's tasks, therefore, remained ambiguous. Under orders from General J. Lawton Collins, OCPW began operations in 1950 as an outlet for ideas on the development of "psy-war" contingencies.[401] As of yet, however, they had not developed an apparatus capable of delivering psychological operations to any potential enemy.

Upon his return to the United States, Volckmann completed his next intellectual achievement, FM 31–21 *Organization and Conduct of Guerrilla Warfare*. Published in 1951, the manual sought to fill the doctrinal gap left by the demise of the OSS. Recommending that "wartime control of guerrilla warfare be exercised by the theater or unified commands," 31–21 called for a Theater Special Forces Commander with "an appropriate size headquarters on the same level as the unified command's Army, Navy, and Air Forces."[402] In total, *Organization and Conduct of Guerrilla Warfare* "was a badly needed, authoritative publication that provided well reasoned methods to organize, control, employ, and disband guerrillas." These concepts were not lost on the Army as control of partisan forces passed from the Eighth Army to the Far East Command before the end of the Korean War.[403]

FM 31–21 particularly resonated with Brigadier General Robert A. McClure, the director of OCPW. McClure himself had an interesting military career. In 1944–45, he had been the head of the U.S. Army Psychological Warfare Branch in Europe* and worked closely with the OSS. As the forerunner to the CIA, the OSS' most memorable accomplishment in Europe was *Operation Jedburgh*. The participants—or "Jedburghs" as they were known—operated in three-man teams. Delivered by parachute, they would establish contact with local French, Belgian, and Dutch resistance fighters and provide a link to Allied materiel. McClure's position as the chief of the Psychological Warfare Branch gave him a front row seat to the planning and operations of the *Jedburgh* campaign.[404]

Influenced by Volckmann's writing, and recalling the success of the Jedburghs in Europe, McClure sought to create a permanent special operations force that would combine the facets of unconventional and psychological warfare. Seeking Volckmann's help, McClure approached him with an offer to become OCPW's Chief of Plans—Special Operations Division. Like Volckmann, McClure believed that reinventing a special operations command for every war was counterproductive. Volckmann agreed to join McClure only after being assured that the Army was serious about creating and maintaining a special

---

*A subordinate command of the Supreme Headquarters Allied Expeditionary Force.

operations force. Joining Volckmann a few months later was Colonel Aaron Bank, a former OSS operative who had served with the Jedburghs in Europe.* With Volckmann as Chief of Plans, OCPW prepared the framework for what would become the Army Special Forces.[405]

OCPW had the option of outlining a force that could follow one of two organizational precedents: (1) the model provided by USAFIP-NL (developing and organizing guerrillas in enemy territory), or (2) the Ranger-style traditions of a "shock-troop" force. Given the nature of what the Special Forces were intended to accomplish, the USAFIP-NL model provided the most logical basis. Aaron Bank later disclosed that Special Forces "have no connection with ranger-type organizations since their mission and operations are far more complex, time consuming, require much deeper penetration [into enemy territory] and initially are often of a strategic nature."[406]

Aware of Volckmann's earlier work, and recognizing the need for a special operations capability, Army Chief of Staff General J. Lawton Collins held a conference at the Fort Benning Infantry Center in April 1951. In doing so, he opened the floor to discussion on the Special Forces concept. Collins, an infantryman himself, favored the Ranger model. In fact, he was quoted saying that, "the Infantry School should consider the Rangers as well as other troops and indigenous personnel to initiate subversive activities. I personally established the Rangers with the thought that they might serve as the nucleus of expansion in this direction."[407] In response, Volckmann—who represented OCPW at the conference—authored a memorandum for the Infantry Center commenting on the Chief of Staff's position.

Volckmann equated the general's use of the phrase "subversive activities" with "special forces operations." He then identified six critical elements of Special Forces operations:

1. The organization and conduct of guerrilla warfare.
2. Sabotage.
3. Evasion.
4. Long-range reconnaissance.
5. Ranger-style raids.
6. Psychological Warfare.[408]

Even though the Special Forces would be capable of performing raids and ambushes in the Ranger tradition, their overall mission would be of a different and far more complex nature.

In regard to the general's comments on indigenous personnel, Volckmann had this to offer:

---

*Other members of the OCPW staff included Wendell Fertig, former leader of the Mindanao guerrillas, and Colonel Melvin Blair, a veteran of "Merrill's Marauders."

> We may visualize the world today as being divided into two major groups or layers of individuals that cover the earth unrestricted by national boundaries. These layers, a red and a blue, are held together by common ideologies. Any future war may well be regarded as an international civil war waged by these opposing layers. The full exploitation of our sympathetic blue layer within the enemy's sphere of influence is basically the mission of special forces [sic] operations. *It is from the blue layer within the enemy's sphere that we must foster resistance movements, organize guerrilla or indigenous forces on a military basis, conduct sabotage and subversion, effect evasion and escape.* We should, through special forces [sic] operations, exploit this layer to assist our ranger and commando operations, and a media for psychological warfare (emphasis added).[409]

Although Volckmann's use of the term "international civil war" may have been extreme, his discussion of the "sympathetic blue layer" was not. Volckmann's conception of Army Special Forces centered on the exploitation of "blue layer" elements, or friendly civilians who could be trained as partisans who could offset the enemy's "home field" advantage. Volckmann's memorandum is important because it spelled out the operational framework for the Special Forces, including its purpose—exploitation of the "blue layer"—and its mission parameters (the six critical elements listed above).

Aside from outlining the operational tenets and roles of the Special Forces, this document is important because it addressed the issue of CIA involvement. Volckmann had written earlier:

> To me, it is basically sound that the military (the Army, since this field falls within ground operations) has the inherent responsibility in peace to prepare and plan for the conduct of special forces [sic] operations and in time of war to organize and conduct special forces [sic] operations. Further, *I feel that it is unsound, dangerous, and unworkable to delegate these responsibilities to a civil agency* (emphasis added).[410]

Whether Volckmann disliked or distrusted the CIA is unclear, but he obviously knew that they were ill-equipped to handle the tasks that were better left to professional soldiers. The Army-CIA alliance in Korea had caused much overlap of responsibility and bureaucratic friction. Furthermore, CIA involvement left military commanders without full control over operations within their sectors.

After forwarding his memorandum to the Army Chief of Staff, Volckmann began work on a study called "Findings and Recommendations re Special Operations Training," synthesizing his ideas and the hard-fought lessons he had learned over the years. Upon receipt of Volckmann's papers, General Collins gave his blessing to the Special Forces project.[411] The Army Special Forces gained their own responsibilities for training and planning special operations—just as Volckmann had wanted. However, the CIA retained its paramilitary capabilities, and bureaucratic friction with the Pentagon over special operations responsibility continues to this day.

If followed exactly, Volckmann's advice may have improved the efficiency of the civil intelligence and special warfare apparatuses. While his advice may not have been followed to the letter, it seems to have made some lasting impact. Today, CIA agents do not supervise military operations and largely serve as auxiliaries to special warfare troops instead of competing with them. Though friction still exists between the military and the civil intelligence community, the distinctions between their responsibilities and physical areas of operation are clearer today than they were over half of a century ago.

Historically, Aaron Bank has been called the "Father of Army Special Forces." At Fort Bragg, North Carolina, memorials dedicated to Bank cite him as the true father of SF. Bank was even named the "Father of Army Special Forces" by a Congressional resolution (HR 364) passed in 2002. There are two reasons why this title has traditionally been given to Bank.

The first reason is because Bank created the Table of Organization and Equipment (TO&E) under which the Special Forces operated. While OCPW determined what structural format the Special Forces teams would follow, Bank suggested a derivative of the Operational Group concept from the OSS.* This was Bank's major contribution to the program. Using this concept, Bank created an organizational table that divided Special Forces units into three tiers. The first incarnation of Bank's TO&E labeled these tiers as *Regiment, District B*, and *District A*. The Operational Detachment-Regiment, was a 15-man group commanded by a captain. The next level up was the Operational Detachment-District B, commanded by a major; followed by District A, commanded by a lieutenant colonel.

Later, the three tiers would be given letter designations—A, B, and C. The finished product would be similar to a conventional brigade, but with fewer personnel. The first tier, the A-Detachment (or A-Team, as it would later be known) consisted of twelve soldiers. One Captain would serve as a Detachment Commander with a 1st Lieutenant as his executive officer. The remaining ten were enlisted men who worked in pairs according to their primary specialty (demolition, combat engineering, combat medics, field communications, and heavy weapons). Three "A-Detachments" comprised a "B-Detachment," commanded by a Major with a complement of nine NCOs. Three "B-Detachments" made up a "C-Detachment" (run by a Lieutenant Colonel) and three "C-Detachments" made a Special Forces Group.

The second reason is because Bank commanded the first Special Forces unit the 10th Special Forces Group at Fort Bragg, North Carolina. As Bank was the first Special Forces Group commander, and was responsible for its TO&E, it is not surprising that he is often heralded as the "Father of Special Forces."

---

*Operational Groups were thirty-man units designed to conduct irregular warfare behind Axis lines.

By any reasonable standard, Aaron Bank was a bright, talented, and extremely competent officer—and his contributions are not to be slighted. Like America itself, the Special Forces has a set of "Founding Fathers"—including Aaron Bank, Russell Volckmann, Robert McClure, Wendell Fertig, and Melvin Blair. Each man made a significant impact on the Special Forces concept; and thus, none can claim sole credit. However, if there must be a "father" of Special Forces, it is clear that Volckmann, not Bank, has the strongest claim to the title.

Volckmann's contribution to the Special Forces concept began with publication of FM 31–20 *Operations Against Guerrilla Forces*. It is important to note that counterinsurgency and special warfare doctrine are two sides of the same analytical coin. Counterinsurgency doctrine is the first intellectual stepping stone to developing a framework for special operations. To successfully conduct special warfare, one must first understand (a) what factors influence guerrilla warfare, (b) what makes guerrilla warfare successful, and (c) how guerrillas can be defeated. These were all concepts articulated by Volckmann in FM 31–20. Per FM 31–21, Volckmann realized that the Special Forces needed a unified, theater-level, command structure which operated under full military authority. This idea holds true today as the US Special Operations Command is now Unified Combatant Command of the US military. The OSS, for its part in World War II, was still a civilian agency and did not take its orders exclusively from the Army.

At OCPW, it was Volckmann, not Bank, who articulated and designed the mission capabilities and operational framework upon which the Army Special Forces would operate. It was also Volckmann, not Bank, who represented OCPW at General Collins' Fort Benning conference and authored the memorandum explaining the strategic purpose of special operations and the mission parameters defined by the six numerated functions. These were also concepts that Volckmann had already codified in his field manuals, both of which he wrote before Bank ever joined OCPW. And while Bank commanded the first Special Forces Group, Volckmann became the Director of Special Operations for the entire US European Command. Moreover, and perhaps most importantly, in a letter dated February 23, 1969 addressed to the History Office at Fort Bragg, *Bank credited Volckmann* for "the development of position, planning, and policy papers that helped sell the establishment of Special Forces units in the active Army.

Even though Army Special Forces operate under Bank's conception of the TO&E, their operations today have more in common with Volckmann's USAFIP-NL. Volckmann did not strictly focus on utilizing the Special Forces for "behind the lines" activities. He also envisioned the Special Forces operating in environments where the front lines had *disappeared*, as had been the case for him in the Philippines. Furthermore, Volckmann's initial memorandum to General Collins and "Findings and Recommendations re Special Operations Training" envisioned a force that would both *train* and *equip* indigenous peoples for guerrilla warfare.

For their part, Bank and McClure shared with Volckmann their experiences in the OSS and the Psychological Warfare Branch. However, Volckmann arguably had a better grasp on the fundamentals of guerrilla warfare and understood these concepts in ways that Bank and McClure never could. Although the OSS and USAFIP-NL both conducted "subversive activities," the OSS operated within an established framework that experienced no discontinuity in its operation. At the start of the war in the Philippines, USAFFE handled all military operations but, after the Fall of Bataan, it ceased to function as a military organization. Volckmann's guerrillas picked up the pieces of the shattered Philippine Army and organized them into the USAFIP-NL, a guerrilla force that operated under fighting doctrines that Volckmann developed as he went along.

Additionally, the OSS did not carry on its missions at a distance from other Allied units. Europe was a densely militarized theater of war with high concentrations of Axis and Allied units. In Volckmann's case, however, the nearest Allied ordnance lay thousands of miles offshore. Also, it was easier in Europe for OSS personnel to blend in with the local population, since both the Europeans and Americans were ethnically white. Volckmann and his American comrades in North Luzon could not duplicate this feat. In fact, this was a condition that highlighted Volckmann's need for civilian support—his Filipino spies could go into places that a white American could not.

Although McClure established OCPW with the expressed desire to maintain unconventional forces, he regarded the Special Forces solely as a means to an end. McClure's primary objective was to establish special operations forces within the Army's existing psychological warfare community and bring psychological operations to the forefront of Army doctrine. Initially, Special Forces were subordinate to the Psychological Warfare Center. Although today this relationship is reversed, in 1951, it was the natural consequence of McClure's leadership. Conducting psychological operations in World War II, McClure regarded them as the banner under which all special operations should fall.* There was nothing hazardous in McClure's setup, but as time progressed, it was evident that a more efficient structure would be one under which Special Forces took the lead. This is not to suggest that psychological warfare is unimportant, it's simply one part of the Special Force equation.

Bank, McClure, and the others at OCPW were a remarkable group of individuals. However, their contributions to the development of Special Forces were neither as far-reaching nor as contemplative as Volckmann's. Had Volckmann not written FM 31–20 and 31–21, McClure may have had no one to seek for adequate help or advice in developing an operational format for unconventional

---

*McClure's focus on the psychological aspect of the program was probably the reason why Volckmann had so much independence in designing the Special Forces component. McClure obviously trusted Volckmann's expertise in guerrilla and unconventional matters.

forces. Furthermore, the Army's doctrine for counterinsurgency did not exist until Volckmann wrote it down. FM 31–20 gave the Army its intellectual, tactical, and operational foundation for counterinsurgency from 1950 until the present day. Likewise, FM 31–21 provided the inaugural framework and operational theory for Army Special Forces.

For the reasons outlined above, the title "Father of Army Special Forces" rightly belongs to Russell William Volckmann.

Portrait of Brigadier General Russell W. Volckmann, 1957. *The Volckmann Family Collection.*

Understanding Volckmann's Legacy

Volckmann was neither the first nor the only American in the Philippines to organize a guerrilla movement; several others fled to the mountains in the wake of Japanese aggression. Yet, the common denominator among the majority of these guerrillas is that they ultimately failed—many of them dying within the first year and a half of combat. As many records were lost during the war, categorizing the other movements remains a difficult task. Furthermore, it is entirely possible that many units kept no records at all, especially considering the scarcity of paper.* When Allied forces returned to the Philippines, the guerrilla records they received were written on a variety of odds and ends: newspapers, leaves, milk and cigarette cartons, and anything else that could be used as a writing surface.** It is also likely that many of these phantom guerrillas either dissolved into larger units or were eventually snuffed out by the Japanese.

The only guerrillas that provide any useful information for historians today are those who left behind some record of their activity. The archival landscape is littered with the names of guerrillas who fought valiantly against the Japanese, but tragically did not survive the war. Where they failed, however, Volckmann succeeded. Among the more notable of the early guerrillas included Walter Cushing, Roque Ablan, Claude Thorp, Marcelo Adduru, and Ralph Praeger. There are several conflicting stories of how each man ultimately met his demise, but their tactical missteps collectively fall into six categories.

First, many of them tried to accomplish too much, too soon. Some began conducting guerrilla operations before the Japanese had even reached Bataan. While their initiative in bringing the fight to the enemy was commendable, it

---

*There were several small, isolated bands of guerrillas that operated in teams of no more than 30 men. Volckmann confirms their existence in his diary but there is no substantial record of their activity.

**The Philippine Archives section of the National Archives II has several such documents. Some have been written on the back of voting ballots and Philippine government job applications. Brigadier General Donald D. Blackburn had many of these in his private collection.

violated what is known as the Principle of Deliberate Delay.[412] In this, they failed to wait until the Japanese had settled into a regular routine of occupation duty and a lower state of readiness.

Second, each of the early guerrilla movements maintained a limited geographic scope. By this, they did not extend their immediate regions. This was not necessarily problematic in the early stages of the war, but to affect any long-term impact on the Japanese, there had to be a synchronization of effort. Operating on a localized basis only facilitated the counterinsurgency efforts of the Japanese. If guerrilla activity became concentrated only within certain areas, the Japanese could easily redistribute their manpower to quell the localized resistance.

Third, these guerrillas had no means to retain any of the prisoners they captured. Rather than burden their operations by keeping track of prisoners, these guerrillas simply released them and moved their operations to another area.[413] This tactical *faux pas* was one of the greatest liabilities to the resistance movement. A released prisoner would do little more than travel to the nearest Japanese garrison and report the guerillas' last known location. Consequently, the Japanese would dispatch entire rifle companies into the landscape to intercept the "banditos." Volckmann, however, not only retained his prisoners, he put them to work on his staff.[414]

Fourth, the early guerrillas had no effective means for dealing with spies and collaborators. With informers indistinguishable from the general population, many guerrillas simply treated the problem as unsolvable and hoped that the "fifth column" would never cross their path. Ralph Praeger, the guerrilla Captain who led remnants of C Troop, 26th Cavalry (Philippine Scouts) in Apayao sub-province, died in 1943 when collaborators betrayed the location of his hideout.[415] Volckmann, however, knew that if he expected to survive the war, he would have to make the collaborators fear *him* more than the Japanese.

Fifth, some guerrillas agitated the local Filipinos rather than solicit their help. This may have been the reason behind Claude Thorp's demise. Thorp, a Lieutenant Colonel, was unique among the USAFFE guerrillas in that he was the only one specifically tapped by a higher authority to conduct guerrilla warfare after the Fall of Bataan. Whether it was MacArthur or General Jonathan Wainwright (MacArthur's second-in-command) who ultimately gave the authorization, Thorp nonetheless disappeared into the Zambales Mountains to organize a resistance among the displaced Americans in Western Luzon. According to Blackburn, however, Thorp's temper and condescending attitude earned him the hatred of the local civilians and the wrath of the Hukbalahap. Disgusted by his attitude, local civilians shunned him and one eventually reported Thorp to the Japanese. If this is true, then Thorp's behavior was undeniably self-destructive—especially in light of USAFFE's humiliating defeat and the circumstances of the Japanese occupation. He was captured in August 1942 and summarily executed a year later.[416]

Finally, many of the resistance leaders' organizational skills were so bad that their guerrilla movements collapsed under the weight of their own mismanagement. A representative sample of this is the Moses-Noble operation.* In his diary, Volckmann never openly indicted the colonels for their lack of planning. Blackburn, however, was never at a loss for words concerning Moses and Noble's missteps. Accordingly, Blackburn indicated that the colonels' mistakes were ones that he and Volckmann strove not to repeat.[417]

The only guerrilla whose fate remains a mystery is Roque Ablan, the provincial governor of Ilocos Norte. Rather than surrender to the Japanese in Vichy-ite fashion, Ablan foraged a nearby Philippine Army camp for arms and ammunition. Arming his governor's staff, he took to the wilderness and began launching raids against Japanese outposts. Although spies repeatedly betrayed the location of his hideouts, he managed to escape the Japanese fury every time.[418] However, after his last escape in early 1943, Ablan simply disappeared. There is no official record of him beyond February 1943.

Cautious not to duplicate the mistakes of his predecessors, Volckmann exploited the geography of North Luzon as a critical element to his success. Hideki Tojo commanded a fearsome army, but it was one that operated on a finite amount of resources. Petroleum, ores, and steel were the Achilles Heel of Japan's war machine. An economic power in their own right, the Japanese relied heavily on Western imports to satisfy their industrial needs. This condition heavily influenced Imperial war policy: to maintain its conquest of the Pacific, Japan had to seize key points of industry without interference from the U.S. Navy. Manchuria and Borneo were the first areas targeted under this policy.[419]

Japan eyed the Philippines for the same reason. There were 7,107 islands in the archipelago, but Luzon was the priority target. The largest of the Philippine islands, Luzon was home to the nation's capital and the heart of Philippine industry—with the northern provinces housing the region's only mining network. What the Japanese had accomplished in Manchuria, they hoped to repeat in Luzon: control of the mineral resources. During the campaign, the Rising Sun scattered throughout the Philippines, but the bulk of the occupation force remained in and around North Luzon.[420]

Strategically opportunistic views of the Philippine Islands, however, were not one-sided. The Allies, too, saw the Philippines as critical. Victory meant denying the Japanese an important resource enclave in the Pacific. If the flow of raw material continued, Japan would still have an outlet for making tools of war. Retaking North Luzon, therefore, meant closure of the nearest Japanese mineral reserve.[421] Unwittingly or not, Volckmann found himself operating in one of the most strategically critical areas of the entire Pacific War.

---

*Colonel John P. Horan (see Chapter 2) also falls into this category.

Volckmann wisely kept his base of operations in the Cordillera Central of North Luzon. He had no concern for the region's mineral resources or what the Japanese could gain from them; the decision to remain in the mountains was a function of pragmatism and utility. The central and southern parts of the island were plains that allowed easy access for Japanese foot patrols. The mountains, on the other hand, provided significant cover and numerous hiding places. The rugged terrain restricted enemy patrols to the narrow network of mountain passes. With enemy patrols often confined to a single column, their movements became slower and made them more susceptible to ambush. Conversely, the Cordillera was ideal terrain for Volckmann and his guerrillas—the mountain crevices and ridgelines offered enviable redoubts against enemy camps and patrol lanes.

In the spring of 1944, General Tomiyuki Yamashita assumed command of the Fourteenth Army. Shortly thereafter, he reorganized the entire defense scheme on Luzon. Drawing his forces away from the coast and the central plains, he consolidated his forces within the Cordillera Central of North Luzon.[422] Yamashita recognized that this action would draw the Americans into a prolonged campaign to dig his forces out of the mountains. It could be done, but not without severe losses to the Americans. What Yamashita did not know, however, was that his new defense plan put him right in the middle of Volckmann's guerrilla network.*

In the radiograms, Volckmann made clear his intentions to continue the guerrilla war as an extension of the conventional fight against the Japanese.[423] As mentioned previously, he did not subscribe to the notions of guerrilla warfare operating on a localized basis, conducting intermittent raids and ambushes while hoping for the Allies' eventual return. Instead, he considered the feasibility of an operation that would employ guerrilla tactics and intelligence in conjunction with conventional forces. In doing so, he discovered the martial nexus by which guerrilla warfare was most successfully employed. Guerrillas were capable of going into places that conventional forces could not go, gathering information that conventional forces could not obtain, and employing assets on the ground that the Allied forces did not have.

Each of the three USAFIP-NL combat operation phases made a critical contribution to Yamashita's defeat in North Luzon. Luzon itself was a vital target for both Axis and Allies. It not only housed the largest of the Japanese occupation force, it was the economic and industrial nerve center of the Philippines. In paving the way for MacArthur and the Sixth Army to land in North Luzon and receive intelligence regarding enemy dispositions, Volckmann and the USAFIP-NL performed an invaluable service to the Allied cause. Through each

---

*This process occurred over the late spring and summer of 1944.

of USAFIP-NL's combat phases, Volckmann eroded the Japanese Fourteenth Army until it was virtually useless as a fighting force.

The first phase of operations set the tone for the rest of the campaign. Defeating the Japanese obviously required a working knowledge of their strengths and capabilities; Volckmann's intelligence-gathering methods reflected this. Aside from knowing the enemy's combat capabilities, one must also understand their logistical and support apparatuses. This is why Volckmann collected information about enemy supply and fuel depots. As Volckmann did not yet have the resources to conduct open warfare against the Japanese, synchronizing strikes and sabotage on key targets had to suffice.

The second phase arguably had the most devastating impact on Yamashita's forces. Although the third phase marked the termination of hostilities and the Japanese surrender, the second phase saw the breakdown of Yamashita's formidable defense structure. Within each of the five regimental districts, Volckmann saw an opportunity to close a vital component of the Japanese war effort in North Luzon. Some of these opportunities were limited in their scope, but others had more strategic implications. For instance, the 11th Infantry—under Blackburn's command—seized the port of Aparri, the last Japanese naval base in North Luzon. As piecemeal as the Japanese resupply would have been, seizing Aparri meant that Yamashita's men were now permanently cut off from the motherland. Incoming Japanese ships would no longer have a safe entry point on North Luzon. Capturing the enemy airfield at Gabu gave the Americans an operational landing zone and refuel station for long-range bombers en route to Okinawa. The creation of this Allied airstrip behind enemy lines facilitated the "island hopping" campaign, for it gave bomber pilots a staging area with greater proximity to the Japanese homeland. Finally, the 66th Infantry's gallant raids in Lepanto-Mankayan wrested from Yamashita's hands the largest mineral reserve in North Luzon.

The third phase was critical in the sense that it not only brought Yamashita out of the mountains, but it highlighted the efficacy of guerrillas and conventional forces in combined operations. General Kruger gave his Division Commanders in Luzon explicit instructions to offer unconditional support to Volckmann's guerrillas and coordinate all offensive maneuvers based on Volckmann's information.[424] This circumstance became one of the intellectual cornerstones for Volckmann's ideology on the Special Forces. While developing the framework for special operations, Volckmann correctly forecasted that, in future conflicts, guerrilla-style units would operate most effectively when combining and synchronizing their efforts with conventional forces.[425] This observation extended not only to combat operations, but to intelligence sharing as well.

Volckmann's legacy, therefore, is one of exceptional leadership and foresight; the impact of his actions stretch far beyond their immediate consequences. Volckmann's ability to synthesize the realities and necessities of guerrilla warfare led to a campaign that eroded a formidable adversary and paved the way for an Allied victory. Had it not been for Volckmann, the Americans would have gone into North Luzon without solid intelligence, thereby reducing their efforts to a "trial-and-error" campaign that would have cost more lives, materiel, and potentially stalled the pace of the entire Pacific War. His actions in this regard saved more lives and facilitated the speed with which the Philippine Campaign was brought to a close. Furthermore, these guerrilla tactics and strategies gave Volckmann a practical foundation upon which to build a cohesive framework for special operations units. Unlike many of our nation's policy makers and military leaders, Volckmann did not develop his positions based on abstract, theoretical notions of what *might* work in a given scenario. To the contrary, Volckmann already had the practical experience to know which methods would produce results.

Authoring two Army field manuals: FM 31–20 *Operations Against Guerrilla Forces* and FM 31–21 *Organization and Conduct of Guerrilla Warfare,* Volckmann codified the Army's first doctrine for special warfare and counterguerrilla operations. Taking his argument directly to the Army Chief of Staff, General J. Lawton Collins, Volckmann outlined the operational concepts for the Army Special Forces. At a time when U.S. military doctrine was conventional in its outlook, Volckmann marketed the ideas of guerilla warfare as a critical and strategic force multiplier for any future conflict.

In the course of writing this book, fellow historians asked me about a publication known as the *Small Wars Manual.* Published in 1935 by the United States Marine Corps, its pages contain guidelines on how to combat irregular fighters in operations other than war. The manual described tactical and psychological considerations not dissimilar from Volckmann's FM 31–20.[426] Accordingly, they asked whether or not Volckmann had referenced the *Small Wars Manual* while developing *Operations Against Guerrilla Forces.* It is possible that he had, but more likely that he had not.

Arriving at this conclusion requires a comparative study of the Army and Marine Corps. Both share a certain degree of operational overlap, but the two services often develop their own doctrines independent from one another. As per their original doctrine, the Marine Corps is a light, lean, and agile force not intended for sustained operations too far from the parent fleet. By virtue of their size and agility, the Marines possess neither the firepower nor the logistical wherewithal to project their forces over large areas for an extended period of time. The Army, by contrast, operates within a framework that calls for sustained combat power and the occupation of key terrain across multiple environments. To accomplish this end, the Army employs a greater logistical and supply apparatus.

The distinction between Army and Marine capabilities undoubtedly influenced the concepts written in the *Small Wars Manual.* "Small wars" represented conflicts that the Marine Corps seemed the most capable of handling. By definition, "small wars" were low-intensity conflicts against asymmetrical opponents and did not require any protracted force commitment. Consisting of small-scale rebellions and punitive expeditions, the *Small Wars Manual* treated these operations in a vein similar to law enforcement. In fact, the manual's protocol directed Marine commanders to work closely with the local police.[427]

Volckmann, however, did not contextualize counterinsurgency strictly within the realms of low-intensity conflict. He saw counterguerrilla operations as part of a larger conflict wherein enemy guerrillas could either: (1) operate in conjunction with regular forces, or (2) become large-scale forces in their own right, capable of sustained harassment against an occupying army. Both contingencies necessitated a force structure beyond what the Marines could single-handedly provide.

Perhaps the Marine Corps kept the *Small Wars Manual* within their own doctrinal community while the Army maintained its conventional outlook. Nonetheless, before FM 31–20, the Army had no established protocol for guerrilla warfare. Reviewing Volckmann's literature on counterinsurgency, it is apparent that he at least *thought* he was starting from scratch. In any event, there is no conclusive evidence indicating that Volckmann ever read the *Small Wars Manual* or even knew of its existence.

As corollary to his work in developing the Special Forces concept, Volckmann made a significant contribution to the development of tactical air support and air control operations. From the practical aspects of his work in Luzon, Volckmann demonstrated the need for coordinated air support to beleaguered ground units. This need was so great that the Air Force not only incorporated the forward air controller concept into its doctrine, but also specifically called on Volckmann to assess the potential of air support in unconventional warfare.* Also, Volckmann was the first to advocate the use of the newly devised helicopter in air-ground warfare. In the wake of the Army Air Forces' dissolution, Army Aviation became the military's premiere rotary-winged force. To Volckmann, the helicopter had two advantages that fixed-wing aircraft did not. Unlike the airplanes that had supported him in North Luzon, helicopters could hover. Also, preparing a helicopter landing zone (LZ) was not nearly as difficult. Instead of the mile-long airstrips that required a full contingent of combat engineers to prepare, creating a helicopter LZ required nothing more than an infantry squad with a few pounds of TNT. Expressing the potential of helicopter-based combat in FM 31–20, Volckmann's ideas paved the way for what is known today as air cavalry.

Furthermore, as America's involvement in Vietnam grew deeper, the Army distilled Volckmann's manuals into one comprehensive guide for fighting the Communist guerrillas in Southeast Asia. This subsequent field manual underwent

---

*In 1963, the U.S. Air Force tapped Volckmann (by then a retired Brigadier General) to lead the Rand Corporation's study panel on the feasibility of air support tactics in counterinsurgency warfare.

several iterations, and became the operational guideline for tactical forces on the ground. His Rand Corporation and FM 31–20 discussions of helicopter support sold the Army on the need for airmobile units. Subsequently, air cavalry saw widespread implementation during Vietnam.

In light of his many accomplishments, however, Volckmann was not infallible. An innovator of any type is bound to make mistakes, and Volckmann was certainly no exception. For instance, killing enemy spies was necessary to survive the war, but Volckmann's methods often went too far. Instead of simply shooting collaborators, Volckmann gave his guerrillas a "blank check" to dispose of them in whatever manner they pleased. Many informers were hanged, mutilated, dismembered, decapitated, and burned alive—one was even beaten to death with a crowbar. Although Volckmann did not participate in any of these atrocities, after the war, some Filipinos lobbied their government to put Volckmann and Blackburn on trial for war crimes. However, the official decree from Philippine President Manuel Roxas—which currently hangs on the wall in Blackburn's home office—exonerated USAFIP-NL and accepted the elimination of spies as a necessary evil in war.[428]

Volckmann also didn't understand the Filipinos' cultural inclinations for vengeance. Often, the indigenous guerrillas would settle their vendettas by claiming that their personal enemies were spies, thereby providing a justification for murder. Volckmann tried to control this by seeking multiple sources to verify someone as a spy, but personal vendettas still accounted for a significant number of deaths.[429] In addition, at times, Volckmann also proved himself as not being the best judge of character. His appointment of Captain John O'Day stands as a testament to this. O'Day had been a miner before the war and held various positions throughout USAFIP-NL, including a brief stint as the commander of the 66th Infantry. On one occasion, he nearly got Volckmann killed as a result of false reporting—for example when he claimed a particular area had been secured when in fact, it had not. When O'Day burned and plundered an entire village because one of the residents was thought to be a collaborator, a fed-up Volckmann relieved him of command.[430] Although Volckmann conceded that eliminating spies was a necessary evil, his termination of O'Day's command indicated that there were boundaries that he would not cross. Clearing the area of spies and collaborators was a priority mission, but Volckmann sought to minimize collateral damage against the innocent.

Robert Lapham emerges as Volckmann's strongest critic. Lapham, a 1939 graduate of the University of Iowa, was an officer in the Army Reserve until his activation in June 1941. Originally assigned as a company commander in the 45th Infantry (Philippine Scouts), Lapham, too, fled the Japanese onslaught in Bataan. Building his group of raiders, the *Luzon Guerrilla Army Force* (LGAF), Lapham began conducting a few small-scale raids in the Central Plains area of Luzon. He and Volckmann had met previously during the latter's trek to North

Luzon. At the time, Lapham was bedridden at his base camp with a high-grade fever. Volckmann indicated that he was on his way north to begin coordinating with the remaining USAFFE elements in Mountain Province. When Volckmann assumed command of USAFIP-NL, he tried to absorb LGAF and organize them into another military district with Lapham as the district commander. Lapham, however, solidly rebuffed him. But instead of punishing Lapham or attempting to force his compliance, Volckmann simply let the matter pass and focused his energies on Yamashita.[431]

Although some of Lapham's grievances against Volckmann are legitimate (i.e. allowing brutal treatment of collaborators and his failure to control subordinates like O'Day), many of them appear to stem from petty jealousies. For example, he castigated Volckmann for keeping his base of operations in the cordillera of North Luzon.[432] He claims that his base of operations in the Central Plains produced better results, but this appears not to have been the case. The Central Plains did give Lapham greater overall mobility but, by the same token, it did likewise for the Japanese. Lapham constantly had to relocate his command posts to avoid the threat of enemy patrols.

Moreover, he claims that Volckmann's record keeping practices were unwise in the sense that it jeopardized the civilians who worked for him. What Lapham did not realize, however, is that Volckmann used the "call sign" system as a means to safeguard their anonymity. Lapham also claims that Volckmann kept records for the sake of his own aggrandizement after the war.[433] Volckmann, however, was a creature of habit, not egotism.[434] Keeping detailed records is a well-established part of military protocol. Volckmann needed to maintain adequate records to validate the claims of his organization, keep track of receipts, and maintain personnel rolls. Finally, even though Lapham indicts Volckmann for his treatment of the Filipino collaborators, he quietly admits that he, too, engaged in similar activities to neutralize threats from the "fifth column."

Even some within Volckmann's own circle have criticized him. Rob Arnold, who commanded the Third District, USAFIP-NL, admits that he was not impressed by either Volckmann or his whole operation. His complaints include a lamentation that Volckmann's GHQ Staff seemed more interested in pursuing relationships with the native women than doing their jobs as guerrillas.[435] But as Ray Hunt (who served with Lapham in LGAF) concedes, "Arnold had a sour nature; he regarded guerrilla operations as senseless; and when he stumbled into Blackburn's camp in the spring of 1943 he was weak and sick."[436] Thus, it remains debatable what motivated Arnold to criticize his leader and the North Luzon guerrilla force—especially considering the tactical victories enjoyed by the 15th Infantry throughout 1945.

After Volckmann left OCPW, he completed a course of study at the Army War College and went on to serve as the Director of the Special Operation Division, U.S. European Command. In this capacity he oversaw the development and implementation of training for Special Forces units in Europe. Also, as part of a Cold War diplomatic mission to Iran, Volckmann prepared a brief for the Shah and his top military commanders marketing the efficacy of special operations forces in a time of war. As a consequence, the Iranian Army adopted its own Special Forces apparatus similar to the American design.[437]

In 1956, at the age of 45, Volckmann became one of the oldest persons in Army history, up to that point, to complete parachute training at the Basic Airborne Course in Fort Benning, GA. This was a requirement needed to assume his next duty position: the Assistant Division Commander of the 82nd Airborne Division. As it were, this was Volckmann's last assignment before retiring. After spending scarcely a year with the 82nd Airborne, Volckmann retired as a Brigadier General in July 1957. Returning to his hometown of Clinton, Iowa, he took over the family business: the Volckmann Furniture Company—a manufacturer and retailer of fine furniture. In 1977, after selling the company's interests to the Ethan Allen Company, Volckmann retired for good. Splitting his time between two homes—one in Clinton and another at a golfing community in Harlingen, Texas—Volckmann quietly lived out the rest of his years. He died on 30 June 1982 at the age of 70.[438]

Overall, despite Volckmann's missteps in the Philippines and those who have tried to discredit or downplay his accomplishments, he emerges as a forgotten hero whose legacy is one of critical importance. Had it not been for Russell William Volckmann, the Allied resistance movement in North Luzon may have very well collapsed by early 1943, and the isolated guerrillas would have been systematically destroyed by the Japanese. Given the comparative resources of the Japanese and American militaries, the Allies would have retaken Luzon eventually, but not without an extreme loss of life and a Pacific War stalled by a quagmire in the Philippines. Had it not been for Russell William Volckmann, the operational framework for the counterinsurgency doctrine and the Army Special Forces may not have ever surfaced. For these reasons, Russell William Volckmann commands a unique and noteworthy place in America's military history.

Volckmann's Citation for the Distinguished Service Cross

Headquarters
United States Armed Forces in the Far East

27 January 1945

DISTINGUISHED SERVICE CROSS

By direction of the President, under the provisions of the act of Congress approved 9 July 1918 (Bulletin 43, 1918), the Distinguished Service Cross was awarded by the Commanding General, United States Armed Forces in the Far East, on 21 January 1945 to the following named officer:

Lieutenant Colonel Russell W. Volckmann, (019537), Infantry, United States Army.

For extraordinary heroism in action in the Philippine Islands from 9 April 1942 to 20 January 1945. Having escaped from the enemy on Bataan on 9 April 1942, this officer made his way through the enemy lines to Northern Luzon, Philippines, where he has since organized, encouraged, and directed sectors of continued resistance and developed detailed information on enemy dispositions and movement throughout the area, thereby assisting materially in the campaign of liberation. In demonstrated exemplary courage and devotion to duty he has inspired the officers and men under his command to perform service of great value under the most difficult conditions.

Entered United States Military Academy from Iowa.

By command of General MacArthur:

Richard J. Marshall,
Major General, General Staff Corps,
Chief of Staff.

The Career Chronology of Russell W. Volckmann

12 June 1934—Graduated from the United States Military Academy at West Point.

1934—Student Officer, Infantry Officer Basic Course, Fort Benning, Georgia.

1934–1936—Rifle Platoon Leader and Company Executive Officer, 3rd Infantry Regiment, 3rd Infantry Division, Fort Snelling, Minnesota.

1937–1938—Student Officer, Infantry Officer Advanced Course, Fort Benning, Georgia.

1938–1940—Company Commander, 9th Infantry Regiment, 2nd Infantry Division, Fort Sam Houston, Texas.

1940–1946—Philippine Islands.

Commander, H Company, 31st Infantry Regiment (US)

Executive Officer and Commander, 11th Infantry Regiment, 11th Division (Philippine Army)

Division Intelligence Officer, 11th Division (Philippine Army)

Commander, United States Armed Forces in the Philippines-North Luzon (Guerrillas).

1946–1948—Headquarters, Army Personnel Division, Washington DC.

1948–1950—Research Fellow, US Army Infantry School, Fort Benning, Georgia. Drafted FM 31-20 *Operations Against Guerrilla Forces* and FM 31–21 *Organization and Conduct of Guerrilla Forces.*

1950–1951—Headquaters, Eighth Army; Executive Officer, Special Activities Group.

1951–1953—Chief of Plans, Special Operations Division, Office of the Chief of Psychological Warfare (OCPW).

1953–1954—National War College, Washington DC.

1954–1956—Chief of Special Operations Division, US European Command (EUCOM).

1956—Basic Airborne Course, Fort Benning, Georgia.

1956–1957—Assistant Division Commander, 82nd Airborne Division, Fort Bragg North Carolina.

1957—Retired at the rank of Brigadier General.

1958–1977—President, Volckmann Furniture Company.

June 1977—Volckmann Furniture Company's remaining interests sold to Ethan Allen Company. Volckmann then split his time between homes in Clinton, Iowa and Harlingen, Texas before his death in 1982.

Promotions

Second Lieutenant—12 June 1934
First Lieutenant—12 June 1935
Captain—15 June 1937
Major—31 January 1942
Lieutenant Colonel—20 November 1944 (temporary)
Colonel—21 January 1945 (temporary)
Lieutenant Colonel—1 August 1946
Colonel—1 February 1953
Brigadier General—31 December 1956

Awards

Distinguished Service Cross (with Oak Leaf Cluster)
Distinguished Service Medal
Silver Star
Legion of Merit
Bronze Star (with Oak Leaf Cluster)
Army Commendation Medal
Korean Service Medal
Asiatic-Pacific Campaign Medal
American Defense Service Medal
World War II Victory Medal

Badges

Combat Infantryman Badge
Parachutist Badge (Airborne Wings)

Notes

Chapter 1

1. Interview with Russell W. Volckmann, Jr., 21 February 2007.
2. Stansberry, Ruth Volckmann, Untitled write-up explaining the nature behind the photograph of the young Volckmann with John Smoller. Smoller eventually went on to serve as a Field Artillery officer with the 13th Armored Division in World War II.
3. Interview with Russell W. Volckmann, Jr., 21 February 2007; Volckmann, "Career Chronology of Russell W. Volckmann," attachment to 21 March 1969 letter to History Office, John F. Kennedy Special Warfare Center, Special Operations Archives.
4. Interview with Russell W. Volckmann, Jr., 21 February 2007; *Register of Graduates and Former Cadets.*
5. Volckmann, *We Remained,* p.3.
6. Ibid; Interview with Russell W. Volckmann, Jr., 21 February 2007.
7. Ibid.
8. Matloff and Snell, *Strategic Planning for Coalition Warfare,* p.2–5.
9. Ibid.
10. Morton, *The Fall of the Philippines,* p.9–12.
11. Ibid.
12. Ibid, p.14–25.
13. Ibid.
14. Matloff and Snell, *Strategic Planning for Coalition Warfare,* p.2–5.
15. Interview with Russell Volckmann, Jr., 21 February 2007; Volckmann, *We Remained,* p.4–5.
16. Volckmann, *We Remained,* p.6.
17. Volckmann, *Guerrilla Days in North Luzon,* p.1–4; Volckmann, *We Remained,* p.7.
18. Volckmann, *We Remained,* p.7.
19. Blackburn Oral History, p.42, MHI.
20. Volckmann, *We Remained,* p.8–9.
21. Ibid.
22. Ibid.

Chapter 2

23. Volckmann's War Diary, 8 December 1941. Hereafter referred to as "War Dairy."
24. Ibid.
25. Ibid.
26. War Diary, 14 December 1941; Morton, *The Fall of the Philippines,* p.100–106. To complete their initial landings, the Japanese divided the 2nd Formosa Infantry within two task forces (code-named *Tanaka* and *Kanno)* each containing roughly 2,000 men. *Tanaka* was the first to land at Aparri, followed by *Kanno* at Vigan.
27. War Diary, 25 December 1941.
28. Ibid, 27 December 1941.
29. Ibid.
30. Volckmann, *We Remained,* p.17.
31. Ibid; War Diary, 30 December 1941
32. Volckmann, *We Remained,* p.18.
33. War Diary, 31 December 1941; Volckmann, *We Remained,* p.18–19.
34. Ibid.
35. War Diary, 31 December 1941.
36. Ibid.
37. Volckmann, *We Remained,* p.21.
38. War Diary, 2 January 1942.
39. War Diary, 3 January 1942; Volckmann, *We Remained,* p.23.
40. War Diary, 3–4 January 1942.

Chapter 3

41. Volckmann, *We Remained,* p.24.
42. Ibid.
43. War Diary, 12 January 1942.
44. Volckmann, *We Remained,* p.25.
45. War Diary, 25–26 January 1942.
46. War Diary, 27–28 January 1942; Volckmann, *We Remained, p.26.*
47. Ibid.
48. Volckmann, *We Remained,* p.27; War Diary, 3 February 1942.
49. War Diary, 1–10 February, 29 February 1942.
50. War Diary, 31 March, 1–9 April 1942.
51. The Diary of Colonel John P. Horan, 19 December 1941–1 January 1942, The Donald D. Blackburn Collection. Hereafter referred to as "Horan Diary. "
52. Volckmann letter to American Forces Pacific Area Command (AFPAC) "Date of Recognition: United States Armed Forces in the Philippines-North Luzon", 26 November 1945, RG 407, Box 468, NARA.
53. Volckmann, *We Remained,* p.41.
54. War Diary, 9 April 1942; Blackburn Oral History, p.67, MHI.
55. Blackburn, "War within a War: The Philippines 1942–1945", *Conflict,* Volume 7–2, p.131.
56. War Diary, 9 April 1942; Volckmann, *We Remained,* p.43.

57. Ibid.
58. War Diary, 10 April 1942; Blackburn Oral History, p.68, MHI; Volckmann, *We Remained*, p.43–44.
59. Blackburn Oral History, p.126, MHI; Lapham, *Lapham's Raiders*, p.11–15.
60. Blackburn Oral History, p.68, MHI; Interview with Edwin P. Ramsey, 3 August 2008.
61. Volckmann, *We Remained*, p.44.
62. War Diary, 15 April 1942. Volckmann records the incident on this date, but indicates that it occurred around this time earlier in the week; Blackburn Oral History, p.72, MHI.
63. Volckmann, *We Remained*, p.45.
64. War Diary, 10 April 1942; Volckmann, *We Remained*, p.46.
65. War Diary, 10 April 1942; Volckmann, *We Remained*, p.47.
66. War Diary, 11 April 1942.
67. Volckmann, *We Remained*, p.48.
68. War Diary, 11 April 1942; Volckmann, *We Remained*, p.48.
69. Ibid; War Diary, 12 April 1942.
70. Volckmann, *We Remained*, p.49; Blackburn Oral History, p.72, MHI.
71. Volckmann, *We Remained*, p.50.
72. War Diary, 13 April 1942.
73. War Diary, 14 April 1942.
74. Ibid; Volckmann, *We Remained*, p.52.

Chapter 4

75. Volckmann does not give many details surrounding his relationship with Moses and Noble. He never mentions them until the entry for 17 April 1942, confirming that he had met them earlier in Bataan. Blackburn, however, indicates that Volckmann spoke with Moses and Noble about his escape plans at least once before the surrender. It appears that Volckmann, Blackburn, Moses, and Noble may have planned their escape as a foursome, but were somehow separated amidst the confusion of the final battle.
76. War Diary, 18 April 1942.
77. In the entry for 17 June 1942, Volckmann writes about learning of Whiteman's death back at Abucay. He had succumbed to fever.
78. War Diary, 18 April 1942.
79. Ibid, 20–21 April 1942.
80. Ibid, 22 April 1942; Harkins, *Blackburn's Headhunters*, 66.
81. War Diary, 23 April 1942.
82. Ibid, 29 April 1942.
83. Blackburn Oral History, p.74–75, MHI; Harkins, *Blackburn's Headhunters*, 50–51.
84. War Diary, 1–2 May 1942.
85. Ibid, 3 May 1942.
86. Ibid, 5–7 May 1942.
87. Ibid, 31 May 1942.
88. Ibid, 3–5 June 1942.
89. Ibid, 15 June 1942; Volckmann, *We Remained*, p.62.

90. Volckmann, *We Remained,* p.62; HQ PHILRYCOM Claims Service, "Fassoth Camp," RG 407, Box 256, NARA.
91. War Diary, 19 June 1942.
92. Volckmann, *We Remained,* p.63.
93. War Diary, 22 June 1942.
94. Ibid, 23 June 1942; HQ PHILRYCOM Claims Service, "Fassoth Camp," RG 407, Box 256, NARA.
95. Why Bernia had been spared from the Japanese onslaught remains unknown. His name appears only briefly in the Philippine Archives section of the U.S. National Archives. The Japanese may have bypassed his plantation because they saw potential value in its resources as well as the influence of its owner. Nonetheless, Volckmann never discusses it. Tragically, Bernia did not survive the war.
96. HQ PHILRYCOM Claims Service, "Fassoth Camp," RG 407, Box 256, NARA; Harkins, *Blackburn's Headhunters,* p.61–64.
97. Ibid.
98. Ibid.
99. Ibid.
100. The only news reports that Volckmann documented were discouraging in nature.
101. Blackburn Oral History, p. 80–81, MHI.
102. Ibid.
103. Ibid, p.81.
104. Harkins, *Blackburn's Headhunters,* p.60.
105. War Diary, 14 August 1942; Blackburn Oral History, p.84–85, MHI.
106. Dizon, "Complete Data Covering the Guerrilla Activities of the Late Colonel Claude A. Thorp", Army G1, RG 407, Box 258, NARA. Some sources, however, indicate that General Jonathan Wainwright (the senior field commander under MacArthur) gave Thorp the authorization.
107. Harkins, *Blackburn's Headhunters,* p.62
108. Ibid.
109. War Diary, 18–19 August 1942.
110. War Diary, 20 August 1942.
111. War Diary, 21 August 1942; Blackburn Oral History, p.88, MHI.
112. Harkins, *Blackburn's Headhunters,* p.69–70; Blackburn Oral History, p.86, MHI.
113. War Diary, 24 August 1942.
114. Ibid.
115. War Diary, 25 August 1942.
116. Blackburn Oral History, p.91–92; Harkins, *Blackburn's Headhunters,* p.78.
117. Interview with Edwin P. Ramsey, 3 August 2008.
118. War Diary, 27 August 1942.
119. War Diary, 29 August 1942.
120. Ibid.
121. Volckmann, *We Remained,* p.75.
122. War Diary, 30 August 1942.
123. War Diary, 1 September 1942.
124. War Diary, 2–3 September 1942; Blackburn Oral History, p.95, MHI.
125. Volckmann, *We Remained,* 78.

126. War Diary, 4 September 1942.
127. War Diary, 5–7 September 1942.
128. Volckmann, *We Remained*, p.80.
129. War Diary, 7–8 September 1942.
130. War Diary, 9 September 1942.

Chapter 5

131. War Diary, 9 September 1942; Harkins, *Blackburn's Headhunters*, 94.
132. Blackburn, "War within a War: The Philippines 1942–1945", *Conflict*, Volume 7–2, p.139, 143.
133. War Diary, 9 September 1942; *A Brief History of the USAFFE Guerrillas*, RG 407, Box 258, NARA; Erieta, "North Luzon Guerrilla Warfare and Governor Roque Ablan's Exiled Commonwealth Government," RG 407, Box 297, NARA.
134. War Diary, 9 September 1942; Volckmann, *Guerrilla Days in North Luzon*, p.18–19.
135. Volckmann, *We Remained*, p.84; Harkins, *Blackburn's Headquarters*, p.98.
136. War Dairy, 10–11 September 1942.
137. War Diary, 12 September 1942.
138. War Diary, 12–15 September 1942.
139. "Ekip" is a transliteration for the Spanish pronunciation of "equip." Volckmann and Blackburn in their respective diaries use "Equip" and "Ekip" in reference to the same barrio.
140. War Diary, 16 September 1942.
141. Harkins, *Blackburn's Headhunters*, 101.
142. Ibid.
143. Harkins, *Blackburn's Headhunters*, 103.
144. War Diary, 20 September 1942.
145. War Diary, 1 October 1942. Volckmann recorded that he lost his .45 caliber pistol while crossing a stream.
146. War Diary, 1–14 October 1942.
147. Harkins, *Blackburn's Headhunters*, 103.
148. Ibid; War Diary, 15 October 1942.
149. War Diary, 22 October 1942; Blackburn Oral History, p.109–110, MHI.
150. Ibid.
151. War Diary, 27 October 1942.
152. Ibid.
153. Harkins, *Blackburn's Headhunters,108*.
154. Volckmann, "Form for Induction into the Armed Forces of the United States," October 1942 (original publication date of the form, used continuously throughout guerrilla war), The Volckmann Family Collection.
155. *A Brief History of the USAFFE Guerrillas*, RG 407, Box 258, NARA.
156. War Diary, 29 October 1942.
157. Volckmann, *We Remained*, 91.
158. War Diary, 9 November 1942.
159. War Diary, 9–10 November 1942.
160. War Diary, 11 November 1942.

161. War Diary, 12 November 1942.
162. Ibid; Volckmann, *We Remained,* p.92.
163. War Diary, 13 November 1942.
164. Ibid.
165. War Diary, 15–20 November 1942.
166. Ibid.
167. Ibid.
168. Volckmann, *We Remained,* p.96. Emphasis added.
169. War Diary, 28 November 1942.
170. Volckmann, *We Remained,* p.97.
171. Harkins, *Blackburn's Headhunters,* 116–17.
172. War Diary, 23, 25 November 1942.
173. War Diary, 26 November 1942.
174. War Diary, 28 November 1942.
175. War Diary, 29 November 1942. Volckmann introduces Herrin on 29 November but does not mention he is Unitarian minister until the entry for 17 January 1943.
176. War Diary, 28 November 1942.
177. Blackburn Oral History, p.118–19, MHI.
178. Blackburn Oral History, p.125, MHI.
179. War Diary, 29 November 1942; Blackburn Oral History, p.134, MHI.
180. War Diary, 31 May and 21 July 1943.
181. War Diary, 4 December 1942.
182. War Diary, 1 January 1943.
183. War Diary, 25–31 December 1942.

Chapter 6

184. War Diary, entries throughout January 1943; General Sato Oki, "Plan of Propaganda," General Orders-14th Imperial Japanese Army, 10 June 1942, The Donald D. Blackburn Collection.
185. Blackburn Oral History, p.127, MHI.
186. Ibid, p.134, MHI.
187. Volckmann, *We Remained,* p.101.
188. War Diary, 7 March 1943; Blackburn Oral History, p.115, MHI.
189. Ibid.
190. War Diary, 27–29 March 1943.
191. Volckmann, *We Remained,* p.111.
192. Blackburn Oral History, p.117–18, MHI.
193. War Diary, 27 April 1943
194. Ibid.
195. Harkins, *Blackburn's Headhunters,* p.145.
196. War Diary, 20 March 1943.
197. Blackburn Oral History, p.121, MHI; Harkins, *Blackburn's Headhunters,* p.143–44.
198. In his later entries (1944), Volckmann indicates sending messages into Benguet and visiting camps there; organizing these camps may have been Fish's handiwork before he died.
199. War Diary, 16–23 April 1943.

200. War Diary, 7 May 1943.
201. War Diary, 19–26 May 1943.
202. War Diary, 9 June 1943.
203. Ibid.
204. *A Brief History of the USAFFE Guerrillas*, RG 407, Box 258, NARA; War Diary, 9 June 1943; Moses and Noble, "Special Orders," 9 June 1943, The Volckmann Family Collection.
205. Moses and Noble, "Special Orders," 9 June 1943, The Volckmann Family Collection.

Chapter 7

206. War Diary, Entries throughout June 1943.
207. War Diary, 9 June 1943.
208. War Diary, Entries 10, 14, 15, 17, 18, 20, 21 June 1943.
209. War Diary, 23–24 June 1943; Harkins, *Blackburn's Headhunters*, p.168–69.
210. Blackburn Oral History, p.164, MHI.
211. Dincong, "Historical Data of the 14th Infantry," RG 407, Box 249, NARA.
212. Volckmann, *Guerrilla Days in North Luzon*, p.45–57.
213. Volckmann, "Reorganization Plan of 1943," RG 407, Box 465, NARA.
214. Volckmann, "General Order 1," 5 November 1943, RG 407, Box 543, NARA.
215. Volckmann, "After-Battle Report: USAFIP-NL G3," The Russell W. Volckmann Papers, Box 4, MHI.
216. Volckmann, "General Order 15," 9 December 1943, RG 407, Box 468, NARA.
217. Volckmann, "General Order 1," 5 November 1943, RG 407, Box 543, NARA.
218. Volckmann, *Guerrilla Days in North Luzon*, p. 44.
219. Ibid, p.18.
220. Ibid.
221. Ibid.
222. Volckmann, *We Remained*, p.147.
223. Ibid, p.152.
224. Ibid, p.153.
225. Ibid.
226. Blackburn Oral History, p.130, MHI.
227. Ibid, p.131–34.
228. Volckmann never provided many details behind his decision to relocate General Headquarters. It appears, however, that the highest concentration of USAFIP-NL forces lay on the western side of North Luzon. Volckmann also stated that news of the growing Allied offensive in the Pacific contributed to his decision. This may indicate that he already had a firm idea of directing Allied forces to the western coast for their eventual campaign against the Japanese Fourteenth Army.
229. Blackburn, "The Operations of the 11th Infantry, USAFIP-NL", Infantry Officers Advanced Course—Fort Benning, GA, 1948, p. 1–3, The Donald D. Blackburn Collection.
230. Blackburn Oral History, p.131–34, MHI.
231. "bargaining chip" quotes mine.
232. Volckmann, "Reorganization Plan of 1943," RG 407, Box 465, NARA.

233. Volckmann, "Memorandum Regarding Financial Regulations, USAFIP-NL", 7 November 1943, RG 407, Box 468, NARA.

234. Volckmann, "General Orders, USAFIP-NL," RG 407, Box 465, NARA.

235. War Diary, 8 February 1943, 27 February 1943; General Sato Oki, "Plan of Propaganda," General Orders—4th Army, 10 June 1942, The Donald D. Blackburn Collection. Oki's orders outline the details of the propaganda campaign scheduled to begin as soon as forces were consolidated and military government established.

236. Ibid.

237. War Diary, 13 March 1943.

238. War Dairy, 8–10 May 1943; General Sato Oki, "Plan of Propaganda," General Orders—14th Army, 10 June 1942, The Donald D. Blackburn Collection; Blackburn Oral History, p.133–135, MHI.

239. War Diary, 11 April 1943.

240. Volckmann letter to all guerrillas "Instructions on Intelligence Gathering," 15 June 1943, RG 407, Box 468, NARA; Concepcion, "S2 Reports", 22 January–2 December 1944, USAFIP-NL Intelligence Files, RG 407, Box 251, NARA. Captain Osmundo Concepcion was Volckmann's chief Intelligence Officer.

241. Volckmann, "General Order 7," RG 407, Box 465, NARA.

242. Volckmann, "G2 Weekly Intelligence Reports: Vol. 1"; The Russell W. Volckmann Papers, Box 7, MHI. Volckmann re-iterated the concept of "special agencies" in FM 31–21 *Organization and Conduct of Guerrilla Warfare.*

243. War Diary, 10 May 1943; Volckmann, USAFIP-NL Newsletter, 26 June 1944, 18 August 1944, RG 407, Box 251, NARA; Volckmann, FM 31–21 *Organization and Conduct of Guerrilla Warfare,* 156.

244. Volckmann letter to USAFIP-NL agents in the Philippine Constabulary, 26 June 1944, RG 407, Box 251, NARA.

245. Volckmann, "Form for Induction into the Armed Forces of the United States," 29 December 1942 (original publication date of the form, used continuously throughout guerrilla war), The Volckmann Family Collection.

246. War Diary, 7–8 October 1943.

247. War Diary, 14 October 1943.

248. War Diary, 15 October 1943.

249. War Diary, 18–22 October 1943.

250. War Diary, 22 October 1943.

251. Harkins, *Blackburn's Headhunters,* p.181.

252. Ibid, p.182.

253. War Diary, entries 25 November, 28 November–18 December, 19–24 December, 25, 26–31 December 1943.

254. War Diary, 1 January 1944; Harkins, *Blackburn's Headhunters,* p.186.

255. Volckmann, "General Orders, USAFIP-NL," 1943–44, RG 407, Box 465, NARA.

Chapter 8

256. Volckmann, "On the Role of Airpower in Counterinsurgency and Unconventional Warfare: Allied Resistance to the Japanese," p.10, Rand Corporation, July 1963.

257. Volckmann, *We Remained,* p.158.

258. "Calendar of Submarine Shipments to Guerrillas", General Headquarters - Southwest Pacific Area, Entry: 27 October 1944, The Donald D. Blackburn Collection; Willoughby, *A Brief History of the G-2 Section, GHQ SWPA—Volume 1: Guerrilla Resistance Movement in the Philippines,* General Headquarters-Southwest Pacific Area, p.88, 1945, The Volckmann Family Collection (also found in RG 407, Box 255, NARA).

259. Volckmann radiogram to SWPA, September-December 1944, "Correspondence with General MacArthur's Headquarters," The Russell W. Volckmann Papers, Box 3, MHI.

260. Ibid.

261. SWPA radiogram to Volckmann, 24 September 1944, "Correspondence with General MacArthur's Headquarters," The Russell W. Volckmann Papers, Box 3, MHI.

262. Volckmann, "On the Role of Airpower in Counterinsurgency and Unconventional Warfare: Allied Resistance to the Japanese," p.10, Rand Corporation, July 1963.

263. Ibid.

264. Volckmann, *We Remained,* p.162.

265. Ibid.

266. Ibid, p.164.

267. Ibid.

268. Ibid.

269. SWPA radiogram to Volckmann, 18 November 1944, "Correspondence with General MacArthur's Headquarters," The Russell W. Volckmann Papers, Box 3, MHI.

270. Volckmann, *We Remained,* p.164.

271. Ibid, p.166.

272. Ibid, p.167.

273. Ibid.

274. Ibid.

275. Volckmann, *We Remained,* p.168.

276. Ibid, "Activities in North Luzon," document of unspecified date, RG 407, Box 542, NARA.

277. Volckmann, *We Remained,* p.170.

278. Volckmann, "Outline of Events, Policies, and Orders Relative to the Apprehension and Elimination of Filipino Jap Spies and Informers", 1946 (unspecified date), The Donald D. Blackburn Collection.

279. Volckmann, "On the Role of Airpower in Counterinsurgency and Unconventional Warfare: Allied Resistance to the Japanese," p.11–12, Rand Corporation, July 1963.

280. Ibid.

281. Volckmann, *We Remained,* p.179.

282. "Calendar of Submarine Shipments to Guerrillas", General Headquarters-Southwest Pacific Area, Entry: 27 October 1944, The Donald D. Blackburn Collection; Volckmann radiogram to SWPA, December 1944, "Correspondence with General MacArthur's Headquarters," The Russell W. Volckmann Papers, Box 3, MHI.

283. Radiograms estimating enemy capabilities, November–December 1944, "Correspondence with General MacArthur's Headquarters," The Russell W. Volckmann Papers, Box 3, MHI.

284. Blackburn, "War within a War: The Philippines 1942–1945", *Conflict,* Volume 7–2, p.149.

285. SWPA radiogram to Volckmann, Box 251, NARA.

286. Volckmann, "On the Role of Airpower in Counterinsurgency and Unconventional Warfare: Allied Resistance to the Japanese," p.12, Rand Corporation, July 1963.

287. Volckmann, *We Remained*, p.188.

288. Ibid, 189.

289. Ibid.

290. Interview with Russell Volckmann, Jr. 21 February 2007.

291. Volckmann, *We Remained*, p.190.

292. Volckmann, "Sketch of Air-Ground Message Pick-up," unspecified date, The Donald D. Blackburn Collection.

293. Volckmann, We Remained, p.190.

Chapter 9

294. USAFIP-NL Intelligence Files, RG 409, Box 251, NARA; USAFIP-NL Battle Records, December 1944–June 1945, 1 July 1945-VJ Day, RG 409, Box 250, NARA; Volckmann, "After-Battle Report: USAFIP-NL G3," p. 2–5, The Russell W. Volckmann Papers, Box 4, MHI.

295. USAFIP-NL Intelligence Files, RG 409, Box 251, NARA.

296. Volckmann, "General Order 14," USAFIP-NL General Orders, RG 409, Box 468, NARA; Volckmann, "After-Battle Report: USAFIP-NL G3," p. 3, The Russell W. Volckmann Papers, Box 4, MHI.

297. Ibid.

298. Sipin, "ENEMY CASUALTIES," Report dated September 1944, RG 407, Box 542, NARA.

299. "Mission," Summary report dated 9 October 1944, RG 407, Box 542, NARA.

300. Volckmann's War Diary, 12 February 1944, 6 June 1944.

301. Duque, "Interview of Major General Toshimitsu Takatsu, Chief of Staff 23rd Infantry Division, Japanese Imperial Army, 20 September 1945" in *Interviews with Surrendered Japanese General Officers,* USAFIP-NL G3, The Russell W. Volckmann Papers, Box 4, MHI.

302. Volckmann, "After-Battle Report: USAFIP-NL G3," p.9–15, The Russell W. Volckmann Papers, Box 4, MHI.

303. USAFIP-NL Situation Maps January–February, The Russell W. Volckmann Papers, Box 6, MHI.

304. Volckmann, "After-Battle Report: USAFIP-NL G3," p.61–62 The Russell W. Volckmann Papers, Box 4, MHI; USAFIP-NL Situation Map—14 January 1945, The Russell W. Volckmann Papers, Box 6, MHI.

305. Ibid.

306. Ibid; Duque, "Interview of Colonel Sotomu Terau, Chief of Staff 19th Division, Japanese Imperial Army, 12 September 1945" in *Interviews with Surrendered Japanese General Officers,* USAFIP-NL G3, The Russell W. Volckmann Papers, Box 4, MHI.

307. Volckmann, "After-Battle Report: USAFIP-NL G3," p.63–67 The Russell W. Volckmann Papers, Box 4, MHI.

308. Ibid.

309. Ibid, 69.

310. Ibid; "Interview of Colonel Sotomu Terau, Chief of Staff 19th Division, Japanese Imperial Army, 12 September 1945."

311. Volckmann, "After-Battle Report: USAFIP-NL G3," p.18 The Russell W. Volckmann Papers, Box 4, MHI

312. Volckmann, "After-Battle Report: USAFIP-NL G3," p.22, The Russell W. Volckmann Papers, Box 4, MHI.

313. Volckmann, "On the Role of Airpower in Counterinsurgency and Unconventional Warfare: Allied Resistance to the Japanese," p.18–20, Rand Corporation, July 1963.

314. Ibid; Volckmann, "After-Battle Report: USAFIP-NL G3," p. 96–101, The Russell W. Volckmann Papers, Box 4, MHI.

315. Volckmann, "Special Order 129," 4 December 1944, USAFIP Letters and Correspondence, RG 409, Box 467, NARA.

316. Volckmann, "After-Battle Report: USAFIP-NL G3," p.75, The Russell W. Volckmann Papers, Box 4, MHI

317. Volckmann, "Special Order 129," 4 December 1944, USAFIP Letters and Correspondence, RG 409, Box 467, NARA; Blackburn, "War within a War: The Philippines 1942–1945", *Conflict,* Volume 7–2, 153.

318. Ibid.

319. Volckmann, "After-Battle Report: USAFIP-NL G3," p.33, The Russell W. Volckmann Papers, Box 4, MHI.

320. Ibid, 35.

321. Ibid.

322. Ibid, 36.

323. Morton, *Triumph in the Philippines,* 560.

324. Volckmann, "After-Battle Report: USAFIP-NL G3," p.63–67 The Russell W. Volckmann Papers, Box 4, MHI; "14th Infantry Operations," USAFIP- NL Battle Records, RG 409, Box 250, NARA.

325. Ibid.

326. Duque, "Interview of Major General Toshimitsu Takatsu, Chief of Staff 23rd Infantry Division, Japanese Imperial Army, 20 September 1945" in *Interviews with Surrendered Japanese General Officers,* USAFIP-NL G3, The Russell W. Volckmann Papers, Box 4, MHI.

327. Volckmann, "Special Order 3," 7 August 1944, USAFIP-NL Letters and Correspondence, RG 409, Box 467, NARA; USAFIP-NL Situation Map—14 January 1945, The Russell W. Volckmann Papers, Box 6, MHI.

328. Blackburn, "The Operations of the 11th Infantry, USAFIP,NL", Infantry Officers Advanced Course—Fort Benning, GA, 1948, p. 1–3, The Donald D. Blackburn Collection.

329. Ibid.

330. Ibid, 6–10.

331. Volckmann, "After-Battle Report: USAFIP-NL G3," p.78–80, The Russell W. Volckmann Papers, Box 4, MHI.

332. Blackburn, "The Operations of the 11th Infantry, USAFIP,NL", Infantry Officers Advanced Course—Fort Benning, GA, 1948, p. 22, The Donald D. Blackburn Collection; Flanagan, *Airborne!: A Combat History of American Airborne Forces,* p. 336–37.

333. Volckmann, "G2 Weekly Intelligence Reports: Vol. 1", May–June 1945, The Russell W. Volckmann Papers, Box 7, MHI.

334. Ibid, December 1944–April 1945.

335. Volckmann, "After-Battle Report: USAFIP-NL G3," p.49–60, The Russell W. Volckmann Papers, Box 4, MHI.

336. Volckmann, "G3 Situation Reports" 15–24 June 1945, The Russell W. Volckmann Papers, Box 4, MHI.

337. USAFIP-NL Situation Map—15 July 1945, The Russell W. Volckmann Papers, Box 6, MHI.

338. Ibid.

339. Volckmann, "G3 Situation Reports" 1 July–1 August 1945, The Russell W. Volckmann Papers, Box 4, MHI.

340. Ibid, 1–15 August 1945; Blackburn Oral History, 204, MHI.

341. *Victory at Bessang Pass*—Macapagal Administration, 1962. Publication commemorates the 17th anniversary of the final victory of the USAFIP-NL. The Volckmann Family Collection; Volckmann, "After-Battle Report: USAFIP-NL G3," p.110–11, The Russell W. Volckmann Papers, Box 4, MHI.

342. Interview with Russell Volckmann Jr.; MacArthur, "Citation: The Distinguished Service Cross," 27 January 1945, The Volckmann Family Collection.

Chapter 10

343. Interview with Russell Volckmann, Jr. 21 February 2007.

344. Interview with Russell Volckmann, Jr. 5 August 2008.

345. "File: Russell W. Volckmann," World War II Prisoners of War Data File: 1941–1946, RG 389, NARA. POW records indicated that Volckmann was officially "Missing in Action" as of May 1942. His status was subsequently updated in January 1945.

346. "MacArthur Tells Volckmann's Work with Guerrillas," in *The Clinton Herald*, 5 March 1945, The Volckmann Family Collection.

347. "Russell W. Volckmann is Reported Safe," in *The Clinton Herald*, 15 January 1945, The Volckmann Family Collection.

348. "Yamashita Trial Set for Manila," in *The Clinton Herald*, 4 October 1945; Clips from RKO Newsreel—26 September 1945 (originally shown at the Rialto Theater in Clinton, Iowa), The Volckmann Family Collection.

349. Duque, "Interview of Major General Toshimitsu Takatsu, Chief of Staff 23rd Infantry Division, Japanese Imperial Army, 2° September 1945" and "Interview of Colonel Sotomu Terau, Chief of Staff 19th Division, Japanese Imperial Army, 12 September 1945" in *Interviews with Surrendered Japanese General Officers*, USAFIP-NL G3, The Russell W. Volckmann Papers, Box 4, MHI.

350. Interview with Russell Volckmann, Jr. 5 August 2008; "Hero Reunited with Family," in *The Clinton Herald*, 8 December 1945, The Volckmann Family Collection.

351. "News Writers Trailed Hero Across the Nation," in *The Clinton Herald*, 7 December 1945, The Volckmann Family Collection.

352. "Clinton's War Hero is Home!" in *The Clinton Herald*, 7 December 1945, The Volckmann Family Collection.

353. Interview with Russell Volckmann, Jr. 5 August 2008.
354. "War Hero is Reunited Here with Wife, Son," in *The Clinton Herald*, 8 December 1945, The Volckmann Family Collection.
355. Blackburn Oral History, p.223, MHI.
356. Roxas letter to Volckmann, 31 July 1945, The Volckmann Family Collection.
357. Blackburn Oral History, p.223, MHI.
358. Interview with Russell Volckmann, Jr.; "Guerrilla Recognition Files," RG 407, Box 465, NARA.
359. Ibid.
360. Interview with Russell Volckmann, Jr. 21 February 2007.
361. Blackburn Oral History, p.222, MHI.
362. Ibid.
363. Ibid.
364. Ibid.
365. Ibid, p.223.
366. Ibid.
367. Ibid, p. 224.
368. Ibid.
369. "Proclamation of Amnesty," signed by the Honorable Kenneth Royal, Secretary of the Army, 12 August 1949, The Donald D. Blackburn Collection.
370. Blackburn Oral History, p. 228, MHI.
371. Ibid.
372. Ibid.

Chapter 11

373. Volckmann, FM 31–21 *Organization and Conduct of Guerrilla Warfare,* p.23.
374. 376 McClintock, *Instruments of Statecraft: U.S. Guerrilla Warfare, Counterinsurgency, and CounterTerrorism, 1940–1990,* p.45.
375. "Russell William Volckmann," *Assembly,* Vol. 47, April 1988, The Volckmann Family Collection. This is Volckmann's obituary from the West Point alumni newsletter.
376. Volckmann, FM 31–20 *Operations Against Guerrilla Forces,* p.2.
377. Ibid, p.24–34.
378. Ibid, p.35–38.
379. Ibid, p.44–46; Birtle, *U.S. Army Counterinsurgency and Contingency Operations Doctrine: 1942–1976,* p.104–05.
380. Volckmann, FM 31–2° *Operations Against Guerrilla Forces,* p.57–63.
381. Ibid.
382. Ibid, p.47–51.
383. Ibid, p.71–74.
384. Ibid.
385. Birtle, *U.S. Army Counterinsurgency and Contingency Operations Doctrine: 1942–1976,* p.104–05.
386. Willoughby, *MacArthur, 1941–1951,* p.210.
387. Ibid.

388. Paschall, *A Study in Command and Control: Special Operations in Korea, 1951–1953*, p.2–3.

389. Birtle, *U.S. Army Counterinsurgency and Contingency Operations Doctrine: 1942–1976*, p.109; Evanhoe, *Darkmoon: Eighth Army Special Operations in Korea*, p.20.

390. Ibid.

391. Ibid, p.110.

392. Volckmann, "Career Chronology of Russell W. Volckmann," attachment to 21 March 1969 letter to History Office, John F. Kennedy Special Warfare Center, Special Operations Archives; Interviews with Russell Volckmann Jr., William Volckmann, and Helen Volckmann, August 5–10 2008; Various personal papers covering 1949–1951, The Volckmann Family Collection.

393. Volckmann, letter to the History Office, John F. Kennedy Center for Special Warfare, 21 March 1969, Special Operations Archives. Letter contains Volckmann's description of how he became involved with McClure and the OCPW.

394. Paschall, *A Study in Command and Control: Special Operations in Korea, 1951–1953*.

395. Ibid.

396. Ibid.

397. Ibid.

398. Interview with Russell Volckmann, Jr. 21 February 2007.

Chapter 12

399. Paddock, *US Army Special Warfare: Its Origins*, p.72.

400. Ibid, p.111–129.

401. Ibid, p.88.

402. "Major General Robert Alexis McClure," *Time*, 14 January 1957; Daugherty and Janowitz, *A Psychological Warfare Casebook*, p.131; "Operational Groups," Exhibition at the Army Airborne Museum, Fayetteville, North Carolina.

403. Volckmann letter, 21 March 1969, Special Operations Archives.

404. Bank, letter to the History Office, John F. Kennedy Center for Special Warfare, 23 February 1969, Special Operations Archives. Letter contains Bank's recollections of his duties with OCPW. In this letter, Bank gives Volckmann credit for formulating the operating concepts of Special Forces.

405. Volckmann, "Memorandum to the Commanding General, Infantry Center: Analysis and Suggestions re Gen J. Lawton Collins' Conference, 5 April 1951", 9 April 1951, RG 319, Box 12, NARA; Paddock, *US Army Special Warfare: Its Origins*, p.122.

406. Ibid.

407. Ibid.

408. Ibid.

409. Volckmann, "Findings and Recommendations re Special Operations Training," Office of the Chief of Psychological Warfare, RG 319, Box 15, NARA.

410. Brown, *Historical Dictionary of the U.S. Army*, p.1, 220; Bank, letter to the History Office, John F. Kennedy Center for Special Warfare, 23 February 1969, Special Operations Archives; Schemmer, *U.S. Special Operations Forces*, p.84.

411. Bank, letter to the History Office, John F. Kennedy Center for Special Warfare, 23 February 1969, Special Operations Archives.

Epilogue

412. Ney, *Notes on Guerrilla Warfare: Principles and Practices*, p.158.
413. "Volckmann's USAFIP-NL," p.5–6, The Donald D. Blackburn Collection. Unpublished text (~15 pages) outlining historical achievements of USAFIP-NL. Volckmann letter to USAFIP-NL District Commanders, "Operating Principles and Procedures, USAFIP-NL," 16 March 1944, The Donald D. Blackburn Collection.
414. Volckmann letter to USAFIP-NL District Commanders, "Operating Principles and Procedures, USAFIP-NL," 16 March 1944, The Donald D. Blackburn Collection. Specifically, Volckmann put his prisoners to work in clerical positions typing memos or performing menial labor jobs.
415. Volckmann, "Outline of Events, Policies, and Orders Relative to the Apprehension and Elimination of Filipino Jap Spies and Informers," 1946 (unspecified date), The Donald D. Blackburn Collection; Volckmann letter to American Forces Pacific Area Command (AFPAC) "Date of Recognition: United States Armed Forces in the Philippines—North Luzon", 26 November 1945, RG 407, Box 468, NARA. Praeger was by no means the only guerrilla to be captured as a result of Filipino collaboration with the Japanese. Volckmann provides the names of twelve (12) other guerrillas who met similar fates.
416. Dizon, "Complete Data Covering the Guerrilla Activities of the Late Colonel Claude A. Thorp" Army G1, RG 407, Box 258, NARA.
417. Blackburn Oral History, 104–09, MHI; Blackburn, "War within a War: The Philippines 1942–1945" *Conflict*, Volume 7–2, p.137–38.
418. Erieta, "North Luzon Guerrilla Warfare and Governor Roque Ablan's Exiled Commonwealth Government," RG 407, Box 297, NARA.
419. Ross-Smith, *Triumph in the Philippines*, p.3–8.
420. ibid.
421. ibid.
422. Volckmann's War Diary, 17 February 1944; Blackburn Oral History, 195, MHI; Volckmann, "After-Battle Report, USAFIP-NL G3," p.9–11, The Russell W. Volckmann Papers, Box 4, MHI.
423. Volckmann radiogram to MacArthur, September – December 1944, "Correspondence with General MacArthur's Headquarters," The Russell W. Volckmann Papers, Box 3, MHI.
424. Krueger, "Memorandum: Procurement, Recognition, Supply, and Disposition of Guerrilla Units," 3 May 1945, USAFIP-NL General Orders, RG 409, Box 468, NARA.
425. Volckmann, FM 31–21 *Organization and Conduct of Guerrilla Warfare*, p.11–12.
426. *Small Wars Manual*, p.17–32.
427. ibid, p.1–9.
428. Blackburn Oral History, p.235–54, MHI; Framed decree from the Philippine President, 1947, The Donald D. Blackburn Collection.
429. Blackburn Oral History, p.235–54, MHI.
430. USAFIP General Order #21, 3 December 1944. RG 409, Box 468, NARA. Volckmann later had O'Day extradited back to the United States but it is likely that O'Day never stood trial or went before any tribunals.
431. Lapham, *Lapham's Raiders*, p.1–11, 148; Volckmann's War Diary, 1–3 September 1942, 8 August 1943.

432. Lapham, *Lapham's Raiders*, p.29–30.

433. Lapham, *Lapham's Raiders*, p.119.

434. Interviews with Russell Volckmann, Jr., William Volckmann, and Helen Volckmann. All three confirm that Volckmann was a man of unfathomable reserve. Rarely did he ever speak of anything that occurred in the Philippines, Korea, or with OCPW.

435. Arnold, *A Rock and a Fortress*, p.209–210.

436. Hunt, Ray, and Bernard Norling, *Behind Japanese Lines*, p.218.

437. Volckmann, "Career Chronology of Russell W. Volckmann," attachment to 21 March 1969 letter to History Office, John F. Kennedy Special Warfare Center, Special Operations Archives; Interview with Russell Volckmann Jr.; Volckmann, "Tehran Breifing: The Potentialities of Guerrilla Warfare," April 1956, The Donald D. Blackburn Collection.

438. Volckmann, "Career Chronology of Russell W. Volckmann," attachment to 21 March 1969 letter to History Office, John F. Kennedy Special Warfare Center, Special Operations Archives; Interviews with Russell Volckmann Jr. and William Volckmann; United States Military Academy, *USMA Fifty-Year Book, 1934–1984*, p.182–83.

Bibliography

Primary Sources

Arnold, Robert H. *A Rock and a Fortress.* Sarasota: Blue Horizon Press, 1979.

Blackburn, Donald D; Brigadier General, USA (Ret). Interview by Lieutenant Colonel Robert B. Smith, USAF. Senior Officer's Oral History Program (Project 83-9). U.S. Army Military History Institute, 1983.

The Donald D. Blackburn Collection. Collection of personal papers, photographs, letters and official documents in possession of Blackburn and family.

Field Manual 31-20: *Operations Against Guerrilla Forces.* Fort Benning (Georgia): The Infantry School, 1950.

Field Manual 31-21: *Organization and Conduct of Guerrilla Forces.* Washington DC: Government Printing Office, 1951.

Field Manual 31-15: *Operations Against Irregular Forces.* Washington DC: Government Printing Office, 1961.

Field Manual 31-16: *Counter-guerrilla Operations.* Washington DC: Government Printing Office, 1967.

Hunt, Ray C. and Bernard Norling. *Behind Japanese Lines.* Lexington: University Press of Kentucky, 1986.

Lapham, Robert. *Lapham's Raiders.* Lexington: University Press of Kentucky, 1995.

Office of the President of the Philippines. *Victory at Bessang Pass.* Macapagal Administration, 1962. Publication commemorating the 17th anniversary of the final victory of the USAFIP, North Luzon.

Peterson, A.H., ed, *The Role of Airpower in Counterinsurgency and Unconventional Warfare: Allied Resistance to the Japanese on Luzon, World War II.* Memorandum 3655, U.S Air Force Project Rand. Santa Monica: Rand Corporation, July 1963. Panel on which Volckmann discussed the vitality of air support to guerrilla operations and made recommendations for future implementation.

Ramsey, Edwin P. Interview conducted by author. 3 August 2008.

Special Operations Archives, John F. Kennedy Special Warfare Center.

File: Volckmann, Russell W.

Letters dated 21 March 1969, 1 August 1975.

File: Bank, Aaron

Letters dated 17 February 1968, 3 April 1968, 27 February 1973.

Records of the Adjutant General's Office, Philippine Archives Collection, National Archives II, Record Group 407.

Box 250. Battle Records.

Box 251. Intelligence Reports.

Box 255. "Guerrilla Resistance Movement in the Philippine Islands." Monograph composed by Major General Charles Willoughby; Radio log of Volckmann's communication with SWPA.

Box 258. "Volckmann's History," Claude Thorpe File, Cagayan- Apayao Forces.

Box 297. Ablan's Guerrillas.

Box 465. General Orders, GHQ, USAFIP, North Luzon. Orders issued periodically from GHQ spanning September 1943-May 1945.

Box 468. More General Orders and Correspondence, USAFIP-NL.

Box 539. Maps of USAFIP, North Luzon Area of Operations, Tables of Organization and Equipment.

Box 543. After-action reports of pilots who conducted strafing runs on targets designated by Volckmann's forward air controllers.

Records of the Army Staff, National Archives II, Record Group 319.

Box 12, 15. OCPW, correspondence and position papers outlining operational concepts and principles for Special Operations Forces.

The Volckmann Family Collection. Volckmann, Russell W. Assorted personal papers— Contains notes, letters, photographs and official documents with Army seal. Spans from 1917 until death.

Volckmann, Russell W. "Guerrilla Days in North Luzon: A Brief Historical Narrative of a Brilliant Segment of the Resistance Movement during Enemy Occupation of the Philippines 1941-1945." Camp Spencer, La Union (Philippines): United States Army Forces in the Philippines, 1946. First Division Museum.

Volckmann, Russell W. "The War Diary of Russell W. Volckmann, 1941-1944." Combat diary composed by Volckmann from 8 December 1941 to 16 June 1944. Entries from 16 June until V-J Day remain unaccounted for. Copy provided by the Volckmann Family.

Volckmann, Russell W. *We Remained.* New York: Norton, 1954.

Volckmann, Jr., Russell W. Interviews conducted by author. February-June 2007.

Volckmann, William. Interviews conducted by author. February-June 2007.

Volckmann, Helen. Interviews conducted by author. August 2008.

U.S. Army Military History Institute, Army Historical Education Center.

"The Russell W. Volckmann Papers."

Box 1. G3 Operations.

Box 2. Duplicates.

Box 3. Correspondence with General MacArthur's Headquarters.

Box 4. G3 Operations (cont'd); USAFIP-NL After-Battle Report.

Box 5. Miscellaneous Papers and Maps.

Box 6. G2 Periodic Reports; Intelligence Summaries.

Box 7. G2 Weekly Reports.

United States. FMFRP 12-15: *Small Wars Manual*. Washington, DC: United States Marine Corps, 1935.

United States Military Academy. *The Howitzer, 1934: The Annual of the Corps of Cadets*. Volume 37, 1934.

United States Military Academy. *The Register of Graduates and Former Cadets*. Volume 200, 2003.

United States Military Academy. *USMA Fifty Year Book, 1934-1984*. 1984. This is a reunion publication for the Class of 1934. Helen Volckmann and Don Blackburn contributed to the memorial page for Russell Volckmann.

Secondary Sources

Birtle, Andrew J. *U.S. Army Counterinsurgency and Contingency Operations Doctrine 1942-1976*. Washington, DC: Office of the Chief of Military History, Dept. of the Army, 2006.

Daugherty, William E. and Morris Janowitz. *A Psychological Warfare Casebook*. Baltimore: The John Hopkins Press, 1958.

Evanhoe, Ed. *Darkmoon: Eighth Army Special Operations in the Korean War*. Annapolis: Naval Institute Press, 1995.

Harkins, Phillip. *Blackburn's Headhunters*. New York: WW Norton, 1955.

Matloff, Maurice, and Edwin Marion Snell. *Strategic Planning for Coalition Warfare, 1941-1942*. Washington, DC: Office of the Chief of Military History, Dept. of the Army, 1953.

McClintock, Michael. *Instruments of Statecraft: U.S. Guerrilla Warfare, Counterinsurgency, and Counter-Terrorism, 1940-1990*. New York: Pantheon Books, 1992.

Morton, Louis. *The Fall of the Philippines*. Washington, DC: Office of the Chief of Military History, Department of the Army, 1953.

Ney, Virgil. *Notes on Guerrilla Warfare: Principles and Practices*. Washington, DC: Command Publications, 1961.

Paddock, Alfred H. *US Army Special Warfare: Its Origins*. Washington, D.C.: National Defense University Press, 1982.

Paschall, Colonel Rod. *A Study in Command and Control: Special Operations in Korea, 1951-1953*. Carlisle Barracks: Army Military History Institute, 1988.

Smith, Robert Ross. *Triumph in the Philippines*. Washington, DC: Office of the Chief of Military History, Department of the Army, 1963.

Index